miraculous
moments

About the Author

Elissa Al-Chokhachy, MA, RN, CHPN, FT, has been work-ing with the dying and the bereaved for almost two decades. She is the recipient of the Boston College Alumni Award for Excellence in nursing and the Dr. William B. Stevens Award for the nurse who enjoys her work the most. Al-Chokhachy is the author of two children's books and is a certified hos-pice nurse and fellow in thanatology. She is currently work-ing on a collection of stories for bereaved parents.

To Write to the Author

If you wish to contact the author or would like more in-formation about this book, please write to the author in care of Llewellyn Worldwide Ltd. and we will forward your request. Both the author and publisher appreciate hearing from you and learning of your enjoyment of this book and how it has helped you. Llewellyn Worldwide Ltd. cannot guarantee that every letter written to the author can be an-swered, but all will be forwarded. Please write to:

Elissa Al-Chokhachy
c/o Llewellyn Worldwide Ltd.
2143 Wooddale Drive
Woodbury, MN 55125-2989

Please enclose a self-addressed stamped envelope for reply,
or $1.00 to cover costs. If outside the U.S.A., enclose
an international postal reply coupon.

Many of Llewellyn's authors have websites with additional information and resources. For more information, please visit our website at

www.llewellyn.com

miraculous moments

True Stories *Affirming that* Life Goes On

ELISSA AL-CHOKHACHY

Llewellyn Publications
Woodbury, Minnesota

First Edition
First Printing, 2010

Cover design by Ellen Dahl
Cover image © Hiroshi Watanabe/Photodisc/PunchStock
Editing by Laura Graves

Llewellyn is a registered trademark of Llewellyn Worldwide Ltd.

Library of Congress Cataloging-in-Publication Data
Al-Chokhachy, Elissa.
  Miraculous moments: true stories affirming that life goes on / Elissa Al-Chokhachy.—1st ed.
      p. cm.
  ISBN 978-0-7387-2122-4
  1. Future life. 2. Death—Religious aspects. 3. Life—Miscellanea.
4. Miracles. I. Title.

  BL535.A44 2010
  202'.3—dc22
                                        2010009685

Llewellyn Publications
A Division of Llewellyn Worldwide Ltd.
2143 Wooddale Drive
Woodbury, MN 55125-2989
www.llewellyn.com

Printed in the United States of America

Dedicated
to
GOD,
The Omniscient One
Known by many names,
Unfathomable,
Far grander than we could ever imagine or comprehend;
The One who reveals Divine essence
In All That Is
And in so many miraculous moments
Which help us remember
Eternity.

Contents

～ 9 *Angels* *231*

～ 10 *Near-Death Experiences* *253*

Acknowledgments

In loving acknowledgment of all who made *Miraculous Moments* possible:

- For those who believed in the dream, the vision, and in me, *thank you.*

- For those who willingly and courageously entrusted me with their innermost thoughts, feelings, and experiences, *I most humbly thank you.*

- For my beloved family members and dearest friends who have stood by me, supported and encouraged me, and have lovingly assisted in the various phases of the editing process, *a huge thank you.*

- To those beloved souls and teachers who are honored within these pages and continue to be present in our lives through their wisdom, guidance, grace, and love, *thank you.*

- And, finally, to those who through their willingness to share these stories have provided invaluable hope and healing to the dying and the bereaved, *my heartfelt thanks to each and every one.*

Introduction

There are two ways to live your life.
One is as though nothing is a miracle.
The other is as though everything is a miracle.
—ALBERT EINSTEIN

THROUGHOUT MY NURSING CAREER, I have been privileged to care for many individuals who were dying or bereaved. I have learned so much from these brave, courageous, and loving souls. The intimate moments shared have moved me beyond words, compelling me to find new ways to bring comfort, hope, and healing. I have carried the vision of *Miraculous Moments* in my heart for almost two decades. The majority of the last eleven years have been focused on compiling this book and its companion book for bereaved parents. Once I made the commitment, I was amazed to discover the commonality of this type of transcendent experience. Many individuals have either had a direct experience or know someone who has. Yet, few people tend to share their experiences publicly.

Over thirty years ago, in a dreamlike experience, my cousin Steffan came to me two weeks after his death. His visit transformed me; it utterly convinced me that life is eternal. The description of this life-changing event is the final story in this book. Thirteen years after Steffan's visit, I found myself employed as a hospice nurse and needing to call on that direct experience in order to help alleviate the suffering of the dying and the bereaved. In my role as a hospice nurse, I frequently help caregivers who need to know that terminally ill loved ones will live on. Faith, hope, and belief in eternal life can provide tremendous comfort to the dying and the bereaved.

Through the years, I have shared my personal experience of Steffan with numerous individuals who were grieving. In return, several of them have entrusted me with life-affirming experiences, some of which have never been shared before. I have found in my professional work that by shattering the myth of death as the final chapter of life, the bereaved are more easily able to move through their grief. Firsthand experiences affirming the continuity of life provide invaluable hope and reassurance; they lovingly remind us that we are never alone.

Physical death does not have to mean the end of a loving relationship. Deceased loved ones can continue to send us love, just as we send love to them. Yes, it is true that when someone dies, our relationship with that individual alters dramatically; the world in which both existed has now changed. But, love does not die simply because of physical death. Love is the essence of life; it cannot die. Love and life are eternal.

Miraculous Moments contains numerous heart-rending stories written by contributors from all walks of life. Every story is true, although some names and demographics have been changed in order to ensure confidentiality for loved ones, patients, and families. Bereaved individuals and health care professionals describe remarkable experiences that occur prior to death (near-death awareness) and afterwards. Signs, visions, sounds, smells, touch, dreams, sense of presence, angels, and near-death experiences have all been included. Every story provides important validation of the existence of life after death.

I applaud every contributor for the courage to join me in this vision. Thank you for your unwavering faith, hope, and trust. May our stories touch the hearts of many. May we raise awareness of spirit in our lives and the existence of eternal life beyond physical death. May we bring hope to the hopeless, healing to all who are hurting, comfort to the dying and bereaved, and peace to this planet. May we never forget to take care of Mother Earth, who makes it possible for us to be here. Finally, may we care for one another, all of life, and remember how truly blessed we are.

ELISSA AL-CHOKHACHY

I

⁓

Signs

*Remember, angels are both God's messengers
and God's message, witnesses to eternity in time,
to the presence of the divine amidst the ordinary.
Every moment of every day is riddled by their traces.*
—F. FORRESTER CHURCH

OUR LIVES ARE FILLED WITH a multitude of occurrences overseen by a force greater than ourselves. Events that may appear as random sometimes have a higher purpose. Signs are sent by spirit to assure us that we are never alone. These messages come in a variety of forms. Occasionally nature sends us the sign, as in the appearance of a beautiful rainbow at a particularly significant moment in the life of the bereaved. Sometimes animals who have a relationship with the deceased present themselves as the messengers. Still, at other times, events that have no logical explanation will occur and directly pertain to the loved one who has died. These synchronistic occurrences are messages. To the casual observer, they may seem insignificant. However, the bereaved experience them with an inner knowing that this is the sign they have been waiting for.

SPECIAL DELIVERY

Jane Harris

⌐────────⌐

The tide was going out and sheets of water were left on the low, flat places near the water's edge. Sunshine touched these places like stretched plastic, wrapped over the sand. As I paused in mid-stride to admire this remarkable scene, I felt transported into a world of my own.

The day was perfect for a walk on the beach with little to distract me. It was semi-deserted and a perfect opportunity to reminisce about my mother, who had died several months earlier. I had conflicted feelings of missing her and not missing her. Grateful for the many gifts she had given me, I called out to my mother so I could thank her. The connection in my heart felt good, as did all the feelings that flowed from it.

I remembered how my mother loved to fish off a jetty in Martha's Vineyard. I was very young and too young to fish with her. In my mind, she was far away, out at the very tip of the island, catching flounder and, sometimes, those unfortunate-looking sea robins. She would bring them back to the beach in a bucket and then bury them in the sand to stop their frantic flopping. I remember those fish being flat, appearing like worn-out, flapping slippers. I believe this was my first taste of death. We ate those fish for supper. At least, Mom and Dad did. I hated the taste of fish for years.

As I walked along the beach remembering my mother and her fondness for fishing, I witnessed a seagull dipping into the sea for a fish. Then, unexpectedly, he flew towards me and dropped his fat, silvery catch right in front of me—he had just plucked that fish from the sea! I was astonished and knew, somehow, my mother had petitioned the seagull to do her a favor.

I had lived by this beach for twenty-five years and had never seen any seagulls pluck fish out of the ocean. Seagulls don't usually feed in that manner. And, oddly, he never came back for his catch. I walked up and down the beach a few more times. Still in a state of shock, I thought about the possibilities that this event signaled. Life after death! The fish had been delivered to me as a special gift from my mother.

Jane Harris and her husband live by the ocean in New England and have raised two beautiful children. As a ceramic artist who merges play, spirit, and skill, Jane's work and play have become one, with unlimited creative possibilities.

ROSES

Elissa Al-Chokhachy

During my journey as a hospice nurse, I encountered a woman named Marge. At thirty-nine years old, she was the primary caregiver for her mother, one of our patients. This young woman was now facing the impending loss of her mother. I had been dispatched to Marge's home to evaluate a change in her mother's condition. After taking vital signs and performing an assessment, I gently informed Marge that her mother was dying. The tears and barrage of emotions that followed eventually led to a discussion of Marge's faith. She recalled an experience associated with her Grandma Nellie's passing some years back.

Marge and her grandmother were extremely close. She loved her grandmother dearly. At twenty-three years old, Marge was devastated when Nellie became critically ill and died shortly thereafter. Young Marge couldn't imagine life without her. Throughout the wake and funeral, Marge was crying hysterically. She prayed fervently, over and over, asking God for a sign. Marge desperately needed to know that her grandmother was still alive.

Grandma Nellie loved roses. A close friend knew this and sent Marge one dozen red roses two days before the funeral in honor of her grandmother. The roses were spectacular; they were in full bloom on the day of the funeral. When Marge returned to her apartment after her grandmother's funeral, she was quite surprised at what she found. Inexplicably, every single rose petal from the dozen red roses had fallen off its stem onto the floor! No one was in her home, and no one had access to her apartment, as Marge lived alone. Also, every window in her apartment had been shut for some time from the chilly autumn temperatures. For this reason, no outside breeze could have possibly been responsible for causing the petals to fall. Instantly, Marge knew the rose petals on the floor were a sign from her grandmother. She was convinced that her prayers were answered—Grandma Nellie was still alive after all!

L'Dor V'Dor:
Messages from Generation to Generation

Cheryl Finkelstein

Although Mom was born in America and was a thoroughly modern woman, she and Dad were raised in immigrant families from the Jewish *shtetls* (villages) of Eastern Europe, and both were able to speak fluent Yiddish. My parents understood and respected the Jewish traditions their families brought from "the Old Country," which were passed *l'dor v'dor*, from generation to generation. One of those traditions was the naming of children after a loved one who had passed away. It was very common, and widely accepted as normal in the shtetls, for deceased loved ones to appear in dreams, bringing some kind of message. And it was pretty routine, in my modern American home, for relatives who had passed away to appear in my parents' dreams, delivering messages from the beyond. I was given my name in just that way.

My parents loved children and had hoped for one of each gender. After my brother Lew was born, they tried for a girl but Mom suffered a miscarriage. When she found she was pregnant again, the doctor's advice for a safe delivery was to stay in bed for nine months, advice she followed dutifully.

One night, my mother was visited in a dream by a deceased cousin of whom she had been quite fond. Cousin Slouveh said she was watching over us both and reassured Mom that she would be safe and that the baby would be safe. "Your baby is a girl," Slouveh said, "and I would like you to name her after me."

Mom and Dad were both thrilled and set out in the morning to inform their own mothers of the good news. The prospective grandmothers, however, were less than pleased. It seemed that Slouveh had died quite young, and the grandmothers felt it would be bad luck to name a baby after someone who had died too soon, but my mother insisted. She had made a promise to Slouveh, who had also made a promise of her own, that she would watch over us. Eventually, a compromise was found; the middle name of Leah was selected, for an ancestor who had lived into her nineties. And so, I was given the Yiddish name *Slouveh Leah*—in English, Cheryl Linda. With this background, it wasn't much of a stretch for me to believe, after my mother passed away, that she would be able to communicate with me. In fact, I assumed that she would.

My mom was eight years younger than my dad and in better health. After Dad suffered a couple of debilitating strokes, she took on the role of caregiver. All of us expected that he would go first. Instead, it was Mom who suffered the stroke from which she never came back.

Mom and Dad had been very clear about their wishes, and both had living wills. After we watched Mom spend a week on a ventilator that was breathing for her, hands tied to the bed because she kept trying to pull out the tube, Lew and I made the decision we knew she wanted and directed the hospital staff to remove the machine. Surrounded by those she loved, her hands free and held by her children, Mom stopped breathing as the hazzan (cantor) from her synagogue, in his beautiful tenor voice, sang her into the next world.

After Dad was resettled in a nursing home close to my home north of Boston, Lew and I put our parents' Florida condo on the market. But first we had to clear it of the contents of their sixty-plus years together, and this was a lengthy and difficult process. Finally, there was almost nothing left. A couple of chairs, a table, and some pictures still on the walls. One of these, a large family portrait that hung over the living room sofa, had been the object of much discussion. Taken the night before my niece's wedding, it was a beautiful rendering of all of us. But the marriage had failed, and my niece was now happily remarried. The family portrait was now something of an embarrassment, an outdated object no one wanted. It was included with the few remaining items, sold as a package to a company coming the following morning to clear everything out.

Alone in my parents' nearly empty apartment, I spoke aloud to my dead mother. "We tried really hard, Mom, to save everything we thought you might want. But, if we forgot anything, you have to find some way to let me know. The guy is coming tomorrow." I waited. No clap of thunder. No bolt of lightning. No sign of any kind. Only silence in the empty apartment. So, I assumed she was satisfied with our decisions and went to bed.

In the morning, a muscular young man, his body heavily tattooed, arrived to remove the few items. He looked around, his eyes settling immediately on the portrait in the living room. "Is that your family?" he asked. "Wow, what a beautiful picture." He examined it closely, identifying me, and inquiring about the others, including Mom and Dad, proudly seated in the front row. Sadly, I told him the picture was among the objects he was to take. He was incredulous that we would sell such a thing, and I found myself explaining to this stranger that the young soon-to-be groom in the picture was the wrong husband, so no one in the family wanted the portrait. But he was undeterred. As he went about his work, he kept talking about the picture, asking questions. "Why would my boss want to buy your family portrait?" he finally asked. Annoyed by his endless questions and wanting to get the painful process over with, I muttered that perhaps his boss wanted the frame. Before I finished the sentence, the young man had pulled out a screwdriver and pried the portrait out of its frame.

Finally, everything else had been removed, and I insisted the young man take the picture. He carried it down in the elevator and placed it in his truck. At that exact moment, my husband arrived. Bob had been attending a conference while we cleaned out the condo and had not been privy to the endless discussions about the family portrait. Seeing it loaded onto a truck, Bob jumped out of his car and angrily confronted the young man. "What do you think you're doing with that picture?" he asked. He was told that the people didn't want it. "The hell they don't," said my husband, who grabbed the portrait from the truck and carried it back up to the third floor. As Bob walked into the apartment with the picture, muttering about "the nerve of this guy, to think we wouldn't want the family portrait," the light came on for me at last.

The previous night, I had asked my mother to send me a message. Then, I had ignored the unlikely messenger. For hours, the very assertive young man with the tattoos had tried to convince me to keep the picture, over and over expressing his incredulity that we would part with such an item and I had paid no attention. Obviously, a different messenger was needed ... someone I might actually listen to—my husband.

The tale isn't over yet; we still had to get the picture home. Bob is a pilot, and we were flying back to Boston in our plane, which has a narrow rear door for cargo. To our amazement, the portrait slipped in with a millimeter to spare on either side, fitting perfectly through the narrow space because the young man had removed it from the frame. Mom, as she always had, took care of everything. The family portrait, which she clearly wanted us to keep, hangs in the room in which I write this story.

Of course, that was not the only message we received from my parents. My niece, who very much wanted children and had encountered some difficulties in pursuit of that goal, found out soon after my father passed away that she was pregnant. She was hopeful but concerned. When her doctor pronounced that the baby's due date would be May 10, Beth promptly burst into tears. Alarmed, the doctor asked if there was something wrong. Beth replied, "It's my grandparents' wedding anniversary and my grandfather's birthday." The doctor, not wanting her to be disappointed, informed her that babies are very rarely born on their due dates. "I know," she said. "The baby will have its own birthday, not theirs. It's a message from them. They are watching out for me and my baby, and everything is going to be all right." And it was. Her son Jalen, named after Dad, was born at the end of April. On the annual family calendar of birthdays and anniversaries, my parents still have the month of May all to themselves.

When we emptied out the condo, I took the box containing Mom's knitting materials. Although lacking in domestic skills myself, I had wonderful memories of the many sweaters, shawls, hats, and whatnot she had made for all of us through the years, and could not bring myself to dispose of her knitting paraphernalia. The box sat for a long time, unopened, in a closet, but when I learned that Beth was pregnant, I decided to knit a blanket for the baby. I thought that if I used Mom's knitting needles, she and I would be making a blanket for the baby together. Little did I know how true that would be.

When I opened the box, I was surprised to find a few rows of yarn, knit in a complicated pattern, on one of the needles. I brought it to a local knitting shop, where a woman was able to find the pattern on a slip of paper in the box. There, in my mother's handwriting, were the instructions. As I left the knitting shop, I asked if the woman could tell from the pattern what this item was intended to be. "Oh yes," I was told. "It was a blanket. This pattern was a very popular one for blankets." And a blanket is what it became.

At Jalen's circumcision, I carried him into the room for the ceremony, wrapped in his new blanket. Several of the photos taken that day of the baby in his blanket show a strange white light. I have never seen anything like it in a photo before or since. And it wasn't in anyone else's photos, only in mine. People tell me it was some kind of reflection from the flash bulb, but I know better. I know it was Mom, letting me know she was there with us, and that she thought the blanket came out great.

Cheryl Finkelstein, EdD, recently retired from a long and rewarding career in public higher education administration. Living on the North Shore of Massachusetts with her husband, she enjoys traveling, reading, taking classes, and raising funds for breast cancer research.

BABA'S FIELD OF FLOWERS

Brianne Duff

I had the distinct privilege of living next door to my husband's grand-parents early in our marriage. My husband's grandfather, Dr. Paul Duff, was affectionately known as Papa, and his wife, Frances Duff, was our beloved Baba. When we were first married, my husband, John, and I lived in a small cottage on their property where Papa had practiced medicine up until he retired. We lovingly referred to our little home as Duff Cottage. Two of our children were born while we were living there and were fortunate to be able to visit with their great-grandparents daily. Our first child, Johnathan, would eagerly await the mail's arrival. Every day, he would run down the long driveway to their estate house and proudly hand-deliver it to his great-grandparents.

Baba and Papa were an amazing couple. Papa was a great story-teller, very much like my husband. Even though Papa would often tell the same story over and over again, Baba would attentively listen as if it were the first time she had ever heard it told. Without fail, she would laugh as hard as ever, as she thoroughly enjoyed hearing Papa's numerous renditions. I admired the depth of their love.

Baba and Papa dressed in their finest attire every day, regardless of whether or not company was due to arrive. Papa would recite poetry and prose, and often quote from classics. Wearing a handsome suit and tie, he stood six feet tall, yet appeared even taller when he wore his Stetson. Baba was equally as formal in her lovely outfits beauti-fully accented with exquisite jewelry and fresh flowers in her hair. She was a woman of few words and often passed the time doing needle-point, crewel, and embroidery. The matriarch of the household, she had her own way of taking care of things. We shared a deep mutual respect for one another.

Baba died at the age of ninety-four. John was a pallbearer for her fu-neral. I did not go to the graveside afterwards, as it was a hot day, and

I needed to get our young children home. Since Baba and Papa had ten children, I knew there would be lots of support for my husband.

When John arrived home four hours later, he told me about the stories his family had shared. One of his cousins had talked for a while about how proper Baba was. Her table was always set "just right." She was beautiful and elegant in every way. Although Baba usually wore roses in her hair, what we learned that day was that her favorite flower was the daisy. After my husband told me this new piece of information about Baba, I strongly felt her presence for the next two days.

Three days after Baba's funeral, I looked out the kitchen window across the driveway to my yard. The hill was covered with hundreds of blooming daisies. I called out to my husband to come and look at the hill. When he did, John smiled in amazement and said, "Baba is present. She is going to remain with us for a long time." Prior to Baba's death, a few scattered daisies had grown in my yard. Each year around the anniversary of her death, the daisies continue to return and bloom randomly. But the hill has *never* been covered with daisies except for on that day. I still get goosebumps whenever I think of Baba's field of flowers.

Brianne Duff, MSN, RN-BC, HNC, educator, and hospice nurse, has practiced the art and science of holistic nursing for twenty-six years. She and her husband, John, have raised three beautiful children who give back to the world through compassionate action.

My Traveling Companion

Jean Bajek

⌒

Although my father was small in stature, his sudden passing left a huge void in the lives of all who loved him. As time passed, my family and I took comfort in our cherished memories. We grew to appreciate that my father, Stanley F. Bajek, left this world the way he'd lived—quietly and peacefully.

The son of Polish immigrants, Daddy's strength was in his gentle nature. By example, my father taught us that anything worth doing deserved to be done well. He encouraged, but never criticized. We felt his pride in our accomplishments without a need for words. A devoted husband and father, he was hard-working and provided well for his family. Daddy also taught us to pay for what we bought. As the fifth of six boys, he highly respected women, and especially treasured finally having a daughter, followed by a granddaughter and a great-granddaughter, too. As his only daughter, I was always Daddy's little girl. All his grandchildren and great-grandchildren loved him and affectionately called him *Dziadziu*, the Polish word for grandfather. He has always been an important part of my life.

Mom and Daddy regularly drove to Florida following his retirement. Never one for the cold, Daddy adored the warm weather and would have enjoyed living in a warmer climate year round. Mom, however, couldn't tolerate the hot Floridian summers, so they never moved from Connecticut. After Daddy's heart surgery in 1984, my parents stayed pretty close to home.

Seven years later, I began visiting Panama City Beach, Florida, annually. In 1999, with the whole family gathered around the table at Christmastime, I excitedly told them about my upcoming winter vacation. I clearly remember Daddy looking directly at me and saying, "You go to Florida and *have a good time!*" I smiled, as he knew I always appreciated the break from the cold Connecticut weather. Daddy passed away in his sleep at the age of eighty-five on January 2, 2001. He never wanted to suffer or be a burden on anyone. And he wasn't.

My life situation changed in 2004, which allowed me to relocate to Panama City Beach. While registering my car at the motor vehicle office, I accepted the car tag randomly handed to me. As I fastened the plate to my car, my heart fluttered as I read the identification: Q015DZ. I instantly thought of Daddy. He was born in 1915 and was known as *Dziadziu*. I immediately remembered that holiday dinner conversation and smiled in acknowledgement. I am grateful that Daddy is still with me. He gives me daily reminders of his presence and rides with me wherever I go.

Jean Bajek, RN, a mother and grandmother, works for a pharmacy in Panama City Beach, Florida. A former child and adolescent behavioral health nurse from Windsor, Connecticut, Jean enjoys writing, photography, and living right next to the Gulf of Mexico.

Our 9/11 Hero

Debora L. Hayes

My husband, Robert Hayes, was a very happy, vibrant person. He was an extremely honest man and a true gentleman. Whether Bob was dealing with presidents of companies, his fellow workers, or his surfing buddies, he was well respected and got along with everyone. My husband often traveled wearing a business suit, and he was known to carry his surfboard alongside, especially if there was an ocean nearby. Bob loved to surf in Puerto Rico and southern France. He was an absolutely wonderful husband, father, and soulmate.

We met at Logan Airport when I was nineteen. Bob was everything to me. We had such a special bond right from the start. He took me to beautiful and interesting places over our four-year courtship. We grew together and shared nine wonderful years of marriage and as best friends.

Bob was handsome, down to earth, and always tan from surfing. Our vacations were usually at places with waves so he could surf. Whenever there was a "nor'easter," Bob would be out riding the waves. As for me, I'm not a surfer. Even though he tried to teach me, my fear of what was in the water prevented me from ever learning. Usually I would stand on the shore, take the pictures, and enjoy watching him surf.

Bob was also a great dad for our two boys. On the morning of his last business trip, Bob did not want to miss our oldest son Robbie's first day of preschool. Robbie was his little buddy, and he had always been there for all of his "firsts." Reluctantly, on that morning, Bob went into Robbie's bedroom, kissed him goodbye, and told him he'd be back in three days. My husband gave me a kiss, said, "I love you," and left for the airport. The date was Tuesday, September 11, 2001.

Approximately three hours later, while Robbie was watching television, the power went off inside our home. Robbie came in and complained that his TV show was off. Shortly after, the telephone rang. It was my mother asking, "Did you hear about the plane crash?"

"No," I replied. "I didn't." Mom knew that Bob was going on a business trip. He had mentioned it at a family cookout on the day before and said he did not want to go. Thinking he had already left, Mom told me that the plane crash was in New York. My heart sank, but it still didn't click that it could be Bob's plane. He had left for Los Angeles early that morning. Little did I know that Bob's plane had been diverted to New York City.

I didn't know Bob's flight number, so I called his employer, a Swiss company based in Massachusetts. As soon as I asked for the information, the receptionist placed my call on hold. I think she knew the answer to my question but didn't know what to say. She picked up the phone, told me that Bob was booked on American Flight 11, and gave me the telephone number of the travel agency to call. The agency confirmed Bob's ticket had been used. His plane, American Flight 11, was the first to hit the World Trade Center towers in New York City. Oddly enough, it crashed at the same moment the electricity went off in our home.

In shock and disbelief, I kept dialing Bob's cell phone over and over, leaving messages, hoping by some miracle that he would call me back. He didn't. I later learned that Logan Airport's cameras, used to videotape all boarding passengers, were not operational on that day. Since there was no proof that Bob had actually boarded, I continued to hold on to the hope that my husband was still alive. The Logan Airport camera malfunction was one of the many problems identified in the 9/11 Commission Report. With so many unanswered questions, there is so much we will never know.

On the morning of September 15, 2001, our four-year-old son excitedly came down the stairs from his room exclaiming, "Mommy, Mommy! I just saw Daddy! Daddy said that everything is going to be okay, Mommy!" That was the only time since the crash that Robbie mentioned anything to me about Bob. It was no coincidence that Bob appeared to Robbie on that day because we had planned a special gathering of family, friends, and neighbors at Alliance Park near our home. There, we held a candlelight memorial service for Bob, even though we didn't have his body or remains. Hundreds gathered to offer their thoughts, support, and prayers. It was reassuring to know that Bob was right there with us.

Everybody at Hampton Beach knew Bob; he surfed there often. Just like policemen and firemen, surfers have their own brotherhood. When a surfer dies unexpectedly, surfers will often hold a Hawaiian paddle-out service. On September 22, 2001, at Hampton Beach, the Cinnamon Rainbow Surf Shop organized a paddle-out memorial service for Bob. Someone made Hawaiian leis out of fresh flowers for everyone. Hundreds wearing wetsuits put leis around their necks, paddled out on surfboards, and made a huge circle in the water. Reverend Chip Thompson, also a surfer and the minister at our church, offered a Hawaiian surfer's tribute. It was truly a celebration of Bob's life. Even though I was pretty numb from everything that was happening, I felt Bob's presence with me when I paddled out to the circle, despite my fears. At the end of the service, everyone threw their leis into the center of the circle, and we all paddled back to shore.

Bob reminds us often that he is in our lives. Every time Robbie has an important "first," something unusual will happen. I remember the day when Robbie, my other son Ryan, and I were driving over to the baseball field for Robbie's first baseball game. The overhead lights in the car kept flickering repeatedly, but it wasn't even dark. I said, "Robbie, what are you doing? Stop it!" "Mommy, I'm telling you. It's not me. *It's Daddy!*"

Shortly after 9/11, my father and I traveled to the crash site in New York City. Since that visit, I continue to smell a strange burning odor, unlike any other scent I have ever smelled before. Sometimes it happens when I am in the car, and other times it happens when I am in my home. Family members have smelled a strange burning odor in my home as well. When it first happened, I contacted an electrician to check out our newly wired house. After a thorough evaluation, the electrician informed me everything was fine. The smell must be Bob's way of letting us know that he is with us, and whenever it happens now, I try not to move; I never want the moment to end. What initially seemed so odd and frightening is now an experience of comfort.

There were several memorials created in Bob's honor, including one outside our home, one in Alliance Park, and one in Blanquefort, France. *Surfing* magazine honored him and two other surfers who died in Pennsylvania that day with a photographic tribute. A friend of Bob's, a pilot in the Army Aces Unit, facilitated the naming of a helicopter used in Afghanistan combat after him. Finally, Bob's name was also included on a 9/11 tribute in Santa Monica, California.

On the first anniversary of 9/11, our community held an outdoor remembrance service on what turned out to be a rainy afternoon. After I spoke a few words on Bob's behalf, the most beautiful rainbow appeared. I know it was sent as a radiant symbol of hope for the survivors of those who had died.

For a few years in a row, 9/11 families were invited to Camp Sunshine in Casco Bay, Maine. Normally a camp for terminally ill children, the staff had decided to hold something special for 9/11 children there. One activity for children and their parents involved writing messages on balloons. Robbie and Ryan wrote personal messages to their dad, as did I. Afterward, with peaceful music playing, everyone went outside with their balloons to let them go. It had been raining while we were writing. By the time all of us got to the water's edge, the rain stopped. Beautiful double rainbows came out the very moment we released our balloons! It was unbelievable! Once again, Bob was with us there in spirit.

Bob is our hero. I will love him forever. I am so grateful that he continues to be in our lives. It is taking us a long time to heal, but we are finding our way. With the help of a little Welsh Corgi named Chance who came into our lives two years ago, my children and I are learning how to love again.

Debora L. Hayes now fills the role of mom and dad for her two energetic, growing boys. They enjoy hiking, skiing, biking, and rafting. Their appreciation for nature helps bring balance and peace into the lives of Deb and her family.

Through the Eyes of a Cat

Elissa Al-Chokhachy

While caring for an eighty-one-year-old man in the hospital dying from congestive heart failure, his daughter, Judith, shared an unusual story. The story concerned the death of a dear friend, Pete, who had died a few years earlier. Judith admitted she had always been skeptical about the existence of life after death, yet Pete's final days had been transforming for her. A mutual friend, Dr. Nguyen, was with Pete when he died. He shared with Judith what had transpired during their friend's final moments.

Pete was lying in his bed. Dr. Nguyen was sitting quietly in the chair beside him when Pete's black cat, Sophie, decided to visit. Sophie jumped up on Pete and then laid down at the foot of the bed next to him. The cat was very attentive and closely observed her master. As Pete took his final breath, Sophie was staring directly at him and continued to stare for the longest time. Then, she slowly moved her eyes from Pete towards the window, as if she were watching someone leaving or who had just left.

Judith mentioned that, ironically, an article on the light spectrum had been published in the *Boston Globe* the week prior. Apparently, research has now proven that humans have a limited ability to see the light spectrum. In contrast, animals have a far greater capacity to view the full range of light. Perhaps Sophie was able to see something invisible to the human eye and was letting Dr. Nguyen know there is much more to life than what he could see ... if only cats could talk!

The Quarter Man

Linda LeColst

⌒

My father, Bill Guerrette, was a handyman with many talents. Taught by his father at a young age how to build cabinets and tables, this resourceful jack-of-all trades could fix just about anything. After forty years of employment at the United Shoe Machinery Corporation, my father retired and went to work part-time for my ex-husband, Donnie, at a local spring water company. For the next fourteen years, Dad answered phones and collected payments from the people who came to refill their water bottles.

It cost twenty-five cents to refill a one-gallon bottle with spring water, and most people paid with quarters. Needless to say, Dad collected hundreds and hundreds of quarters over the years. In 1999, when the U.S. Treasury Department began releasing the "Eagle" quarter series with the names of states printed on them, it was no surprise that Dad started collecting them. His fascination developed into a game and personal challenge to fill entire rolls of quarters from each state. While at work, Dad would always search through the quarters collected that day and on days he wasn't there. Whenever any of our family members or myself stopped by to see Dad, we automatically emptied out our pockets, just in case by some chance we might have a quarter Dad needed. Quite pleased with his efforts, Dad was excited about his steadily growing quarter collection.

When Dad became ill with lung cancer, he was forced to retire from the job he had grown to love. Following his surgery, I regularly visited him at the rehabilitation center where he was recuperating. On one particular day, I was amazed to see how peaceful Dad looked, especially since he had been so uncomfortable after his surgery. Donnie, who was visiting at the same time, agreed. Dad excitedly told us about a spectacular dream that he had experienced the night before. While looking directly into Donnie's eyes, Dad spoke about lots of people he had seen in the dream. Then, Dad described the most "beautiful, beautiful, beautiful" lights he had ever seen. As he slowly said the word "beautiful" three times, Dad closed his eyes, squinted and then tilted his head upward. My father had a look of wonder and amazement on his face. Then, he questioned if either of us had ever had a dream like that. We hadn't, the conversation changed, and Dad did not mention it again. Two weeks later, on December 22, 2002, my father passed away.

On the evening of my father's death, the whole family went over to my parents' house to be with Mom and to help one another through our first major family loss. While there, we noticed strange electrical things beginning to happen in the kitchen. The overhead light flickered on and off, the coffee maker started percolating, and the oven turned on by itself. The first of several signs from Dad, these occurrences happened within hours of his death.

On Christmas morning, I prayed, "Dad, please send me a sign that you have crossed over and are doing okay." A few hours later at my mother's house, my brother, Bill, came up from the cellar, the place where Dad had spent endless hours building. Once upstairs, Bill noticed something bothering him in one of his shoes. He took off his left moccasin and was surprised to find a quarter inside the shoe. My brother rationalized that the quarter must have slipped through a hole in his pocket.

"Is it a state quarter?" I asked. Bill answered, "Yes, the quarter is from Rhode Island." Suddenly, I realized this could be the sign I was asking for. Bill reached into both pant pockets, checked for holes and found both intact, and his eyes opened wide in amazement. He couldn't believe what had just transpired. I explained that *Dad* must have been down in the cellar with him, and *Dad* must have placed that quarter in his shoe. Initially, Bill was quite taken aback by the concept, as he was never one to believe in the idea of a spirit world.

Later that evening, when Bill was describing the quarter incident to his wife, he reached into his pants pocket to retrieve the quarter.

He was surprised to find the coin now missing. Family members stopped what they were doing to search the entire house, yet the elusive quarter was nowhere to be found. It was becoming apparent to all of us that the Rhode Island quarter had left in the same mysterious manner it had arrived. In my heart, I knew it was a clear sign from the man who had passionately collected quarters all the latter years of his life. Later, I chuckled to myself, saying, "Okay Dad, you can give Bill all the quarters you want, but I want hundred-dollar bills." Little did I know I would soon find a crisp, one-hundred-dollar bill in my Christmas gift envelope from Mom and Dad.

While at work a year later going through some of my father's things, Donnie happened to find an envelope containing $5 worth of state quarters Dad had been collecting. Inexplicably, three of the quarters in that envelope were released *after* Dad died: two on his mother's birthday and one on my younger son's birthday. The United States Treasury Department releases state quarters five times a year. How is it that quarters released a year and a half after Dad's death found their way into that envelope? And how was it that all three of those quarters happened to be on significant days for our family members? Dad, I think you're up to your old tricks again. Thanks for your great sense of humor, for continuing to make us smile, and for letting us know you're okay.

Linda LeColst, a single mom of two grown sons, raises Silver Persian cats. Through the blessing of one special kitten, Miss Wings, many angels have been brought into her life and into the lives of others.

THE MISSING BUCKET

Barbara Scuderi

Sometimes a person comes into your life and you don't fully appreciate the impact and influence she has on you until she's gone. It was an unusually hot day in August more than twenty-five years ago when I first met my neighbor, Zelna. Expecting my third child, I had just moved into the house across the street from her. She arrived at my doorstep with a loaf of freshly baked bread, and from that moment on, we became fast friends.

Even though she was twenty years older than me, Zelna and I shared many interests—walking the beaches, shopping for flea market bargains, and sewing. Her wonderful sense of humor inspired me and often lifted my spirits. Zelna astounded me with her constantly positive outlook on life. She had the capacity to see the joy in an otherwise sad situation. I especially recall a difficult time in my life when she wrapped her arms around me and consoled me with her humor, saying, "Who needs men anyway?" I was going though a divorce, raising three children on my own, and holding down a full-time job.

Zelna always welcomed me into her home for a comforting drink of Ovaltine and soothing conversation. She never expected anything in return for her kindness and generosity, and always gave of herself to her family and friends. She often did the unexpected just to see the delighted expression on someone's face. At my surprise forty-first birthday party, she truly gave me a gift of love. Zelna knew I loved to sew, but that I did not always finish complicated sewing projects. Unbeknownst to me, she had found an unfinished blouse I had put aside several months before. Zelna brought the blouse to her house to complete and wrapped it up as my birthday gift. That gift meant more to me than anything I have ever received—before or since.

On February 14, 1990, I took my dog Riley for his usual afternoon walk. On our return home, I noticed that Zelna's front door was open, with my nineteen-year-old daughter, Lisa, standing there in her bare feet. She yelled to me, "Mom! Mom! Something's happened to Zelna!"

I raced to the door and saw that Zelna had slid off her chair onto the floor. Lisa quickly told me that Zelna's son, Richard, had called our house looking for me. He had been talking to his mother when she dropped the phone; Richard asked Lisa to please check on her. Lisa was just getting out of the shower when Richard's phone call came in. She dressed hurriedly, immediately raced across the street, found Zelna on the floor, and called 911—help was on the way!

It appeared Zelna wasn't breathing; I would have to use my knowledge of CPR to help her. Just at that moment, the paramedics arrived at the door and quickly went to work trying to revive her. Lisa and I watched as they carried her outside on a stretcher to the waiting ambulance. That evening, I waited anxiously to hear any news. Several hours later, I was told that Zelna died from a massive cerebral hemorrhage. It was Valentine's Day, the day when we remember the people we love most.

My sister Donna and I are generally skeptical by nature. We are not believers in psychic predictions, UFOs, or other unexplained mysteries, as neither of us has experienced any of these occurrences in our lives. The summer after Zelna died, Donna and I decided to search for sand dollars at a local beach. At seven o'clock in the morning, the beach was deserted, and it was an unusually clear, calm day with a gentle surf. We had walked about a half-mile carrying our sand buckets when we spotted a huge snail coming out of its shell. It was approximately eight feet away from us, just below the surface of the water. We left our empty buckets on the sand and went to investigate. After spending no more than two or three minutes watching the snail, we turned to get our sand buckets. Donna and I were surprised to see that my bucket was gone!

Initially, we thought perhaps the surf had taken it out to sea, but the surf was too gentle. We searched and searched the water yet still found no pail. Next, the two of us looked for seagulls, thinking one of them may have lifted the bucket in its beak and flown away with it, but there were no seagulls in sight. Other than the two of us, no one else was on the beach. Donna and I were totally mystified and continued to search for an explanation.

Nine years later, we still don't know what happened to that bucket. Deep down, I feel Zelna was playing one of her practical jokes. How she loved to do the unexpected! I can still see her laughing every time I walk by that spot on the beach!

Barbara Scuderi, retired elementary school teacher, lives with her husband, Joseph, and dog, Scooter. In addition to tutoring and writing monthly book reviews for her church library publication, she enjoys reading, gardening, quilting, and playing in a bocce league.

A Birthday to Remember

Leila Milley

———

As the youngest of four daughters, I had so much fun growing up with Mom. She loved to travel. Mom always took me wherever she went as her "traveling buddy." She worked hard all year long to vacation with her four girls on Cape Cod every summer. We could always count on Mom dragging one of us out of bed each morning for an early sunrise walk to the beach. Although sunrises never seemed that exciting to me as a kid, Mom was always thrilled. She was like a small child opening up a brand-new gift each time. In Mom's eyes, everything was so much better at the Cape.

While we were there, we always celebrated somebody's birthday, even Mom's. If anyone ever asked Mom how old she was, she always responded with "forty-two," her favorite age. As the years passed, Mom's age never seemed to change. I remember one time when my ten-year-old nephew, Barry, asked, "Gram, shouldn't you be forty-three by now?" Mom laughed so hard; she never forgot that story.

Following retirement, Mom's health steadily declined over the next fourteen years. Our social, carefree mom no longer wanted to leave the house. She became homebound and oxygen dependent, and eventually needed to be transitioned into a lovely nursing home nearby. Several months later, Mom was admitted to hospice. During my last visit with her, I asked the hospice nurse how much time Mom had left. The nurse explained that she would let go when she was ready, but that she might be waiting for closure to move on. It was time to say goodbye.

I sat down next to Mom and took her hand in mine. Not knowing what to say, I just started talking. "Mom, I love you. We all love you, and we know you love us. You've been such a great mom. I don't want you to worry about us. We'll be okay. You can let go now. I'll keep you in my heart forever." Saying all this to my mom was the hardest thing

I've ever had to do. But, after I said it, a great sense of relief came over me. I felt lighter and more at ease. I wasn't shaking as much anymore. Once I had said everything I needed to say, I just cried and cried. As I did, Mom's hand squeezed mine even tighter, and then it relaxed. Mom opened her eyes and gave me a nod, as if she understood.

Sometime during the night, I had the most amazing dream. Mom came to me. I only saw her face, just her face, as if it was a close-up picture that someone had taken of her. She looked twenty years younger. Her hair was permed just the way she always wore it. And Mom had this *beautiful* smile! Her skin was smooth, and her face was bright. Mom looked so happy and calm. She looked just like the mom I had remembered. Then she said goodbye. While still smiling, Mom slowly disappeared into the dark. That vision would be my last beautiful memory of my mother. That same morning, Mom died at sunrise, her favorite time of the day. Although my sisters and I had been taking turns holding a bedside vigil, our mother chose to take her final journey during the few moments one of us had left the room.

Do I know if Mom is with me? I can absolutely say yes. A year after she passed away, as I approached my forty-second birthday, I found myself filled with sadness, missing Mom. My birthday turned out to be a beautiful, sunny day. During dinner, I tearfully shared with my husband and daughter how empty and strange it felt to be turning forty-two. Mom had been forty-two for as long as I could remember. Now it was my turn.

Following dinner, we left the restaurant and headed home. Out of the blue, it started to rain. Then, all of a sudden, right in front of me, was the most beautiful double rainbow I had ever seen. It was so vibrant and so crystal clear; it was unbelievably amazing! Instantly, I knew it was Mom wishing me a happy forty-second birthday! For years, we had been involved in an organization called the Order of the Rainbow for Girls. For Mom to send me a double rainbow on my forty-second birthday was absolutely incredible. My heart was so happy!

All I could do was cry and say, "Thank you, Mom! Thank you for my birthday gift!" I wanted to absorb every single ounce of that moment. Even my husband said it was the brightest rainbow he'd ever seen.

When people pass from this world, do they send signs letting us know they are still with us? Well, whenever I see a seagull or hear the ocean waves, I think of Mom. When I'm up before the sun and get to watch it rise, I can feel her smile. And when I see a rainbow, I know it's Mom shining down on me, watching over me, and protecting me. In that moment, I look up at the heavens and say, "Thank you, Mom. I love you, too."

Leila Milley lives with her wonderful husband, Peter, and daughter, Sarah, the sweetest and most joyful child any parent could wish for. She gives thanks to her guardian angel mother and father who lovingly protect and guide Leila and her entire family on earth.

The Moose Sighting

Sandra McDonough

⌐⟶

Occasionally, a special person enters your life. For me, that person was Harold Roy Bonnyman. My mom married "Bonny" after she retired and moved from suburban Massachusetts to the small town of North Sandwich, New Hampshire. Bonny and my mother owned and operated an antique shop in a one-room schoolhouse. He was well respected in the community and affectionately known as "Silk Hat" Bonnyman for the black top hat he wore as a charismatic auctioneer. The two lived happily together in their secluded antique farmhouse with its hypnotizing mountain views and serene marshland across the street.

Bonny was a welcome addition to our family. This endearing man soon became the only grandfather my children ever knew. Every summer, our family would spend a week swimming in nearby Squam Lake, attending an auction, walking in the woods, and fishing with Grandpa. Bonny kept a journal of every single fishing trip as well as the number of fish and types of fish that had been caught. My children loved going back each summer and reminiscing with Grandpa about the previous summer's catch.

Bonny was also an avid moose watcher. Whenever we visited, he would tell us lots of stories about his many moose sightings. Faithfully, he kept a journal of each and every moose that had visited the marsh, along with the date, time, and duration of its stay. Bonny also kept an ongoing list of all the people in town who had never seen a moose before, as he wanted to make sure that everyone would have the same opportunity as he.

Whenever Bonny spotted a moose, he would immediately contact the friends and local townspeople on his list who hadn't seen one before to please come quickly to his house. If by chance they were lucky enough to be home for Bonny's "moose alert" and were able to quietly and skillfully coast their cars down the road in time, they would be treated to an awe-inspiring view of a magnificent beast or two grazing in God's country.

Each time our family visited the farmhouse, we would be filled with anticipation in the hopes that we, too, might see one of Bonny's moose. However, the exuberant sounds of my three young children playing, screaming, and blowing moose-calling horns seemed to keep the timid creatures away from the marsh. Moose have keen hearing capabilities and apparently they wanted no part of the lively goings-on at the old farmhouse. It would be many years before I was privileged to behold one of the beastly creatures in living color.

Because everyone knew Bonny was fascinated with moose, he became the recipient of many "moose" gifts over the years. His collection of moose paraphernalia steadily grew, boasting "Herkimer" the stuffed moose, moose shirts, moose hats, moose books, and moose towels, just to name a few.

As time went on, the old farmhouse eventually became too much for Mom and Bonny to manage, so they moved to a quiet little neighborhood near the center of town. Their pleasure-filled days of sitting on the carriage-shed porch, watching golden sunsets, and waiting for moose to graze in the marsh had come to an end, along with the memorable moose sightings. The new home had woods in the backyard, but no mountain views and certainly no marshland for moose to visit.

Bonny's health was in decline, and after seventeen years of marriage to my mother, he passed away just a few months short of his ninetieth birthday. We held a beautiful memorial service for him, which was attended by his family and many friends. Because it was January, Mom held on to Bonny's ashes in an urn in her living room while she waited for the frozen winter ground to thaw. She would give Bonny a proper burial in the spring. My family and I made lots of phone calls to help support Mom during those long, lonely days, and we visited whenever we could.

On Easter Sunday of that same year, my husband, children, and I drove to New Hampshire to have dinner with Mom just to be together as a family. On that very day, an amazing thing happened. Mom and I were in the kitchen, cleaning up the dishes after a lovely Easter dinner. Her kitchen is designed with a large bay window offering a beautiful view of the woods behind her house. I happened to look out the window and couldn't believe my eyes. Out of the woods came a huge, dark-brown moose lumbering right into my mother's backyard!

Standing over six feet tall, the moose walked right through her garden and stopped for a few seconds to look at us through the kitchen window! His dark, beady eyes stared at us, and we stared right back at him. He almost seemed to be saying, "Do you see me? Because I'm going to stand here until you do." The moose didn't stay long. He nodded his head at us, took a stroll around to the front of the house, nodded his head again, and then disappeared back into the woods; we were awestruck.

Mom and Bonny had lived in that little house for more than five years. They always remained on moose alert in the hopes of having another sighting, but had never seen a moose on the property. Three months after Bonny's passing, our entire family was sent our very own moose sighting on Easter Day!

Now, I'm not positive, but I think Mom agrees with me that Bonny sent that moose just to check in on us. He wanted to let us know that even though he's missing us, he's doing just fine. Thanks for sending the moose, Bonny. We love you too.

Sandra McDonough, an aide in the Walpole school system, has been married to her husband, Bill, for thirty-seven years. With three grown children and a grandson, Luke, Sandy has a passion for reading, long walks, and traveling.

BLACKBIRD HAS SPOKEN

Dannielle Genovese

———

It was a beautiful, clear day, and I was looking through the sliding glass door into my backyard when I noticed a few blackbirds landing on the trees and grass. As I gazed out the window, the telephone rang. It was my close friend Walter, who had called to tell me that his father-in-law, Fred Nava, had passed away after a brief illness. Just as he finished telling me the sad news, some movement caught my eyes, and I was astonished to see the entire yard filled with a large flock of blackbirds. I couldn't remember ever having seen blackbirds in my yard before. I remember thinking this might be Fred's way of making a farewell visit to my husband and me on his journey to eternity.

Both Fred and Walter had accompanied me on a trip to Ireland in 1998. I was teaching high school at the time and took students to Europe each year. I needed chaperones and was delighted to offer them an opportunity to share our Irish adventure. Fred was an extraordinary man with a keen sense of humor and a love of people that embraced everyone he met. Having known him for many years, I knew my students would enjoy his company. What I hadn't realized was how easily he would charm everyone he encountered with his big smile and sharp wit. As a result of our time together, we became even closer than before, and I continue to relish every minute spent in his company.

The highlight of the trip to Ireland was a stop made at Connor Pass, a steep cliff overlooking the Irish Sea. Our bus left us off at the edge of the cliff where an Irish farmer approached us with some very young lambs. He offered to let us have our pictures taken holding one of them. I gave him a small donation, took a baby lamb into my arms, and nuzzled it with my face. Someone snapped a picture, and we continued on our way. In that moment, I remember how happy and complete I felt. It was truly the most special moment of the trip.

Now, as the news of Fred's death sunk in, my memory recalled that special time we had spent together. Sadly, I realized it was time to say goodbye.

The wake and funeral were held a few days later. My husband and I lived several hours away from Fred's home, and were only able to visit the funeral home the morning of his mass. A display of pictures had been set up on a table. Much to my surprise, delight, and sadness, I noticed a picture of me holding the lamb. Fred appeared in the photo, slightly to the left, looking directly at me. His face was wreathed in a warm and loving smile. That picture said so much about our friendship and the kind of man he was. It was the first time I had seen the picture; I was deeply moved.

We paid our respects, followed the cars to the church, and took our places in the pew. As the mass began, music filtered throughout the church, and we were invited to sing the opening song, "Morning Has Broken," with the soloist. I gasped and then shuddered as we started singing the second line, *"Blackbird has spoken…"* I realized that it was not a mere coincidence that the blackbirds landed in my yard at the very moment I heard the news of his death. Fred had found a way to communicate his living presence to me.

There is no doubt in my mind that those we love move on to a better place. I am even more certain that they still watch over us with their continuing love and concern. Sometimes, if we are lucky and listen carefully, we are reminded of their loving presence in the smallest wonders of nature.

Dannielle Genovese, a retired high school social studies teacher, is having fun creating works of art. Married to Paul for over forty years, she is the mother of two daughters, grandmother of five, and enjoys volunteering for hospice and the community.

Having Fun in the Sun

Lisa Brown

From 1988 to 1994, I was employed as an oncology nurse at a large metropolitan hospital in Boston. As a nurse caring for individuals with cancer, I found it easy to form close bonds with my patients and their families, especially the ones who returned regularly for treatment. This was particularly true with one memorable patient and his wife over a two-year period.

I liked Rick and his wife right away. Rick was a gregarious guy who loved to tell jokes and laugh. He had recently been diagnosed with lung cancer and had just been admitted to our oncology unit in February of 1991 for chemotherapy.

During one of the first times I cared for Rick, we talked late into the night. He was having difficulty breathing, and I was trying to help ease some of his anxieties and fears. Our conversation naturally came around to the subject of smoking, as well as the number of years he had smoked. I mentioned that my husband was a smoker, which was frustrating for me since I had daily reminders of its devastating effects whenever I worked. Wishing that the hands of time could be turned back, Rick said, "Wouldn't it be great if your husband could see me now?" Ironically, the next morning when I returned home, my husband told me about a terrible dream that he had just experienced during the night while I was working. In the dream, he found himself having difficulty breathing and literally woke up feeling scared and out of breath.

Over the next year, Rick was admitted frequently for either chemotherapy or for treatment from its complications. During one of those hospitalizations, Rick shared with me about a special trip to the Caribbean that he and his wife, Rita, had just planned prior to him becoming sick. They were so excited to tell me about it, as the two of them were very much looking forward to gambling, sipping on cool, refreshing alcoholic drinks, and basking in the sun. Rick and Rita were determined to go on the trip and as soon as he was discharged, they did.

Unfortunately, their Caribbean vacation was cut short. Rick began experiencing severe back pain, and they had to return home three days earlier than planned. The two of them went straight from the airport to the emergency room and Rick was immediately admitted to the hospital. I received a call from the ER and then escorted Rick and his wife to his room. However, I realized fairly quickly from their behavior and from the smell that filled the elevator that they had most probably partaken of several alcoholic beverages on their plane ride home.

Once in his hospital room, Rick immediately pulled out a t-shirt that he had purchased for me from the Hard Rock Café. He also asked if I had received the postcard he sent. I laughed and replied, "No, Rick, you just got back. The postcard would never have arrived by now." Well, he said laughing out loud, "You probably won't get it anyway... because it has naked bums on it!"

Weeks passed and with each hospitalization, Rick became progressively sicker. During one of his admissions, I remember Rick daily pinning a plastic button onto his hospital johnny that read, "Wake me up—I'm a lot of fun!" Even though he was someone who liked to joke and kid around, it was during that admission that Rick realized he was dying. It was also during that time that Rick made the difficult decision and choice to die at home rather than at the hospital. However, Rita did not support his decision and became quite angry. She didn't want her last memory of Rick to be lying dead in their house and then to have to live in their home with that memory.

A few days before Rick's scheduled discharge from the hospital, alcohol was found in his room by the cleaning staff. Since alcohol use is strictly forbidden in the hospital and a health risk for patients, I needed to address the situation. I told the staff that I preferred to be the one who spoke to Rita about the problem, which I did. Unfortunately, the conversation did not go well. Rita became quite irate, highly emotional, and yelled at me for accusing her of drinking in her husband's hospital room. It was an extremely uncomfortable situation for both of us, and our relationship was strained from then on.

The day for Rick's discharge finally arrived in early November of 1992, a few weeks prior to Thanksgiving. Sadly, I pushed him in a wheelchair down to the hospital lobby and outside the exit doors. Rick and I were both crying, knowing we would never see each other again. However, Rita avoided all eye contact. She busied herself transferring Rick's belongings into the back seat, as I helped her sick, frail husband into the car. Once Rick was in the car along with all his belongings, Rita slammed the car doors and angrily drove away.

I read in the newspaper a few weeks later that Rick had died. I mailed off a note of condolence to his wife, Rita, even though I knew our relationship had been strained. I never heard a response.

On February 12, 1993, one of the nurses from the oncology unit happened to ask if I had ever heard from Rita. I replied unhappily, "No," and went on to share how uncomfortable I felt about how everything had ended.

The next morning, Rita happened to telephone the hospital oncology floor. She spoke with the unit secretary and asked if I was scheduled to work on Valentine's Day. The secretary told her I wasn't working on Valentine's Day, but I would be coming in that afternoon. Rita thanked her for her assistance and hung up the phone.

As scheduled, I arrived at work, got reports on my patients, and went straight to a mandatory unit meeting. When I came out of the meeting, the unit secretary presented me with a gorgeous bouquet of flowers and a card that read, "To Rick's other sweetheart. Love, Rita." I was overwhelmed with joy and comfort! Making a mental note to call Rita as soon as I had the chance, I began to do assessments on each of my patients for the evening.

Approximately thirty minutes after receiving the flowers from Rita, my unit coordinator called me to the front desk. He handed me an interoffice envelope and said, "This just came for you." Intrigued, I opened up the large manila envelope and found inside a postcard addressed to me at the hospital. It had a picture on it of three women's rear ends, all wearing thongs and postmark stamped from the Caribbean. The card read, "Lisa, don't worry about me. I am having fun in the sun! Rick." I was floored. Somehow, I knew in my heart that Rick was looking down on me, having fun in the sun, and absolutely loving having one last laugh on me.

Lisa Brown, APRN, MS, BC, is currently a psychiatric nurse practitioner. Her extensive background in oncology involves caring for patients diagnosed with cancer and HIV.

THE BLUE HERON

Jean M. Wood

⎯⎯⎯

"Oh, honey, I'm so lost! I don't know anything anymore, and I'm getting worse!" For several years, Mom had repeated those words with considerable frustration and deepening loss, especially during the last six months of her life. An extremely vibrant and independent woman, my mother, Ellamae Morrison, struggled with chronic obstructive pulmonary disease, a respiratory disorder that severely limited the quality of her life. Mom came to live with me after she fell in her home at the age of ninety-three. Despite concerted efforts by her health care team, Mom's care eventually exceeded what I was capable of providing. Sadly, I made the dreaded decision to place her in a hospice unit at Memorial Hospital in Albany, New York, in order to maintain my own health; I would have much preferred for Mom to remain in my home under my care.

Because I had left the hospital for a brief period to get some sleep, I was not with my mother when she died. Although she had passed, her body was still warm to my touch when I arrived. Mom was quiet now. None of that dreadful, labored breathing… the loud, desperate struggle for breath that had left me unable to sleep night after night in my home and at the hospital. Months of knowing this moment would come had not prepared me for the intensity of the pain ripping through me. Surprised by the physicality of my grief and the loudness of my sudden, uncontrollable crying, I found myself bereft. I missed her presence already.

I sat down next to Mom. I talked to her, rubbed her forehead, her hair, her hand. I paced. I sat in the chair near the bed and called to her softly, "Mommy, I need to know that you're still here with me!" In that moment, a feeling of total calm filled my being. The torrent of my deep sobbing ceased. Stillness surrounded us both. I experienced a profound sense of wonder and awe, a peace within my mourning; I was grateful my mom's presence.

During her funeral, I felt her presence again. The cemetery was silent, each person quiet, somber as we gathered around the grave. When my friend began to play the flute, birds I had not known were there erupted into raucous singing. Their accompaniment to my mother's favorite hymn, "Amazing Grace," was joyous. Their exuberance made me smile. The birdsong was a gift, assurance of my mother's nearby presence.

I slept for three days following Mom's burial. There had been very little time for sleep during the months that preceded her death. My body and psyche needed time to rest. From the time of the funeral and for several days afterward, awake or asleep, one phrase from "Amazing Grace" would not leave me. *I once was lost but now am found... 'twas love that set me free,* played over and over in my mind; I simply couldn't make it stop. As I lay in my bed one morning, looking out at the sky, thinking about Mom, I suddenly understood! Mom was giving me a message. She'd been in such anguish, such turmoil, feeling lost for so long. Now, she was found; she was finally free! I felt awe and wonder and a newfound sense of gratitude. I took sustenance from the unquestionable message from Mom.

Although my mother loved all birds, there was one bird in particular that we both especially loved—the blue heron. I had spent time with a blue heron once in New Hampshire and had written a poem about the experience in my book *Prisms—A Book of Poetry*. Although Mom liked all my poems, the one about the heron was way up there on her list. She was my biggest fan. After her death, numerous heron sightings began to occur for those who loved her most. Her cherished friend Hannah, who drove Mom to all my book signings and readings, was startled when a blue heron flew directly in front of her car on the day of the funeral. Hannah knew it was Mom's way of letting her know everything was okay.

Another heron experience reminded me of my mother's dry sense of humor. My friend Diane and I were traveling on a nearby highway in her minivan; I was the pampered passenger, enjoying the scenery as she drove. As I reached for a snack from the back seat, Diane began to scream and cuss; the van swerved wildly. "What happened?" I asked. Diane angrily explained that a huge blue heron had flown so close to the windshield that it had almost hit the car! She was not favorably impressed.

The heron visitations continued with rather remarkable frequency. On the anniversary of my mother's death, I visited the place where we had buried her. As I pulled into the cemetery, my soul ached. I had very few regrets about how I had parented my mother as she grew old, but it bothered me that there were times when I could have stopped to visit her amidst the demands of my life and didn't. I felt guilty about that and wanted to talk to her about it. I rounded a curve by the cemetery pond. There, immediately before me, I encountered a blue heron sitting in the middle of the road! Behind the heron to the left was the small path leading to our family plot.

I had to brake the car and stop quickly. The heron was looking squarely at me, quiet and unmoving, as if anticipating my arrival at that time in that exact spot. He was neither startled nor frightened by my car mere feet away. I eased myself from the car, continuing to marvel in this prolonged and sacred moment. The heron sat there returning my gaze. There was no question in my humming mind that my mother was saying, "I know, it's okay; I loved you then, and I love you now." Mom was releasing me from all I might have done differently or better in my years of caring for her.

It's been six years now since she died. Blue herons continue to bless me with their unobtrusive appearance, their stillness, and sense of quietude. Each time, I am filled with awe. I know in those moments that I am in the presence of the Divine and my mother. Mom comes to encourage and reassure me, and to draw me close, just as she had throughout my life. I find myself uplifted and upheld, urged to hold on and be filled with faith. With immense joy, humility, and gratitude, I return to those moments often. May the serenity of the blue heron touch your heart and bring comfort to your journey, as it has to mine.

Jean M. Wood, author of two poetry books, Prisms *and* Given Love, *is also the author/playwright of* Journey Shared—A Chronicle of Healing, *her friend's experience with breast cancer. Jean is nearing completion on two new books on fibromyalgia.*

A Clear Sign

Elissa Al-Chokhachy

On the evening of August 18, 1998, my cousin Brent and I were reminiscing about days gone by. He had come to visit me from Tennessee. I was excitedly sharing news about a project I was working on to help the dying, the bereaved, and individuals facing the loss of a terminally ill loved one. I had started to compile a book of various types of firsthand experiences reflecting the miraculous unending nature of the human spirit. I asked Brent if he would be willing to include in this book his remarkable dream following the death of his brother, Steffan, whom we both loved dearly. Brent agreed. That night, while sitting in my family room, he allowed me to tape-record his recollection of that most vivid experience.

After we were done, our conversation switched to our beloved Uncle Ralph and the time Brent had spent helping his wife care for him during his last days. Uncle Ralph was a Presbyterian minister who died in 1994. He was a kind, gentle, and loving man who was very dear to both of us.

I was looking directly at Brent when, all of a sudden, the chandelier ten feet behind him flashed on to full brightness! And then, just as abruptly, it shut off. No one was near its dimmer toggle switch on the wall. We were alone in the house.

"Did you see that?" I blurted incredulously.

"Yeah, I saw it!" Brent replied curiously. "It looked like a flash or something..."

"It was the chandelier that turned on and off, by *itself*!" I exclaimed. "I was looking straight at it!"

Through the windows of the French doors next to us, Brent and I could see the clear, starlit night outside. There were no clouds in the sky or evidence of precipitation that might have created a sudden flash of light inside my home. I knew in my heart I had just received a tremendous gift from Uncle Ralph and/or Steffan. It was a clear sign letting me know I was headed in the right direction creating this book.

My cousin and I were given a direct experience that life is much more than it appears to be. There was no logical explanation for the chandelier operating itself. It had never happened before and has never happened since. A few weeks prior, I had printed out the title of the book, *Miraculous Moments,* and had placed it in a three-ring binder. I trusted that the stories and experiences would come to me. How affirming to have one occur in my own home.

2

The Light

Death is not extinguishing the light.
It is putting out the lamp because the dawn has come.
—RABINDRANATH TAGORE

EXPERIENCES OF THE LIGHT ARE extraordinary. How is it possible that light bulbs are able to turn on and off by themselves? And how is it that coded messages from a lighthouse are able to beam in at just the perfect time? The light is many things to many people. Dying individuals may experience the light as part of nearing death awareness, which occurs during the last few days of life. The dying, as seers, occasionally share with us visions of what they see. One woman described the light as warm and comforting; any of her prior worries were completely replaced by the profound awareness of God's love. Miraculously, revelations from the dying are able to bring much comfort and hope to the bereaved.

God's Love

Elissa Al-Chokhachy

⟡

Catherine was a vibrant, independent woman in her mid-sixties. She was a hospice patient diagnosed with colon cancer. Her courage and her determination were admirable. Each day, she disciplined herself to take a one-mile walk around the block; Catherine was not going to give in to her disease.

Eventually, Catherine's health deteriorated and she became bedridden. One weekend, her daughters called hospice to report a change in their mother's condition—she seemed vague and distant. I drove to Catherine's home to evaluate the situation. After a thorough assessment, I gently informed her two daughters that Catherine was in the early stages of actively dying. I offered emotional support and prepared the daughters for the upcoming changes. Afterwards, I went back into Catherine's bedroom to say goodbye.

During my assessment, I had been struck by how unusually calm, peaceful, and alert Catherine seemed. When I questioned her about any pain she might be experiencing, Catherine told me she had none. I wondered what I could do in order to help her before I left. Although I had never done this with any other patient, I spontaneously felt moved to say, "Catherine, if you ever find that you're afraid, just look for the light."

Catherine cheerfully replied, "Oh, I do!" Astonished and laughing, I questioned, "You do?"

"All the time," she said confidently. I remembered her daughters reporting that their mom had been seemingly far away for the last two days.

"Catherine, what does the light feel like?" I asked.

"It feels very warm ..." she said, as she smiled sweetly at me. "And it lets me know that there is nothing to worry about." Occasionally, in my work as a hospice nurse, I am blessed to witness transcendent moments such as this. Although some dying patients actually verbalize the things they are seeing, others seem to traverse a much quieter, more solitary, inward journey. Had I not commented about the light, I doubt that Catherine would have shared her inner experience with me. I decided to inquire further, "What is the light, Catherine?"

"For me or for you?" she asked precociously. Surprised at her response, I chuckled and said, "For you, of course!" Her eyes sparkled as she looked straight into mine. Catherine radiated a beautiful peace as she lovingly replied, "It's God's love for me!"

GIFF'S COMFORTING LIGHT

Penny Wigglesworth

My husband, Gifford Wigglesworth, had a twinkle in his eye that melted everyone. He was so full of love, but didn't like to show it publicly. Tall, handsome, and huggable, we called him the Big Bear. He loved our four children, ten grandchildren, and me unconditionally. We were married for forty-one wonderful years.

Giff had a very simplistic view of life. He believed that when a person is born, a candle is lit; when the person dies, the candle is blown out. Life was as simple as that. My views were markedly different than his. Belief in life after death continues to play a huge role in my volunteer work with hospice and the community. Since my husband's passing, I have been sent numerous signs that strongly reaffirm Giff's presence in my life.

My husband died unexpectedly in Naples, Florida, four months after his seventieth birthday celebration. In the middle of the night, he hadn't felt well, took an antacid for indigestion, and went back to bed. I asked if he was all right because his skin felt clammy. Giff reassured me that he was fine, and we both went back to sleep. The next morning, my husband woke me to tell me that he was feeling much better. I felt relieved. Then, ten minutes later, everything changed. I found myself calling 911 and doing CPR on my husband. Giff was gone so fast.

Although we were together when he died, his sudden death was so traumatic. Friends, neighbors, and one of our sons immediately surrounded me with their love and support. That evening after everyone left, I went upstairs to our bedroom. All alone, I climbed into bed, turned out the lights and started to cry. Just knowing I had to be strong for our four children, my tears accelerated into hyperventilation. Meditation could not calm me down. Suddenly, the bedside lamp next to me turned on all by itself. Instantly, I knew it was Giff! I could feel his comforting presence. Convinced he was with me, I was able to go right to sleep with the room now filled with his light.

The next morning, I felt a kiss on my cheek as I awoke. I thought to myself, *Oh Giff, don't wake me up now. I finally just got to sleep*...But then, I remembered everything that had happened. Despite all our efforts, my husband had died. I was stunned, shocked, and devastated by everything that had transpired. The following day, my son Gifford Jr. told me he had the most amazing dream of his father. In the dream, he had seen a huge computer screen with words written in capital letters on the screen. They said, "I'M OKAY. TELL EVERYBODY I SAID HI." Despite young Gifford's numerous efforts to teach his father otherwise, Giff always used the capital letter lock whenever he typed on the computer.

I returned to our winter home in Marblehead, Massachusetts, and relived his death over and over. Thoughts kept racing through my mind. Did I do enough? Did I do CPR right? Should I have taken Giff to the hospital when he talked about indigestion? Maybe he would still be alive today...Then, that night, I had a dream about Giff. Appearing a bit younger and without any gray hair, he was wearing a navy blue golf shirt and khaki pants. I started to cry frantically. "I couldn't save you. It's all my fault that you died." My husband looked directly into my eyes and said reassuringly, "It's not your fault. It was my time." That same night, I was awakened to the bedside lamp spontaneously turning on next to me. Once again feeling comforted, I said, "Thank you, Giff," turned off the light and went back to sleep.

The last time I felt the comfort of Giff's light happened later on my birthday, December 29, in Naples. This was the first time I had returned to the place where he died. Even though friends encircled me with their love and support, it felt too hard to stay. I began inwardly making plans to leave first thing in the morning. That night, as I looked up at the stars through our bedroom window, I struggled to get to sleep amidst the tears. One more time, the bedside lamp next to me suddenly turned on all by itself, exactly as it did on the night Giff died. Instantly, I felt so cradled by that warm light and the knowledge of Giff's presence. Feeling reassured, I remember thinking… *Of course, I can do this. He's always with me, no matter where I am.* I stayed for four more months.

I did have one other reassuring dream with Giff. I was standing at a party, and my husband was standing directly behind me. Giff was tall, dark, handsome, and young again. He was wearing a dark-colored suit with a tie. I asked, "What are you doing here, Giff? I thought you died." My husband replied, "We never die, Penny. Love never dies."

Penny Wigglesworth, a wife, mother, and grandmother, is the author of Penny Bear's Gift of Love. *As the founder of the all-volunteer, nonprofit Penny Bear™ Company and the Circle of Hope, Penny and numerous volunteers provide outreach to others in need.*

BEAMS OF LOVE

Martha A. Brine

⁓

And we are put on earth a little space
That we may learn to bear the beams of love.
—WILLIAM BLAKE

Shortly before 2 AM on December 23, 1995, the telephone rang at my seaside home north of Boston. The caller announced that my mother, Esther Brine, had passed away at the Abbott Nursing Home. Mom had spent the last three and a half years of her life ravaged by the steady progress of Alzheimer's disease. As her body traveled backwards in time, she began to lose capacities in the reverse order attained. Clear, insightful statements came less and less frequently. And, when they did come, they were often so searing in truth that I began to call them "Edicts from Esther." Inside her tangled brain, amidst the static of nonsensical chatter, the edicts were somehow able to emerge and deliver a clear, direct message for all present at their rendering.

As her disease steadily progressed, Mom no longer knew the names of those who loved her longest and best. She became the very thing she had foretold four years earlier when she said, "I feel as though my mind is trapped inside my body, unable to get out." When Mom's quality of life deteriorated beyond measure, our family made the difficult choice not to prolong her life unnecessarily; no extraordinary measures would be taken. Now, with the awakening phone call from the nursing home, all of these memories descended in a rush, heralding the second, more final death of my mother's physical body. The disease had obliterated the person I knew and loved. That had been the first cruel death. Now, physical death removed the last remnants of the shadow of her former self to which we clung.

As I sat in the darkness of my living room, I felt a profound sense of loss. Suddenly, I noticed a light repeatedly flashing on the wall behind me. I looked out the window in search of its source. Could it be from the blinking lights on my indoor Christmas tree reflecting on the window? No, I had switched the lights off several hours earlier before falling asleep and being awakened by the ring of the telephone. Was it a flashing light from a passing police cruiser coming up the hill outside my home that had pierced the blackness within? A look out the window revealed no such vehicle driving by.

However, the seascape vista from my second-floor flat on Ocean View Road revealed a flickering beam in the distance from a lighthouse twenty miles away on the south shore of Boston. Only a crystal clear night such as this could make it visible. I instantly sensed my mother's spirit with me in that flashing beacon, clearly reassuring me of her warmth and continued presence from another dimension; everything would be all right. The glowing light on the living room wall let me know Mom was still very much there for me. In the midst of my aloneness, it deeply warmed me with a real sense of comfort.

When the light of the day arrived that morning, my rational self questioned how a light so far away could have possibly reflected itself on an interior wall in my home from such a distance. Perhaps it was just a dream or the response of an overactive imagination in the wee hours of the morning. Surely there was no reasonable explanation for this sudden burst of brightness amidst the physical and emotional blackness of hearing the news of her death.

Days later, while at work, I received a poem entitled "Time and Tide," written especially for me on the occasion of my mother's death. It was composed by my colleague Jean Hodgin, an English faculty member, who made a point of marking important events at our college with her gift of meaningful verse. The lines were full of nautical imagery of the seagull soaring above the waves, the sound of the tidal roar soothing my sorrow, and the solace found in the wintry waves of memories washing over me.

Time … and Tide
I stood and watched a soaring bird
Caress the wind above the sea,
And wondered if she could have heard
The tears that welled inside of me.

As long I wandered on that strand
And let the soothing tidal roar
Efface the mourning mood at hand,
I knew my heart would ache no more.

There came a solace, dear relief,
Engendered by each wintry wave,
And in its wake, I knew no grief
For I had memories to save.

—JEAN HODGIN

In speaking with its author, I relayed how comforting and meaningful her words and seaside images had been. They were so much in keeping with my initial thoughts at the time of my mother's death. I shared with her about the blinking lighthouse and the comfort it had provided on that memorable night. I also mentioned how the Minot's Ledge Lighthouse could be seen flashing on cloudless nights from the Swampscott coastline.

My poet friend, who knew both the lighthouse and its call signal, asked if I knew what the one-four-three rhythmic blinks of its beacon meant. I wasn't aware that each lighthouse blinked its own signature code. I also didn't know the message sent out from that particular lighthouse. My friend revealed the coded message from the Minot's Ledge Lighthouse means "I love you!" Instantly, I knew that the flashes of light seen on that cold December night were indeed from my mom. Esther, the woman who gave me life and taught me the meaning of love, would always be there to light my way.

Several years later, the last full moon of the century happened to fall on the evening of December 22, 1999. On the next day, the fourth anniversary of my mother's death, the *Boston Globe* newspaper highlighted a magnificent color photo on its front page of the full moon behind yet another lighthouse, the Scituate Light. That photograph taken by Tom Herde is available through the *Boston Globe* store as one of its best and classic photographs. The description reads, "The last full moon of the century rises over Scituate Light. A rare alignment of perigee and winter solstice has not occurred since 1866."

Coincidentally, Minot's Ledge Light, the source of her first message, was built to replace Scituate Light in 1860. Although the Scituate Light structure remains preserved as a memorial to the past, its light was darkened seemingly forever once the Minot's Ledge Light was lit. My mother's "I love you" message came through loud and clear once again! This time, it came through a new medium where the picture was worth a thousand words—or, better yet, *three* priceless words from my mom.

A dozen years have passed since I received that arousing phone call announcing my mom's passing. I still live in that same place. I gaze out the same window that first revealed the vista and blinking light and provided so much comfort the night she left this earth. Over time, I have grown accustomed to not hearing any more edicts from Esther other than in the silence of my heart or in the sea of memories that her name and face evoke.

My mother always loved the ocean much more than the countryside or the mountains. It only seems appropriate that she selected lighthouses as her medium of choice. Mom's beams of love have surely guided me every step of the way. They are reminders of her ongoing presence in my life.

Yesterday, after having spent the past several weeks researching lighthouses, I stopped at the local post office to mail some letters. While standing in line, I happened to overhear a customer in front of me asking for the latest commemorative stamp. "Do you have any of those new lighthouse stamps?" she questioned. I couldn't believe my ears! I had never heard of a lighthouse stamp, much less seen one up close. I think it was Mom's razor-sharp way of letting me know that I had her stamp of approval for this story. Thank you, Mom. I love you, too.

Martha A. Brine, EdD, has been a public and private school educator and administrator in both Jamaica and the United States. As a member of a book club for over fifteen years, Martha enjoys reading, traveling, and writing prose and poetry.

The Final Gift

Mary Ellen Whalen

My dad and I always had a special bond. This bond deepened as he became more ill and frail in the later years of his life. The time we spent together during those final years brought the two of us to a place where we became quite comfortable discussing the subjects of dying and death. I sensed through my father's outer disguise of bravado that he had an inner fear of dying, as well as of the unknown. Fortunately, I was at a place in my own spiritual maturity where I felt confident that death was only a doorway to a place most people refer to as heaven.

Dad was a quiet and gentle man by nature. Never a deep conversationalist, he skated the surface of almost every subject he discussed his entire life until he entered this final phase. During this time, Dad actually encouraged me to share my view on what I considered to be a very peaceful and beautiful event, the crossing from this world into the next.

As I shared my thoughts and feelings, I observed that my father became visibly more comfortable about the whole idea of dying. It was during one of those profound moments of openness that I found the courage to invoke a promise from him.

"Dad?" I asked. "How about you coming back to visit me after you pass to let me know what it's like and how you're doing?" My father smirked at me, just as he always did whenever I said something or did something that he found particularly humorous.

"Okay," Dad agreed, as the two of us laughed together at such an unusual request.

A few years later, my eighty-three-year-old father was dying from liver failure and congestive heart failure in Peoria, Arizona. For several weeks, Dad lay quietly in his hospice bed, seemingly unaffected by all those around him. Other than kissing me hello and goodbye, my father did not want to eat, drink, or talk. I would quietly sit next to him in order to be a beacon of light, hope, faith, and love, as well as to spiritually comfort Dad during his last few days and hours.

It was during those quiet moments that my father unknowingly let me be privy to the most amazing time of my spiritual learning process. Even before he left this earth, Dad was already keeping his promise. With no prior knowledge or experience in this area, I witnessed a process that the dying individual goes through as he or she prepares to leave this world.

On Tuesday morning, May 6, 2003, I had arrived at the hospice house to visit my father. The home was surrounded by a tranquil desert setting and staffed by the most caring of individuals. Before entering my father's room, one of the visiting ministers stopped to tell me about something that had been written on my dad's chart by one of the night nurses. Around 4 AM, the nurse had found Dad reaching upward toward the ceiling with both his arms and eyes wide open. When she asked Dad if he was seeing someone, my father nodded yes, smiling.

Later, the same morning around 10:30 AM, I was sitting next to my father in his room. He suddenly lifted himself up in bed and looked toward his left. I questioned, "Dad, is there someone there?"

"Yes," he whispered.

"Do they want you to go?"

"Yes."

"Dad, do you want to go?"

"No." I reassured Dad that it was okay and not to be afraid.

The next day around 3 PM, I witnessed my dad looking upward and holding his two hands out in front of him in a cupped position, almost as if he were holding a cup. Then, Dad began to drink from his cupped hands. I closed my eyes and, to my wonder, saw a heavy, luminous, green liquid being poured down my father's throat as he drank. About ten years before, Dad's voice box had been surgically removed for cancer of the throat. I had the sense that whatever Dad was drinking was some sort of healing potion for his throat.

At 11 AM on the following day, a lovely scene was shown to me. As I sat quietly with my father with my eyes closed, I saw Dad in a beautiful European flower garden with a sparkling water fountain in the center. Close by was a beautiful limestone rotunda of ancient proportions and stature. Through the opening, lots of beautiful rays of bright white light were streaming outward. My dad was walking calmly around the outer perimeter of the garden looking inward toward the light. At that time, Dad made a conscious decision not to go into the light, but rather to continue walking around the outer courtyard.

Another scenario followed within seconds. I found myself looking at a Western town setting, similar to the setting in *Gunsmoke*, my dad's all-time favorite TV program. Dad was considering which path would be the best for him to take. My father was looking at a horse, as he was contemplating the possibility of riding off into the sunset. Then, Dad decided it would take too much effort to get on the horse, so he chose a horse-pulled buckboard with a bed in the back. My father climbed onto the buckboard and laid down to rest. I was sitting right next to Dad in this scenario, as the male driver for the buckboard began to drive away. Then, the vision ended; Dad had decided the buckboard ride was just too bumpy.

As I was looking out through the window in my father's hospice room, I was immediately brought into a third scenario and awareness. I noticed that his room was beginning to fill up with a brilliant white light that caused all physical elements in the room to fade away. I was suspended in time, but understood that I was being gifted with a rare insight into my father's spiritual journey. I very quickly became aware that the light I was being shown was the very same light that my father might choose when it was time for him to leave this earthly realm.

On the next day, the telephone rang while I was sitting next to Dad in his hospice room. I picked up the receiver, said hello, but heard no verbal response. Instead, what I heard was the sound of someone gasping for air. I called the receptionist to find out about the call that she had put through to my father's room. Strangely, even though she had been handling the switchboard at the time of the call, the receptionist assured me that she had not forwarded any calls to Dad during that time.

A little while later, around 4:15 PM, Dad suddenly sat straight up in bed with his eyes open and started communicating with someone above him. He looked down at his left wrist, the same place where his wristwatch had always been for decades. Although his watch was no longer there, Dad nodded yes, as if he were in agreement of the timing of whatever he was being asked. I closed my eyes and saw Dad's light body (soul) being lifted up out of his physical body from a lying position to a sitting position. My father's light body did not go all the way into the light, but rather it was returned back into his physical form.

The next morning around 2 AM, my father passed from this world very quietly, in the same gentle manner he had lived. It was Mother's Day, the only day during the year that Dad consistently sent a greeting card to me throughout my adult life. Dad bid his final earthly farewell that morning. How comforting for me to know that God welcomed my father into His light and love on Mother's Day. I wonder if my mother, who had died forty-four years earlier, was there to greet him.

Exactly two weeks later on Sunday morning, I saw my father one more time in a dream. Dad appeared in good health about twenty to thirty years younger and walking with a cane. My father smiled at me. I asked, "How are you, Dad?"

My father acknowledged my question with his familiar shoulder shrug and a small smile, as he was never one to give superlatives. I took this to mean that everything was okay. He appeared peaceful and somewhat happy. This was our only verbal exchange.

Then I touched Dad's shoulders to pull him close for a hug. My father felt warm, flabby, and kind of squishy. Suddenly, a large television screen appeared to my right in the room. On the screen and surrounded in a multitude of butterflies was a figure of a person waiting patiently and silently for my father. It was at that point that my dad went out of view, as did the person, the television screen, and the butterflies. I awoke remembering every detail of what we had shared and felt so comfortable with my father leaving.

I knew in my heart that Dad had come back to fulfill the promise he had made several years prior. This was my father's final spiritual gift to me. Thank you, Dad. I love you, too.

Mary Ellen Whalen has been blessed with success in business but prizes her personal relationships with family and friends the most. Her greatest life pleasure is spending time with her wonderful husband, their two grown sons, and two special little grandchildren.

PEACE

Elissa Al-Chokhachy

⌒

Tom was a sixty-year-old hospice patient whom I visited several times. He struggled with throat cancer, had a tracheostomy, and was constantly suctioning himself. Tom rarely slept, as he was afraid that he would drown in his own secretions. The head of his hospital bed was kept bolt upright, and he paced his room restlessly morning, noon, and night.

Tom struggled with neck pain that intensified during the lengthy dressing changes and treatments. His pain was managed with large amounts of morphine he took every one to two hours as needed. Because Tom had to be seen twice daily, several nurses visited him. The dressing changes were difficult, as Tom would repeatedly plead, "Don't do it. I can't take it. Please, just let me go."

During one of my visits about four weeks before Tom died, his brother told me that Tom was confused. When I questioned what had happened, his brother said, "Tom was talking about our dead father this morning. He said he was in the room with us." Interestingly, I found Tom very clear, lucid, and free of any confusion or hallucinations while visiting him.

Two weeks later, the nurse who visited Tom four times each weekend shared some interesting information. Because Tom's dressing changes were so heart wrenching, this nurse had noticed tension building up within her body prior to each visit. She found that meditating each morning for one hour in advance helped keep her emotionally balanced and centered. During her Saturday morning meditation that weekend, she witnessed an unusual burst of light and heat, significantly stronger and more intense than she had ever experienced before. She realized that something had shifted in her body. The anxiety over Tom's impending visit was gone, and she knew somehow that everything would be all right.

When the nurse arrived at Tom's house, she found him sitting in bed. "Come on in," Tom calmly beckoned. "I'm ready for you." His nurse was stunned, as she would normally have to coerce him into the bed in order to do the dressing change. This time, there were no attempts on Tom's part to prolong the inevitable. Also, he had stopped the constant pacing which normally psyched him into an overwhelming state of tension, anxiety, and worry. This was a totally different Tom. As the nurse looked at him, she noticed a huge beam of light radiating from him. She sat down next to Tom, held his hand, and listened as he enthusiastically relayed the morning's events.

At exactly the same time the nurse was meditating earlier that day, Tom had suddenly found himself immersed in a beautiful, indescribable light. His deceased father came to him and told him that they would be together soon, and he was not to worry; it would not be too much longer. Tom was so relaxed that he told jokes throughout the entire dressing change. He was excited to think that he would soon be reunited with his dad.

Later that day, Tom told his significant other that she needed to call everyone on the phone that morning to tell them what he had experienced. His significant other was quite upset with his request, so Tom made the phone calls himself. From then on, Tom never got out of bed. He no longer worried; he stopped incessantly suctioning himself. And, for the first time in years, Tom allowed himself to sleep. Within a week and a half, Tom died. His pain and suffering were finally over. Tom's dad—and the light—had brought him peace.

3

Visions

I saw them with my bodily eyes as clearly as I see you.
And when they departed, I used to weep
and wish they would take me with them.

—St. Joan of Arc

THE DYING WILL COMMONLY SPEAK of seeing deceased loved ones during the last few weeks of life, another example of near-death awareness. These visions erase the fear of death and pave the way for a peaceful transition; they also provide a comforting peace. Remarkably, bereaved individuals also describe life-changing visions of their deceased loved ones who have passed from this realm to the next. Seeing their loved ones appearing happy, healthy, young, and healed again provides tremendous hope and reassurance that life is eternal.

For My Dad, with Love

Marilyn Freeman

I love to remember summers in Maine with my family. Sun-bleached hay first bends flat, and then quickly tosses its seed heads about in a wild dance led by the northwest wind. Cloud shadows race across our blueberry fields and on up the ridge. Looking up into miles of blue sky, I have to squint at the bright sun playing hide-and-seek through white snowbanks of clouds. Two ancient elm trees wave their branches above my head in the wind, and the familiar cawing of the crows is quickly carried away by the gusts. An old worn piece of rope clothesline stretches between the barn wall and the rough trunk of one of the elms, the line empty except for a few weathered clothespins. There, through the propped-open side door of the barn, I can see the old red tractor, its hand-sharpened mowing blade nicked from hitting rocks hidden in clumps of sweet fern growing in the fields. The exhaust pipe is still a little crooked, and the worn seat is padded by Dad's old shirt. When I move inside the barn and breathe deeply, I can smell the scent of long-ago oil spills, barn boards, sun-ripened blueberries, and years of stored-away hay.

As I write this, I find I become more than an adult woman in her mid-sixties. I am the wife of a wonderful, loving man and blessed with a son (now almost forty) who shares a similar gift of integrity and focus with the grandfather he never knew. Yet, my mind also sees me as a teenager whose father died unexpectedly just weeks before my high school graduation. But mostly, while wandering among my memories, I am again a child of the summers spent at our blueberry farm in Maine. I am a daughter sitting with her father underneath the pine trees that scent the air along the dusty Cedar Swamp Road. We don't need to talk much as we chew on pieces of sweet grass and take turns whistling bird sounds and listening for the echoing answer of the song sparrow's call. Maybe all this is why Dad chose that familiar farm setting in which to reassure me that all was at peace with him after he died.

I graduated from high school a few short weeks following my father's sudden death from a heart attack in April 1964. Mom never let on how hard it must have been to gather both her energy and courage to speak with so many people she recognized at my graduation ceremony. When Dad died, my oldest brother was twenty-two and living at home; my other brother was twenty and serving out at sea on a Navy submarine. There was something numbing about our just making it through everyday routines of living without Dad. Remembering those difficult days, I now know how much pain his death brought Mom, and how she kept most of it from us so we wouldn't worry about her or how we all would live our lives without him. We three kids entered adulthood quickly that spring.

Every summer growing up, for as far as memory stretches itself, my parents, two brothers, a dog and cat, usually a grandparent, and I packed up six weeks' worth of living supplies and traveled to our family's blueberry farm about twenty miles northeast of Bangor, Maine. We three children spent hours hanging on the back of the old tractor as Dad showed us how to carefully mow the rough terrain in the fields. We learned how to rake, pitch, and store hay, and how to cut and spray the never-ending clumps of alder bushes—all of which continually threatened to take over the hard-earned berry crops.

Dad could only take a couple of weeks off and occasional weekends as vacation from his job as a chemical engineer back home in Massachusetts. When he did join us, most of his time was spent outside trying to keep the old homestead in working repair. I could hardly wait for my legs to get long enough to reach the gas and clutch pedals on the tractor. As he did in turn with all three of us children, Dad would let me sit in his lap and drive, while he patiently manned the pedals. I realize now how much more quickly he could have finished his work had he chosen not to teach me.

Whether standing on the back "hitch bar" of that old tractor or learning to drive it, I learned to love the play of light and shadows on the fields from the sun and clouds, and the way the wind would flatten the hay as we mowed in one direction, and stand it up when we returned in the other rows. Conversation between Dad and me wasn't possible over the clacking pulley-and-belt system that ran the cutting blade... but it wasn't necessary.

Before he left for the fields each morning, Dad usually wore a worn, wool plaid shirt against the dampness of the early-morning fog, and an old cap with a visor to shade his eyes from the sun's glare as the day wore on. That shirt became a seat pillow of sorts as the sun burned through the mists and the rising temperature forced Dad to remove it. I loved and respected the set of his jaw, the way he clamped his usually unlit pipe in his teeth or held it in his hand, and the squinting focus in his gaze as he worked hours on end.

And so it was, a couple of months or so following his death that spring in 1964 — the timing is hazy to me now — that my dad came to me to say goodbye and to let me know that everything was okay with him. Was it just a dream? I don't recall being asleep. Was it a vision? I'll probably never know for sure. But what I *do* know, with absolute certainty in both my mind and my heart, is that somehow I *clearly* saw myself back at the farm, standing by the clothesline on the little knoll that overlooks the widest, most windswept part of the blueberry fields that stretch in the direction of Great Pond Mountain. As the wind blew the clouds around and the sun burned down from the bluest sky I can ever remember, there, in the distance, halfway down the fields and silhouetted against the mountain ridge beyond the Cedar Swamp Road and the woods, was Dad on the old red tractor. The wind drowned out the idling sound of the engine as he stopped, stood up, and turned around to face back towards me. And there, pipe in hand as always and dressed in the same old plaid wool shirt, he took off his cap, smiled a wide, happy smile, and waved his arm back and forth to recognize that I was standing there...his un-ending reassurance gifted to me...and his goodbye completed.

So long for now, Dad; give Mom a big hug for me. And, Dad... thanks for everything. I love you.

Marilyn Freeman has been happily married to her best friend, Nick, for forty-three years. A lifelong resident of Marblehead, Massachusetts, and proud mother of their police lieutenant son, Matthew, Marilyn enjoys quietly helping people through her volunteer outreach at church and in their community.

TANIKA

Glenda Whiddon

———

I knew her as Tanni. At three years old, I had not mastered English well enough to pronounce "Tan-eek-kah." And, even though I am only able to see Tanni in dreams now, her gentle touch and soft song continue to echo deep within the river of my memories.

Tanni was my nurse. When I cried at night, she was there. When I was hungry, Tanni would hold me until my mother could bring me milk. When I was frightened or lonely, it was Tanni who comforted me and sang to me with a voice that surely came from the goddess of the earth herself. My mother and father made sure that Tanni was always with me. Each night before Tanni came in to stay with me, Momma would tell me stories of how Tanni used to be her nurse. She assured me that nothing bad would ever happen, as long as I trusted Tanni to take care of me, and as long as I did all the things that Tanni asked.

For the first three and a half years of my life, I can't remember ever feeling lost or alone. Unlike most children, I wasn't afraid of the dark. Instead, I welcomed it. For it was during the darkness each night that I would hear the slow creaking of Tanni's rocker and be able to listen to Tanni's stories about the children of her youth who played upon the prairies of the great Cherokee Nation.

When I turned four, my mother told me that Tanni would not be able to come as often. I remember I cried and cried until Tanni came that night and held me...and told me the story of Nochie, the Great Spirit who in the beginning, was both earth and sun. But because Nochie wanted a friend so badly, he decided to split himself into two pieces. When he did that, he gave up a part of himself. And, just like Nochie, Tanni told me that she, too, had given up a part of her life so that the two of us would never be separated, as long as one of us remembered the other.

I saw less and less of Tanni after that, but each time I did, I held her tighter than the time before. Even as a young child, I learned to understand the meaning of separation, loss, emptiness, and the inevitable grasp time has on all of us. I learned this lesson long ago and carried with me for the next forty years—or so I thought.

Then, something remarkable happened. Nine years ago, I was crying silently, as I held my dying mother's hand. Momma slowly opened her eyes, and I could tell she recognized me. My mother motioned for me to come close. As I did, Momma whispered a name I hadn't heard in a very long time—Tanika. I smiled, despite the ominous situation we both were facing. I couldn't help but smile, as that name had always brought me comfort. I held Momma's hand tighter and replied, "Momma, Tanika's not here." My mother pressed my hand to her breast and with the slightest of smiles said, ever so quietly, "Tanika has always been with you, and she has never been with you. Tanika is your spirit; Tanika has always been your spirit."

As I started to say something, memories suddenly began to flood my mind and thoughts…I realized in that moment that I had never actually seen Tanika in my bedroom at the *same* time as my mother or father…I had never heard the songs of the Indian children playing until *after* Momma had turned out the lights. And, I never felt safe at night until after the creaking of Tanika's rocker magically lulled me off to sleep. At first, I couldn't fully comprehend the depth of what Momma was saying. Then, I remembered…I remembered that Tanika was the name of my great-grandmother who had passed away *before* I was born. Tanika was a medicine woman. She was my childhood nurse, mentor, protector, and my great-grandmother. Tanika has always been with me and never been with me. Tanika is my spirit and has always been my spirit.

Glenda Whiddon has a deep passion for life and a love for knowledge instilled by her grandmother, a Native shaman. One of the most profound life lessons she learned from Momma was "knowledge is not always truth, but truth is always knowledge."

A Mom's Love Lives On

Karen Veronica Hurd

In my lifelong career as a second grade teacher, I have only once had the privilege of having three children from the same family in my class. In this particular situation, both parents were very involved in their children's education, especially their mother, Rose. If ever I needed a chaperone for a field trip, she was there. If I needed a room parent, Rose was there, too. She was a dedicated mother and supportive parent whom I could always count on.

When I had her eldest child as my student, I witnessed Rose's consistent involvement in her children's education. Two years later, I was privileged to have her second child in my class. At this point, Rose felt very comfortable with me. Whenever a parent was needed, she volunteered. However, also during this time period, Rose was diagnosed with cancer. Surgery was done posthaste for a brain tumor. With two hundred and fifty students enrolled in our school, we were fortunate to have an extremely supportive environment of children and families to assist Rose and her family.

Homemade meals were provided, and her children were carpooled to various activities. Just name it, and our school and community was there for this family in need. I felt privileged to be able to be there for Rose, as she had been there for me as a classroom volunteer. Her family continued on in their activities, and Rose continued to be present in her children's school.

I cherish the memories I have of Rose reading the first book in the *Harry Potter* series out loud to my students. We were all amazed at her strength and her ability to remain active in her children's education. Throughout that time, Rose was holding on to life for all that it was worth.

During the summer, Rose's family kept us updated by e-mail on her condition. We all knew that Rose's fight was coming to a close. When classes began in September, Rose was still hanging on and fighting for her life. I couldn't believe it when this remarkable woman attended our Open House. No longer able to stand, Rose came to see me in a wheelchair. As we hugged each other hello, we both knew that it was also our final goodbye. I did not weep when I heard the news that Rose had died. I was blessed to get to know her as a woman, a mom, a parent, and a friend. Who could ask for anything more? Rose's presence enriched our entire community. This dedicated mother touched the lives of so many. The following year, much to my surprise, Rose's third child was assigned to my classroom. I felt so honored to have an opportunity to help and teach her youngest daughter. In my heart, I knew I would take special care of this child.

During a read-aloud one beautiful autumn day, I chose a book on loss and grief in order to be able to initiate a classroom discussion on the subject with my students. Although I don't remember the title, when I completed reading the story, I looked up and saw Rose standing by the sink in my classroom. She was standing in the same place she always stood so many times before while checking in on her child. Rose looked healthy and vibrant, just as she did before becoming ill. I was so moved by her presence. This loving and dedicated mom was just checking in one more time, making sure that all was well with her child. In that moment, I knew in my heart that Rose's love for her children still lives on.

Karen Veronica Hurd is an elementary school teacher in Northampton, Massachusetts. Practicing Usui Reiki since 1989, she became a Reiki Master in 1999 and a Karuna Reiki Master in 2003.

A Promise Kept

Libby Potter

I was raised in a small New England town with liberal Protestant religious roots. My active youth group, which encouraged faith-based activities, significantly influenced my teenage years. Occasionally, I explored the topic of death with my paternal grandmother, who owned and operated a private nursing home in her house for more than forty years. One day, I happened to be visiting Grammy when two patients died within hours of each other. At fourteen years old, I observed from a distance the necessary procedures surrounding the care of deceased patients, but made sure to stay out of the way.

Later, after the patients had been transported to their respective funeral homes, Grammy and I talked about death. Calm and peaceful, Grammy explained that she wasn't afraid to die. She had lived a long life, worked hard, and most of her friends had already passed on. Whenever she sensed a patient was dying, Grammy made sure that she or one of her nurses stayed with the patient until they passed. Repeatedly, she experienced a great sense of peace surrounding the death. Although I felt uncertain about the concept of death, I never forgot the calmness and peace in Grammy's face and voice as she spoke.

In the late 1960s, mandatory state laws required all nursing homes be brought up to code with the installation of in-house sprinkler systems and fire escapes. Not only would changes be costly, it broke Grammy's heart to think of her beautiful home being ripped apart in order to install the necessary piping in the ceilings and walls. Grammy had worked hard to set up a home environment for the elderly, with oriental carpets on almost every floor and beautiful paintings and drapes on the walls and windows. As a result, Grammy made the decision to convert her private nursing home to a boarding house. As patients died, they were replaced with live-in boarders. By the summer of 1970, the professional nursing staff was gone, with only a cook and laundry attendant remaining. Grammy's nursing home became fully operational as a boarding house for elderly women.

The following summer, Grammy began experiencing her own health problems. She was hospitalized after a heart attack, and while in the cardiac care unit, Grammy had to be resuscitated after a second myocardial infarction. Coincidently, I was working in the outpatient department of the same hospital and felt fortunate to be able to visit her every day. When Grammy told me that she wished she had not been resuscitated, I felt frightened. Yet at the same time, I didn't want my Grammy to be in any pain.

Fortunately, Grammy recuperated and was well enough to be discharged home. During one of our subsequent conversations, I blurted out a question that even surprised me. "Grammy, after you die, if it's at all possible, would you *please* let me know that you're safe?" Grammy was initially taken aback by my question, but then smiled. She chuckled and said, "If I can, I will." All the members of my family took turns staying with Grammy. She died a couple of months later in September of 1971 during a brief hospital stay at the age of seventy-eight. I was nineteen years old.

About four weeks later, I happened to be alone in her twenty-five-room home that had served both family and numerous patients over the years. As I walked through the large, vacant dining room into the kitchen and stepped into the back entryway, I had a distinct feeling that someone else was in the kitchen. The feeling was warm, strong, and safe. I stopped in the doorway and slowly turned around toward the pantry. There, standing in the pantry doorway nearly twenty feet away, was Grammy! She was wearing a multicolored, floral full apron on top of her pink-and-white striped seersucker day dress. Amazingly, I could also see the doorjamb and pantry directly behind her. Grammy was translucent! She was smiling, and I could feel a penetrating peace and calm in the room. I smiled back. As I began to speak, the vision faded. In a matter of three seconds, Grammy entirely disappeared. I was thrilled! Grammy had kept her promise. I knew that my Grammy was safe.

Twenty years passed before I felt safe enough to share this story with anyone. It happened that my brother, Richard, and I had been talking about our deceased father. Richard had never doubted the existence of life after death, but had been having an extremely hard time since our father died in 1988. Somehow, the conversation led into a discussion of Grammy. When I shared my story about Grammy's appearance, I was surprised by his response. Richard recalled a telephone call he'd received a few months after Grammy died. Her house had been sold, and the new owner had telephoned with a peculiar request. "Richard," he said. "*Come get your grandmother!*" As it turned out, the new owner had been feeling her presence ever since he had moved into the house. Not only did I have an experience that let me know Grammy was all right, the new owner of her house did, too!

Libby Potter, a nutritional microscopist, currently works with a new concept of health and wholeness based on the Ph Miracle research. As a result of numerous mystical experiences, Libby enthusiastically embraces eternal life awareness and communication from beyond the veil.

I'm Still Missing You

Maryjane W. Seeley

Jesse Robert Seeley, Jr. was a fun, lovable guy. He was my soulmate. We were married for thirty-four years. A former Marine, my husband was capable of doing just about anything. Jesse was fifty-seven years old when he passed away from congestive heart failure. My mother died seven months later. I can't begin to describe the heartache and loneliness that I felt from their combined losses. However, two weeks later, the most amazing thing happened. My husband and my mother came to visit me!

I was sitting out on the porch around 11 PM the first week of February 2003. Strings of Christmas lights were providing a soft, pretty light as they outlined the porch windows and doorways. Sitting in my usual corner seat in front of the rectangular wooden table, I was daydreaming, watching the cars go by and missing the two of them. My left hand and arm were holding my head up, supported by the table in front of me. I was beginning to feel really tired, so I laid my forehead on top of my crossed arms to rest for a few moments.

All of a sudden, I heard voices faintly behind me, and the sounds got closer. I thought to myself, *I know darn well the kids aren't here...* By now, I was sitting up in my chair, but I was not feeling fully awake. Just as I turned around to see who was there, I recognized their voices and couldn't believe my eyes. There in front of me was my husband... and my mother! Jesse said, "Sweetheart, you need to go back and get into bed. Hanging your legs down like that, you know what it does to your back." My mother chimed in with the same message, and then said, "Hi sweetheart."

"Mom! Jesse! I've missed you guys so much!" I was so excited to see them both. Before she died, my mother was literally hunched over, barely able to walk. Now, she strolled onto the porch wearing a yellowy-gold caftan and walked very tall and straight. She also looked about fifteen years younger. Jesse looked exactly the same as he did when he died, with his big, beautiful blue eyes and his balding head. My husband was wearing a brand-new pair of dark blue jeans and his favorite green, blue, and white plaid flannel shirt. They both looked extremely healthy and were smiling at me. Mom looked happier than I'd seen her in years.

Jesse came around to my left to where he normally sat. My mother stood right next to me on my right. In awe, I kept looking back and forth at the two of them. I was so happy! "I'm so glad you're back!" I said. "I've missed you so much! I love you guys. *I'm so glad you are back!*"

Then, the two of them just disappeared right in front of me. I cried tears of joy. The intense love that I felt from the two of them during that experience was incredible. I was happy for them, but at the same time, I wanted them back. I desperately missed the two of them. Seeing Jesse and Mom one more time made me want to see them even more.

I had been depressed and lonely for months. I wanted to be with my husband so much that I had actually been praying to die. About three or four months ago during my nightly prayer time, I heard a message from God. He told me it wasn't my time and to stop praying for my life to end. Because I had been trapped in my own grief and despair, I hadn't been able to share in the special moments with our kids. I was missing out on them. I knew Jesse wouldn't want me to live like that either. On that night, for some reason, the message sunk in. And, for the past few months, I have been happier than ever since he died. It's been five long years, and I can finally laugh; I can find humor in things again. In the past, I had always lived for my children. Now, I have it all back. They are my everything.

Over the years, my daughter's best friend, Trudy, frequently visited us. She lived with us one summer and even called us Mom and Dad. After Jesse died, my husband came to Trudy in a dream. He was dressed in his Marine Corps uniform. Jesse told her that *everything was going to be okay now.* That visit helped Trudy to come to resolution about his death; it helped me as well.

I still miss Jesse terribly. Sometimes, I have dreams of him. In one dream, we were holding each other on the couch out on the porch, which we never did in real life. It was so vivid and clear; it felt so wonderful. Every night, I tell my husband that I love him and that I miss him still. There is no one else. I look forward to the day when we are finally together again.

Maryjane W. Seeley, LPN, is a mother of three daughters and retired nurse who assisted on the development committee for the subacute unit of Exeter Health Care in Exeter, New Hampshire. Janey's family and her husband mean everything to her.

I Remember Mama

Anne Bruno

⌐────────⌐

While visiting my mother on Mother's Day in 1989, I noticed a beautiful glow radiating from her. Having worked in the medical profession for years, I recognized this glow as one I had seen on several patients facing imminent death. I reflected on this new awareness, wondering if, on some level, Mom was preparing for her own death. At the end of the visit, I asked my twin eleven-year-old daughters if they noticed anything different about Nana. They both said in unison, "She was looking really pretty!" This confirmed my suspicions, and I began emotionally preparing for my mother's death.

Mom was seventy-two years old. Basically, she was healthy, although she had survived five heart attacks over the years. My mother was high-strung, very private, and borderline antisocial. She liked to keep to herself and maintained only minimal contact with the outside world. When she did speak, though, Mom was an embellisher. She felt a great deal of pride in the little things her grandchildren accomplished. If Johnny made the honor roll, Mom would proudly boast, "Did you hear? Johnny made straight A's this quarter!" She was also very proud of her home, and she kept it sparkling clean and well-organized.

Two weeks after Mother's day, Mom was hospitalized. Our family was told, "It doesn't look good." She probably wouldn't survive the night. We telephoned the priest, and my mother received her last rites. On May 20, 1989, surrounded by her family, Mom died quietly. Although I had left the hospital just minutes before her death, I was grateful that Mom had a good death, one that was mercifully quick, with minimal suffering.

One afternoon about two weeks later, I was standing alone in my house when I experienced a state very difficult to describe. I was neither awake nor asleep. Without apparent reason, my surroundings disappeared, and I found myself in a semi-trance. I felt as if I had been lifted up into the sky, or perhaps, transported into a different dimension. There, in front of me, was my mother! She was wearing the brightest white floor-length gown I have ever seen. The quality of the whiteness was extraordinary. It was so clean and brilliant, bright white, similar to the sunshine glistening off freshly laden snow on a bright, sunny day.

"Wow!" I remember thinking to myself. "Mom, look how bright you are!" Mom wasn't really standing, but rather hovering, when I noticed that my twin girls had appeared next to her in the vision. She gave each of them the biggest hug, squeezing them ever so tightly. Then, she turned to me, smiled sweetly, and said, "Everything's okay." Mom waved her right hand and bade her final farewell with a simple, "Bye." In her glistening white gown, my mother floated backwards. I watched her slowly fade away, like the ocean tide rolling out. I hadn't been with my mom at the actual moment of her death. I think that's why she came to say goodbye.

Whenever I think of this experience, I get all teary-eyed and over-whelmed with the feeling, "Wow! She's all right!" I am filled with amazement that Mom and all the others who have gone on are really okay . . . and that someday . . . I too, will be fine when it's my turn to go.

Anne Bruno, LPN, a retired nursing home and VNA nurse, recently completed her family genealogy dating back to 1690. Occasionally, Anne is gifted with a memorable experience after visiting the grave of a deceased relative.

Brilliant in Sepia

Denise Kahn

~

Our host drove us out to Coyoacán, a lovely little suburb of Mexico City. Two of my friends were with me. We visited the center of town, where the architecture reminded me of Spain. Huge clusters of multi-colored bougainvilleas decorated rustic houses and whitewashed walls, as fruit and vegetable markets deliciously filled our senses. I remembered how much Dad loved Mexico and its people, and I was quickly following in his footsteps. He would have enjoyed this evening promenade with its energy, smells, and especially the music that filtered out of every other cantina. I still picture him coming home from work, turning on the record player, and putting on his favorite Mexican singer friend, Tito Guízar, with his velvet voice. He would grab my mother and dance an amazing rumba, mambo, or cha-cha right there in the living room. Young me was fiercely proud, as Mom and Dad always put on a delightful impromptu show.

The atmosphere in the main plaza was light and happy, the weather balmy and perfect. It was a Saturday night early in November, just a couple of days after the Festival of the Dead, a glorious fiesta honoring those who have passed away. During this celebratory festival, Mexican families and friends honor the deceased by going to the cemetery and having a picnic right on top of the tomb, tablecloth and all, with the departed loved one's favorite foods and music, amidst dancing and laughter.

My friends had flown with me to Mexico City. I was putting the last touches on a book I had just finished translating for its author, our host, from Spanish to French. As a thank-you, the three of us had been invited to stay a few extra days and visit some local sites. Bells rang out from a small church in the middle of the square. We decided to go in. Our host opted for a cantina. The house of worship was packed. The three of us lit candles, squeezed ourselves onto a wooden bench, and I said a prayer for Dad. I so wished he could have been there, right next to me, enjoying this land and its people.

We were the only *güeritas,* an endearing Mexican term for light-skinned gals. Everyone was cordial and gracious, and we were each handed a red rose. We listened to the organ playing in the background. The woman on the keys had a lovely voice, and all the people singing in the church made up a fantastic choir. I relished the moment, as I come from a long line of concert pianists, opera singers, and music. I was in heaven.

About halfway through the mass, as I was taking in all the details of the church, the locals, the décor of flowers, and the altar, I noticed a huge cross in the front of the church with a wooden sculpture of Christ attached to it. The organ player had stopped playing, and the priest was talking. But, for some reason, I couldn't hear the clergyman...I was still hearing music... *Where was it coming from?* I couldn't figure it out. It became apparent to me that I was the only one hearing this divine melody.

As I was looking toward the front, my eye caught a sepia-colored shadow forming on the right next to the Christ. It grew larger and became the actual size of the cross! *What was this?* I looked around. No one else seemed to notice. Was I the only one seeing this growing shadowy figure? Was I losing it?

I closed my eyes and felt an amazing warm and *loving* glow throughout my body. I kept my eyes closed a few minutes longer, torn between opening them and not. If I did, I worried that the exquisite feeling would go away, and I never wanted it to leave. I decided to gamble. I opened my lids—and gasped! There he stood, bigger than life, bigger than even the Christ on the cross—brilliant and glowing inside the sepia cloud was Dad! The translucent, brownish hues reminded me of an old photograph. I kept staring. I had never seen him like this. He looked about twenty-five, built strong like a boxer, with thick waves of very blond hair. He was barefoot, wearing a casual shirt and shorts, one foot propped on the barrier behind him on what looked like a pier with the ocean flowing below; he looked very much at ease. Every little girl thinks *her* dad is the best-looking man in the world; young Dad was confirming this. Here was this gorgeous guy who looked very much like John Wayne—tall, handsome, athletic, and with a grin that had always made my heart smile. His eyes looked at me adoringly, and even though I was looking back at them through the sepia hues, their baby-blue color was unmistakable.

The night at the hospital when Dad finally succumbed to a devastating illness, a saying of St. Francis de Sales flowed into my head: *"There is nothing stronger than a gentle man, and nothing more gentle than a strong man."* That was Dad. Everything he did was with the greatest, most gentle love and finesse. He was my statue. I looked up to him, adored him, and respected him. He was a father every child would have been blessed to have. And now, here he was, bigger than life itself, seemingly alive and smiling. Dad was talking to me, communicating from the other side! His lips were moving, yet the smile never left his face. He wanted me to know how very proud he was of me in what I had accomplished so far in life, and that I was embarking on my mission to make this world a better place. Dad gave me one last smile, winked, and reminded me that he would always be with me. Then, he faded away, along with the brilliant sepia cloud. What a blessing, what a joy to be with him once again.

I suddenly realized the mass was over, and the melody I had been hearing stopped. My friends and the parishioners were trickling out of the church. I moved with the crowd. Once outside, I looked up at the ebony sky. Millions of stars winked at me, and I wondered which one Dad was sitting on, smiling from our little tête-à-tête. I hollered internally at the sky, *Give me a sign, Dad, some sort of confirmation.* And he did. For no reason whatsoever, and with not a cloud in the sky, it started to drizzle. So did my eyes.

Denise Kahn, mother of a Marine, born in France to an American father and Greek mother, speaks six languages fluently. At work, she assists travelers on a major European airline and also enjoys writing, travel, music, and good friends.

LITTLE GRANDMA

Julie Evans

One afternoon about two weeks after my mom passed away, I was driving home with my two-year-old son, Bryce, and my nine-month-old daughter, MaryKate. Bryce fell asleep during the car ride. Once we arrived home, I picked my young son up, carried him inside the house, and laid him down on the couch. Slightly awakened, he was facing the back of the couch, resting quietly.

About a half-hour later, Bryce sat up and told me that he had just seen Grandma. I asked him if he'd had a dream about her. "No," he replied. "She was standing on the couch. Grandma said, 'I love you, Bryce.'"

His voice rose as he continued, "It was *little* Grandma!" Bryce made a point of emphasizing how small she was by showing me with his thumb and pointer finger her actual size. I asked Bryce if Grandma had said anything else. He said, "No, that was all." Bryce was two months away from his third birthday and knew my mother well. When Bryce told me so matter-of-factly that he had seen his grandma, I thanked my mother for coming to him.

To this day, I wish Mom would show up while I am on the couch, or in the kitchen, or lying in bed, to say she loves me. I know she does. She told me often in the past she did. I am thankful Bryce was able to have that experience. Although Bryce no longer remembers it, I tell him the story every once in a while; I remember it well. I will always be comforted to think of the time when *little* Grandma showed up to tell my son she still loves him.

Julie Anne Evans, wife of Brad and mother of Bryce, MaryKate, and Brody, works as a rehabilitation therapist at the Atascadero State Hospital. Julie and her husband volunteer often as coaches for their children's sports activities and enjoy camping with their family.

APRIL FOOLS

Carol Costello

I'll never forget the day when my pragmatic, self-reliant, resilient, and supremely rational father confided to me that he had seen my deceased mother the day before. It was April 2, 2003, and I assumed my father, who claims no faith in the supernatural, would provide a plausible explanation for my mother's appearance. Although, like my father, I don't follow any organized religion, I do attempt to pay attention to my spiritual self. Somehow, his words did not shock me; I was surprisingly unsurprised.

The best mother on earth, Mama had died two years earlier on a cold December evening. Her eleven-year-long battle with Alzheimer's disease had left her bedridden for the last three. Seemingly overnight, the loving mother that I had known and cherished as a young woman became trapped and lost in realities sometimes horrific, sometimes mellow, and totally unfathomable. Gone were the days of Mama's endless warmth, her teasing, playful ways, and the endless April Fools pranks for which she was notoriously known. A tenuous and difficult situation for all, my most persistent and steadfast father managed to lovingly care for Mom at home throughout all the years of her illness.

I stood waiting for him to explain what he had seen. When he didn't continue on his own, I asked quizzically, "How did she look?"

Dad said softly and calmly, "Beautiful. She looked *really* beautiful." "Beautiful" was not a word common in my father's vernacular. Years before, when I had asked how Mom had looked to him after four years of courtship and fifty-two years of marriage, he answered, "The same." My mother's appearance had drastically changed, especially in the last ten years of her life, yet, my father continued, "She never changed in my eyes."

"Beautiful? Really?" I was amazed.

"Yes," he replied, as he went on to describe what had happened. "I was sitting here at the kitchen table, as I always do. I had been dozing. I looked up, and she was there, where you are now, standing across the table from me and looking at me!"

Forcing my logical self into posture, I questioned, "Were you still asleep, do you think?"

"No," he stated assuredly and slowly continued, "I asked her, 'Sarah, what are you doing here?' And then, she was gone."

"This happened yesterday? Are you sure, Dad? Yesterday?" My father nodded affirmatively. I waited a moment, as I thought about it, and then laughed out loud. "Well, Dad, she got you again!"

"What do you mean?"

"Yesterday was April first, Mom's favorite day!" I reminded him. "It was her chance every year to trick you and trip you up! She got you yearly and delighted in her mastery!"

He admitted, chuckling, "You're right! She always used to fool me with some silly prank each year."

Hoping he might share some funny memories with me, I asked, "What sort of prank would she pull, Dad?"

"Oh, I don't remember, really... just something foolish." But, I imagined a scenario in my mind similar to what I had remembered hearing in the past with my mother shaking my father in bed early in the morning on April Fools' Day saying, "Joe, Joe, are you awake? We overslept! It's nine o'clock. Wake up!"

My unsuspecting, time-controlled Dad, who never needed an alarm clock, would awaken in a start, hurriedly roll over, and rustle through the tangled sheets only to check the clock and discover that it was 7 AM, his normal wake-up time. Meanwhile, Mom would announce, grinning, "April fools!" And, as soon as Dad saw the real time, Mom would erupt into a fit of mischievous, contagious laughter, because once again, she had successfully fooled her very smart and much-too-serious husband. I loved her resounding laugh, those memorable April Fools pranks, and the joy, laughter, and love that my mother brought into our lives for so many years.

Dad, I don't know if your eighty-four-year-old body laden with drugs for heart disease, diabetes, and insomnia affected your vision. I don't know if visions are a sign of insanity, of drugs, or of God. Perhaps, it really was Mom who had come to play one final April Fools joke when you least expected it, after she was gone. But what I do know is that somewhere in my being on the day you shared with me that you had seen her, I believed you. And I know I was happy for you, awed, and a bit envious that Mama had come to you and not me.

Carol Costello, MA, teaches English, Spanish, and ESL at North Shore Community College. Married to Walter for thirty-eight years, she is the proud mother of Sarah and Elaina and the proud grandmother of Anthony, Chloe, and twins Eve and Elle.

DAD AT THE DRIVE-IN

Susan Beetem

My father, Max, was my idol. He was a strong, muscular, five-foot-five man with thinning salt-and-pepper hair and a mustache. Dad's skin was always tanned because he loved to be outdoors. I loved spending time with him in his workshop or out in the yard while he tended to his many fruit trees. My father was an engineer and very talented in his own creative, artistic way. Dad was always making things for me, from jewelry to furniture to play equipment to even clothes. I would tell him what I wanted; Dad would whip up a pattern and sew it for me. All I had to do was choose the material.

I was the youngest of four. The older three children were from my father's first marriage. They were eighteen to twenty-two years older than I. When I was born, my older siblings already had babies and toddlers of their own. Needless to say, my nieces, nephews, and I all grew up together.

My sister and brothers were always pointing out that, when they were growing up, they certainly weren't spoiled like me. Back then, Dad was working full-time days and going to school nights studying to become an engineer. He didn't have the time or the money to spoil them. However, he thoroughly enjoyed spoiling his grandchildren. He spent lots of time with all of us—playing, teaching, motivating us to do well in school, go to college, and become people we would be proud to be.

Just a few days short of my eighteenth birthday, my father died of a stroke on January 27, 1970. He'd had a few mini strokes in the past but had always recovered. I was a senior in high school at the time. The whole school, especially my classmates and close friends, were very supportive. It was so hard on me, as I remember watching my father's condition worsen over a period of a few weeks. Mom and I got the call from the hospital late that night—Dad was gone. I couldn't believe it. I couldn't believe I would never hear his voice or see his face again.

A few months later, I was at a drive-in movie with my boyfriend and some other friends. We were sitting in the car waiting for it to get dark, laughing and joking. I was staring at the screen only half engaged in the conversation, when suddenly I saw my father's face. He was huge! His face took up the whole screen. Dad was smiling at me! It was the same ear-to-ear grin he would always smile when he was very proud of me. His face remained there on the screen for maybe thirty seconds or so, and then it slowly faded away. I didn't dare mention what I'd just seen to anyone in the car, because I was sure they'd think I'd lost it. Besides, I was in denial myself—I couldn't possibly have seen my dad!

That was the first experience I'd ever had. Half doubting it and not fully understanding what I'd seen, I spent the next few years telling myself that I didn't really see Dad on that screen. But the fact is, I did. I know that now. I was fully awake and had all my senses about me. Yes, I *did* see my father on that screen. He was there, showing me one more time how proud he was of me!

Susan Beetem, RN, an emergency and operating room nurse for over thirty years, raised two children, Max and Stef, with her husband, Jeff, in the foothills of Albuquerque, New Mexico. The luckiest mom in the world, Sue adores her children and special friends.

4

Smells

Smell is a potent wizard that transports you across thousands of miles and all the years you have lived.
—HELEN KELLER

DURING THE LAST FEW DAYS of life, the dying occasionally tell us that they smell roses, beautiful bouquets, and occasionally, perfumes. Smells trigger memories long forgotten. Oftentimes, people are associated with particular fragrances, such as perfumes, colognes, and aftershaves. Still others are associated with the aromas of things they enjoy. How does one explain the unexpected fragrance of roses on a beach when there are no roses around? How does one explain the smell of food cooking when there is no one in the kitchen? When the identifying scent of a deceased loved one spontaneously occurs, it provides loving reassurance that we are never alone.

Morning Toast

Libby Potter

———

Jake was the son of a ship builder and the ninth of ten children born in the late 1800s. His mother died shortly after the birth of her youngest child, leaving the older siblings with the responsibilities of the home and younger children. Their father passed on when Jake was twelve or thirteen. Jake was forced to leave school and move a considerable distance with his siblings to join their older brothers. He began working in a clothing mill which eventually became the family business, and Jake ran it as his own.

Remembering his early childhood years living near the ocean, Jake purchased waterfront property at the age of thirty-seven in the remote seacoast town of Scituate, Massachusetts. He recalled what he had learned in his younger years about tides, storms, southern exposure, and northern protection. When he chose the property, he placed his house accordingly.

Jake continued to live and work in the city, gradually building his waterfront home in his spare time. He married Molly in his mid-forties, and together, they raised three children. At age sixty, Jake sold the clothing mill and retired with his wife and children to their waterfront home. Jake and Molly lived self sufficiently in their home for nearly thirty more years. They took great pride in managing the gardens, fruit trees, and lawns, and enjoyed fixing and puttering around their house.

I knew Jake during the last ten years of his life. As he had completed only eight years of schooling, he felt blessed and modestly pleased with his life accomplishments. In the final two years of his life, Jake's family knew he was beginning to fail. He experienced significant weight loss, fluid in his lungs, and was hospitalized for evaluation and treatment. Many times over the years, Jake made his wish known that he did not want any life-support measures or hospitalizations. Both he and Molly were convinced that when people went into the hospital, they rarely came out. The hospital was a place to die without dignity. Jake was astonished when he actually returned home from the hospital the two times that he went.

Over the course of the last year and a half, Jake lost nearly sixty pounds while receiving regular chemotherapy treatments. Though the word "cancer" was never spoken in my presence, I feel comfortable assuming that Jake had some form of the disease. Molly wanted to choose a burial site with her husband, but Jake refused. When questioned why, his response was chilling: During World War I, there was a plague that killed many young men where he was serving. His job was to dig graves for the dead. At one point, he was instructed to dig his own grave to ensure a place for himself, since he had caught the fever. Obviously, Jake survived the plague, yet swore he would never again choose his resting place.

After he transitioned into retirement, Jake's morning routine was to get up around 4:30 AM and prepare toast for breakfast. Afterwards, he would begin his chores or projects for the day, return inside to puff his pipe, and then share breakfast with Molly. In the last year of his life, Jake had entirely stopped smoking his pipes and cigars. He often commented that he wished he had never smoked at all. The complications he faced at that time erased all the pleasure and status that he once had derived from this luxury.

Splitting wood several times a week was his ongoing exercise. On the day that Jake passed, he had a mission to reassemble a table saw that had been taken apart nearly a year and a half before. He felt that no one else would know where all the parts were. Although he was thin and frail, this proud man refused my help that morning. Jake completed the task by mid-afternoon, walked back to the house, had a light supper, and went to bed at 6 PM. This was unheard of. He died very quietly while talking to Molly around midnight that night.

Nearly nine months later, I visited for the weekend and woke up at 4:30 AM to the smell of toast. I assumed that Molly was downstairs in the kitchen. When I finally got up around 7:30 AM, Molly was still in her bedroom. I dressed, went downstairs, and waited for Molly. As she entered the kitchen, she was wearing her blue full-length velour bathrobe and slippers. When I asked if Molly had been downstairs earlier that day to have some toast, she smiled and motioned for me to come closer. "It's Jake," she whispered, letting me in on her secret. "I smell his toast nearly *every* morning. When I'm dressing and making my bed, I often smell his pipe smoke, too." Smiling, feeling a sense of contentment, she said, "I know he is still with me. I speak with him every day."

EAGLES AND ROSES FROM DAD

Candice M. Sanderson

I moved from Paducah, Kentucky, to Naples, Florida, in the early '90s. My first walk on the beach at Park Shore was breathtaking. The beach, right on the Gulf of Mexico, was beautiful. My twenty-one-year-old son, Phil, and my eight-year-old daughter, Cassie, ran ahead of me, racing to see who could reach Doctor's Pass first.

Before long, my children rushed back to tell me they'd just seen a bald eagle land right in front of them on the beach. I immediately thought of my father, their grandfather, Corbin Meriwether. Dad had such a great love for eagles. I remember all the times he would take my sisters and me to Lake Barkley State Resort, right outside Cadiz, Kentucky, for organized eagle hikes. For hours, we would traipse through the frozen wilderness during the bitterly cold month of February in the hopes of spotting an eagle's nest. And, if we were lucky and not frozen solid by the time we got there, we would get a brief glimpse of an eagle soaring overhead.

As Phil and Cassie breathlessly described their eagle sighting, I immediately thought of my father. If only Dad could have been with us at that moment to be able to see the eagle up close... no snow, no ice, no hours of hiking... right here, right now!

Since that first experience on the beach, I've tried to make beach walking a part of my daily routine. On one occasion, I happened to notice the smell of roses while walking in the sand along the water's edge. The aroma was so intense, as if the entire gulf was filled with thousands of roses. I decided to walk inland and away from the shoreline to try to find where the roses were located. I must have walked at least a quarter of a mile, combing the area while still smelling them. For some reason, I wasn't able to find their elusive source.

A few weeks later, I was walking along the same beach when I smelled the fragrance of roses again. What a vibrant, alluring scent, but … where was it coming from? Just as I had done before, I searched the entire area from the shoreline inland, but I still couldn't locate those roses. The same peculiar and inexplicable event happened a dozen or more times after that.

One evening during February of 1998, I was feeling sad and lonely. My son had graduated from college and was living in Nashville, Tennessee. My daughter had stayed overnight with a friend. I felt all alone and missed my children. I missed my husband, who had died of cancer in 1987, and I sorely missed my father, who had passed away in 1990. I began crying and begging for a sign from my husband and my dad. I needed to know that they were still around.

After fifteen or twenty minutes of intense crying, I was both physically and emotionally drained. I pulled myself together and slowly got up. I walked into Cassie's bedroom, searching for an item I had recently misplaced. I immediately stopped in my tracks. There, lying on the floor, were two photographs. How could this have happened? Where did they come from? I had just been in my daughter's room not thirty minutes before, and there was nothing lying on her floor!

I slowly approached the photographs and picked them up. One was a family photo taken fifteen years prior, and the other was even older … it was a photograph of a single red rose. Thoughts raced through my mind. It took a few moments to make the rose connection. Then, I remembered … I remembered the red rose in the photograph was one of my father's experimental roses that he had raised back in Paducah, Kentucky!

Annually, Dad devoted a small corner of his flower garden to raising several varieties of experimental roses, each beautiful and unique. My father always planted his roses in a protected area, tucked away in the corner of the garden close to the front door of the house where we grew up. Occasionally, when I returned home and entered the front door, I would be greeted with their fragrant and luscious aroma, a very special welcome, indeed.

I smiled as I looked at the photograph of the single red rose, reliving the memories of all my father's rose gardens throughout the years. Suddenly, images of being on the beach and repeatedly smelling fragrant roses came back in a flash; I had an epiphany! Of course, it had been Dad all along! He had been trying to tell me he was still with me. Why hadn't I thought of it before? Each time I'd smelled those mysterious roses, I had always left the beach mystified, never being able to explain what had happened. The mystery had been solved and finally, everything made sense. It was my father letting me know he was still by my side.

Once I made the rose connection, I looked again at the two photographs in my hand. The second photo was a family picture with my husband, father, son, and me. I looked at my husband's face and my father's face in this fifteen-year-old photograph. Both appeared to be looking straight at me and smiling. I felt such a sense of peace. Stillness and tranquility washed over me as I gazed into their eyes. I could actually feel in my heart that both my husband and father were telling me that they were with me in spirit and always had been.

I felt so happy and so uplifted. I knew that my prayers had been answered. I walked out of the room and, for some odd reason, went directly into my bedroom to a large picture hanging on the wall. Even though I had lived in the apartment for over five years and had moved this framed picture multiple times to various locations, I had never taken the time to look at it closely until that night. I felt as if an invisible hand had guided me to look at that picture. I peered closely as I examined the painting, and then I gasped... the artist's name was signed Vivian Angel! Yes, of course! Two angels, indeed, had already visited me that night to give me such warm and comforting messages of love.

A couple of weeks later, I smelled the roses again on the beach. This time, I stopped, smiled, and said aloud, "Thanks, Dad, for sending the message. Thank you for being with me." I looked up at the sky and, lo and behold, there was the bald eagle again. He was flying directly over my head. I watched his majestic flight straight down the beach, right in front of me. As soon as the eagle reached the condominium where I live, I watched in amazement as he made a ninety-degree turn and flew directly over my top-floor apartment!

In the blink of an eye, I was immediately transported back to that first walk on the beach when my children had seen the bald eagle at Doctor's Pass. Speechless, as I watched this magnificent winged creature, I began to laugh; I finally got it. Both the eagles and the roses were signs from my father, letting me know that he is with me, watching over me, protecting me.

Candice Meriwether Sanderson, MS, is a school psychologist and mother in Naples, Florida. Being a perpetual student in spiritual matters has led her to study angels, meditation, prayer, Reiki healing, dream interpretation, psychic development, and journaling about spiritual experiences.

Loving Presence

Ann Moore

In late December 1997, just after hearing the news that her fifth grandchild had been born in Philadelphia, our mother suffered a massive stroke. Although our physician father had always made the medical decisions for our family, he was now seventy-two years old, brokenhearted, and immobilized. The decision for our mother's surgery was left entirely to my three siblings and me. We opted for surgery. Mom had a craniotomy and remained on a ventilator for several days in the ICU to help her breathe. Once extubated, she lay in a semi-comatose state. When my sister whispered that she could let go and stop fighting, Mom murmured back, "I'm not ready to leave my children." And she wasn't. Weeks later, our mother was discharged to a rehabilitation facility nearby.

Our family rallied around my parents. My sister Julie, a speech pathologist, managed all aspects of Mom's rehab; she made sure the various specialists viewed her as a total person. My brother Eddie visited our mother every day and helped build my father's confidence. My other brother Matt, busy with his newborn, drove home from Philadelphia to lend his support. I moved from Schenectady with my two children to help Mom with her physical therapy and to keep house for Dad. With my daughter enrolled in all-day kindergarten, my three-year-old son soon became the major motivator for Mom during her physical therapy sessions at the rehab. Our father, mute and lifeless, sat by our mother's bedside until it was time for him to go home.

Three months later, the christening was set for Matt's new baby. Julie stayed with Mom while the rest of us journeyed to Philadelphia with Dad. Again, we were the caregivers—directing Dad to the gate, to his seat, handling his bags, prodding him to keep up as he shuffled through the airport. Finally, at Matt and Susan's house, Dad came to life as he held his new grandson in his arms. He raved about my sister-in-law's pasta fagioli, exclaiming that it was nearly as good as his mother's.

While waiting for our return flight home at the airport, Dad, who never drinks, suggested that we have a beer and a hot dog at Nathan's. As he happily munched away, Dad dwelled on the weekend; he marveled at the change in my brother since the birth of his son. As he sipped his mug of beer, Dad repeated what he had written to me in a letter while I was still in college, "It's all in the children, Ann. It's all in the children. I'm so glad that Matthew has a child."

A few days later, Dad awakened me to inform me that he thought he was having a heart attack. He was immediately transferred by ambulance to the same hospital where he had worked for so many years. Once again, Julie, Eddie, and I huddled in a hospital corridor where we soon learned that Dad needed open-heart surgery. Matt later joined us and the four of us surrounded our father with our presence and our love. Dad asked me to record his bequeathment of his personal possessions, which I did as the four of us stood next to his gurney. Then our father was wheeled into the operating room for a quadruple bypass.

Although Dad survived the surgery, he was unable to wean off the ventilator. He remained in the ICU for five more months as a result of developing one complication after another. Mom endured a blood clot of her own and was transferred back to the same hospital. My siblings and I would wheel her in to visit Dad each day. Mom, frail and tiny in her wheelchair, unable to see him, would reach up with her good arm to pat his hand. Dad, high up on his cardiac bed and unable to talk to Mom, would mouth words and reach down to hold my mother's hand. Both of my parents lit up when one of their children or grandchildren entered their rooms; it was hard to leave them at the end of the day.

Sadly, Dad became increasingly confused and died five months later. I was away on vacation in Maine with my husband and children the night Dad died. We drove home for his funeral. It was difficult to see my mother wheeled up to her husband's casket. Who would have ever thought that she would have out-survived him? Our mother mumbled in grief to Dad, "It's not fair, Leo. Why did you leave me?"

After his burial, I stayed on in Erie to help with various matters. On my last day there, a flock of Canada geese flew over our home. Dad, an avid bird watcher, had always emphasized that the species was named *Canada* geese, not Canadian geese. I clearly felt my father's presence as the birds flew overhead. Later that same day, after the first leg of my flight home, I briefly deplaned in Pittsburgh. I looked up and realized that I was in the exact location that my father and I had waited for our flight together just a few months earlier. I glanced across the corridor and saw the Nathan's sign. Compelled, I walked over to where we had sat. Suddenly, I smelled a strong odor. It was the identical sick smell of my father's ICU room at the hospital. A strong wave of peace rushed over me, and I instantly realized that my father was right there with me! Filled with gratitude, I told him, "I love you, Dad!"

There was one other significant time when my father let me know of his presence; it related to my daughter, adopted in 1991. At the time, my new baby and I had stayed with my parents in Pennsylvania for ten days in order to complete her adoption paperwork. Afterwards, they drove us home to Schenectady. On the way home, a beautiful double rainbow emerged from the sky. My father turned to me and somberly announced, "That is a sign that this child will be truly blessed." However, twelve years later, when my husband left me, I was devastated. Most of my emotions were in turmoil about how our two children would cope and if I could survive the financial worries, hurt, and despair. One day, I tearfully drove to the junior high school to pick up my daughter from a practice. As I pulled into the parking lot, a spectacular double rainbow emerged from the sky. Once again, I immediately felt my father's presence assuring me that everything would be fine and that we would get through this. Thankfully, we did.

My mother survived for seven more years in her home under my sister's loving care and management. Eventually, her fighting spirit waned, and she grew depressed. My sister rescued a dog named Jake and brought it home to see if Mom could be brought out of herself. Right from the start, Mom and Jake became bonded. In April of 2005, Mom suddenly became ill and died five days later. Our entire family had planned to be home the very same weekend. It was almost as if Mom had orchestrated her own sendoff. Her passing was spiritual and comforting, as we watched this wonderful woman die with dignity and finally let go of the family she loved so dearly.

On the Saturday before her death, Jake would not enter her room, a place he faithfully guarded. The next Monday, most of Mom's children were out doing various errands. My sister and her husband sat with my mother. Jake suddenly went into her bedroom and laid under his mistress's bed. Fifteen minutes later, Mom passed away. Jake got up and lapped at my sister's hand submissively. We all knew that Mom waited to give a final special goodbye to her three caregivers—Julie, Frank, and Jake. It was her tribute to them for their years of sacrifice, devotion and love.

Ann Moore lives with her two beautiful teenage children, Tori and Brennan. Several challenges, including four unexpected family deaths and a divorce, brought her family closer. With each successive passing, Ann's spirituality grew and confirmed that there is life after death.

Waiting for the Tulips to Bloom

Becky Childers

Duane K. Morgan was a tall, fit man with grayish blue eyes and gray-ish hair. Strong in his own beliefs and common sense, my father had a wonderful sense of humor. He dearly loved his family, my mother, and all five of his daughters. Dad was married to Mom for fifty-one wonderful years. When he was only sixteen years old, my father en-listed in the Army and immediately became a part of the Occupa-tional Forces in Korea. At nineteen, he was sent to fight on the front lines. Because supplies were limited when the war broke out, soldiers were inadequately dressed. Their feet would sweat from wearing the issued boots and then freeze from the harsh winter conditions. As a result, numerous soldiers developed frostbite and nerve damage to their limbs. My father was one of thousands of men who were cold-injured during the first part of the Korean War.

Twenty-seven years after his discharge, Dad began experiencing cold sensitivity and excruciating nighttime leg cramps. When he first shared with me that his feet were frostbitten in the war, I decided to research further. I soon learned that frostbite was quite common during those years in the service. When I shared this with Dad, he started telling me about the various men with whom he had served. Inwardly, I made a personal commitment to find them. Not only did I locate many of his war buddies, I also discovered that every one of them was suffering from identical feet and leg problems. With strong encouragement, Dad finally agreed to be medically evaluated. The doctors confirmed his cold injury and instructed him to fill out the appropriate compensation forms. I forwarded the information to all the other guys in Dad's battalion. Sure enough, they were found to be suffering from cold injury, too.

Then Dad developed a facial droop, leg weakness, and muscle twitching. Diagnosed with ALS, commonly referred to as Lou Gehrig's disease, on his seventy-first birthday, Dad was also diagnosed with CREST syndrome, a form of scleroderma. After hearing the shocking news and such a horrible prognosis, Dad plummeted into a deep depression. Over the next few months, he began to stumble and fall.

Knowing that Dad had very little time left, my family and I organized a reunion with sixteen of his war buddies in Reno, Nevada, during October of 2002. Everyone was overjoyed. The last time they had seen each other was on the evening of November 27, 1950, when they were attacked by the Chinese forces near the Chosin Reservoir. One special surprise involved one of their critically wounded comrades, Garabed. Dad had held Garabed's head tightly on the front lines to control the bleeding while they waited for the medics to arrive. Dad worried for years that his friend had died from the head trauma. Yet Garabed was at the reunion, alive and well. Dad was astounded. I never saw my father cry so hard as when he was reunited with Garabed. Those two unforgettable days together were a once-in-a-lifetime opportunity.

One month later, Dad's speech became garbled, and he began to fall more often. None of us thought Dad would make it until Christmas. But, Dad had set a goal for himself. He wanted to see the red and yellow tulips bloom that he had planted the year before. Fortunately, that winter was warm and sunny, and Dad was able to spend a lot of time outside on the porch enjoying the fresh air and birds that he loved. In the spring, I was awarded the Hometown Hero Award for my work with the veterans. Because Dad was too weak to attend the ceremony, we watched a videotaped copy together at home later that night. Dad was so proud of me. Shortly thereafter, my father's red and yellow tulips in the front yard finally bloomed.

A few weeks later during his last visit with Dad, my husband walked up to him, gave him a kiss, took a few steps away, and then turned around to take one last look. When he did, Dad opened his eyes briefly. In the darkened room, my husband was amazed to witness the most *indescribably* beautiful shade of iridescent blue coming from deep within my father's eyes! Then, Dad closed his eyes, and the light was gone. A short while later, my father died. My twin sister called to tell me the news. I felt a great sense of relief that Dad had died at home, because that was his wish. But, I felt tremendous sadness in losing the father whom I had loved so much. My husband, daughter, and I returned to the house to see him. Dad looked *so* peaceful. His hands, formerly bent and crippled from the scleroderma, were now finally relaxed and beautiful; Dad looked like his old self. On our way home, the three of us witnessed the most beautiful rainbow. We knew it was Dad letting us know that he was doing okay.

Over the last couple of years since his death, my family and I have experienced several signs from Dad. The most clearly definable sign has been the repeated occurrence in our home of an overwhelming smell of Golden Burley tobacco that Dad smoked in his Dr. Grabow briar pipe over the years. Because it has such a distinctive odor, it is easily recognizable. For me, it is such a wonderful experience to have my nose suddenly filled with the overpowering cherry smell of Dad's tobacco. My family and I have grown accustomed to its occurrence and are actually soothed by its presence. We smile in acknowledgement whenever it happens, and say, "Hi Dad."

Eight months after my father died, I had the most wonderful dream. It felt more like a visit because Dad seemed very real. During the dream, I was headed to my parents' home. Mom was visiting my sisters in Oregon, so I wanted to make sure that everything was okay at the house. I walked into the living room of my parents' home, and it was dark. I remember telling myself that it felt so lonely being there without Dad. Then, I clearly heard Dad's voice, "Hey, working girl!" "Working girl" was his nickname for me, since I always seemed to be working long hours and involved in numerous projects. I turned around quickly to see Dad leaning against the wall by the front door with his arms crossed and one leg crossed over in front of the other. I was so happy to see him, but I also had the awareness that my father was gone. Dad appeared to be in his late fifties, and he looked extremely happy. Stumbling over my words because I knew he was gone, I asked, "Dad? How are things? How are you?"

Incredibly happy and with a big smile on his face, Dad said, "Everything is wonderful!" Then, I woke up completely immersed in a feeling of total peace. I *knew* my father was okay and had come to tell me that everything was great. Even better than that, Dad was whole again! I can't begin to describe how much joy I felt in my heart to have had a visit with Dad standing, talking, healthy and clearly happy! Wherever he is, I know my father's tulips have surely bloomed. And, I am certain he couldn't be happier.

Although Dad may not visible, he is surely still with us. Before the last visit with him, my husband believed that once you died, you died. Scott was not raised in a religious home. Yet, as a result of all that transpired, he now believes that God is real, and there is something more that exists beyond physical death. Although Scott still struggles to understand the extraordinary light he saw in my father's eyes, incredibly, he is no longer afraid of death. Because the two of them were extremely close, it is fitting that Dad showed Scott "the light," and amazing that the experience was able to change Scott's attitude towards God and life hereafter.

As for me, I continue to volunteer my efforts with the veterans around the United States in my dad's honor. I have talked to many people about the various occurrences that have happened since the time of his death. There are no words that could possibly describe the inner transformation that has occurred within my husband and me; we are forever changed. I'm so grateful for all the gifts we have received from Dad and for all the reminders that he continues to bring.

Becky Childers resides in northern California with her husband and daughter. In addition to designing crystal and beaded jewelry, Becky continues to assist Korean War cold-injured veterans in honor of her dad.

5

Sounds

Music is well said to be the speech of angels.
—Thomas Carlyle

Melodies are often associated with special events. Meaningful words and music can fill our hearts with love and joy. The voice of a deceased loved one can evoke an emotional response as well. Has the memorable voice of a deceased loved one brought you comfort or soothed your sorrow? Has the bark of a deceased pet ever given you pause? The comforting sounds of music, voice, and song bring hope and healing to the dying and to the bereaved.

TENDERLY

Sally Miller

My husband of nearly forty-seven years, Dick Miller, passed away after a two-and-a-half-year battle with lung cancer. He was brave, strong, and never complained, despite the various difficulties and severity of the treatments he received. Dick and I had shared a magical marriage filled with constant love and mutual respect. We raised three daughters together, and we were lucky enough to see them become successful in their careers, marriages, and in motherhood. Proud parents and grandparents, we were truly blessed.

From the moment Dick received his terminal diagnosis, we were together twenty-four hours a day. I never left his side. And, at the end of Dick's courageous journey, my beloved husband died in my arms. Over the past year since his death, I have found myself totally overwhelmed with grief. We were supposed to grow old together. I couldn't imagine doing it alone.

As much as possible, I have tried to fill my time productively. Even so, I have found myself extremely sad and lonely. Yet, I have noticed that I have become more spiritual. I am now more open to the possibility of an afterlife. Since Dick's death, I have noticed many meaningful *coincidences* that have blessed me with the feeling that my husband is still in my life. The most recent connection took place during a vacation in February of 2003 I shared with my entire family.

Dick was an ardent boater and fisherman. He adored the ocean. Over the years, we shared many wonderful times with our family on our thirty-two-foot powerboat, *Sequel*. Even the grandchildren looked forward to visiting Papa's boat. However, without Dick to share it, the boat no longer had meaning for me. I found myself faced with the sad task of selling it.

When the broker handed me the sale check for *Sequel*, I promised myself that I would use the money I received in a special way. With my daughter Betsy's help, I planned a Disney cruise vacation for the entire family. What could be better? With our grandchildren ranging from ages three to fourteen, there would surely be activities for everyone. Dick would be so pleased that our family had come together on a boat to honor him. I scheduled the trip to coincide with our wedding anniversary, as a way to honor our marriage and help me through what I was sure would be a difficult day.

The cruise was an ideal choice. It was a five-day cruise from Florida to the Caribbean. We all enjoyed the luxuries of being aboard an amazing ship, the atmosphere of the "wonderful world of Disney," delicious food, and wonderful accommodations.

On June 19, the morning of our anniversary, I awoke with a special sadness. I was missing Dick terribly. Fortunately, the sadness was tempered by sharing a room with my seven-year-old twin granddaughters, Elise and Claire. I was determined not to be sad for them. Once we were dressed and ready, I took each girl by the hand and walked to the breakfast buffet, knowing the rest of the family would be joining us soon.

As the three of us entered the breakfast area, I heard music playing over the intercom system. However, instead of the usual Disney songs that had been continuously playing throughout the cruise, I recognized a melody that held incredible significance in my life. They were playing *our* song, "Tenderly," the song that Dick and I had chosen for our first dance together at our wedding forty-seven years earlier. I thought I was hearing things—it seemed unreal. I hadn't heard that 1940s jazz melody in years.

The children and I finished going through the buffet line and joined the rest of the family on the west deck. My daughter, Heidi, walked up to me and whispered knowingly, "Mom, I heard the music they were playing." I knew then that I had, in fact, heard *our* song. My whole family and I were moved by Dick's presence that day and the special anniversary gift he had given to me. Remarkably, my beloved husband had turned a difficult experience into a tender one I will treasure always.

Sally Miller, a retired anesthesia department office manager, enjoys writing short stories and is working on an autobiography. Sally and her husband raised three incredible daughters who married three wonderful sons-in-law and blessed them with six amazing grandchildren.

LYEVA

Yulia Vershinina

Lyeva was a reddish brown dachshund my parents owned when I lived with them. His name in Russian meant "lion." Very nervous and possessive, our doggy was a little terror. He spent most of the day barking at even the slightest movement or noise he heard. Lyeva's bark was distinctive and something hard to forget. It was high-pitched, loud, and irritated most of the tenants in our building.

In 1999, I moved from Saint Petersburg, Russia, to the United States in order to pursue my studies. I called home often. As usual, I could always hear Lyeva barking in the background at every little distraction. My parents would joke with me over the telephone, telling me that I had left them with a "special gift" when I moved to the U.S.

Despite his crazy temper, my parents adored Lyeva and had secretly hoped that our little doggy would live until he was at least fifteen years old. To their disappointment, our little terror passed away last year unexpectedly from congestive heart failure at the age of twelve. It left my parents in a state of shock and disbelief.

Following his death, something strange started happening. Whenever I called home, I could hear the sound of Lyeva barking in the background. It was definitely our little dog's bark, as it was the same familiar high-pitched piercing tone that I'd always heard, except it sounded further away. The first time it happened, I asked Mom if there were any other dogs barking in her building at that time. She told me no, there were none. Then, I questioned if she could hear any barking at all—I didn't mention Lyeva's name to Mom, as I didn't want to upset her. Even though Mom couldn't hear any barking, I could.

For the next six months or so, every time I called home, I could hear Lyeva barking on the phone. I guess our little terror wanted us to know that he was still with us. Gradually, the barking sounds completely disappeared. And, even though his bark had sometimes been annoying, I had grown accustomed to that sound. I still miss his bark and our little doggy Lyeva.

Yulia Vershinina was born and raised in Saint Petersburg, Russia. With a bachelor's degree in Cognitive Science and Linguistics and a master's degree in Organizational Psychology, Yulia works as an organizational development consultant and teaches communication skills at North Shore Community College.

No Need to Worry

Keri Bodwell

⌒

In the summer of 1997, I met my dear friend Lillian Hart. My husband and I were in the process of building our dream house in the countryside of Vermont. The house was to be our great escape from the "big city" pace we had become accustomed to throughout our thirties. Lillian's house was directly across the street from ours. Every afternoon just after one o'clock, we would notice a small, frail figure emerge from her gray, neatly kept Cape. Lillian would then begin her slow, arduous walk down the long, dusty driveway. She appeared quite elderly. Seemingly, the reward that lay in the mailbox each day must have been worth the great effort it took for Lillian to get to the road and back.

By the fall, my husband and I had completely moved into our new home. Lillian and I had already become fast friends. She was no longer making the long journey to the mailbox. Each day, I would pick up the mail for her and deliver it. In return, she would invite me in for afternoon tea. I looked forward to our daily visits. Although there was over a forty-year span between the two of us, it wasn't felt. We shared a deep love of travel, current events, faith, and most particularly—our families. It was during one of those intimate afternoon teas that Lillian first made a mention of her younger sister, Kate.

Although the two sisters lived opposite lifestyles, it was quite obvious there was a deep bond and love between them. Referring to her sister, Lillian whispered, "It is a connection that has lasted even beyond death." Intrigued, I coaxed my new friend to tell me more about her relationship with Kate. She willingly obliged.

The two sisters couldn't have been more different: Lillian was a pious, church-going woman who lived by high moral standards and ethics. From a young age, she had a love for Christ and all of his teachings. Kate, on the other hand, was a woman full of passion for life, with less concern for her own morality—or anyone else's, for that matter. This worried Lillian terribly. Throughout their lives, she found herself repeatedly praying for her sister's soul to be saved.

When Kate died, Lillian's concern for Kate's salvation turned to dread. Questions plagued her. Was Kate in a loving place? Was she paying a price for her zest for life and her liberal behavior of youth? Would she have to pay a debt for behavior that only hurt her? Lillian began to pray with even more fervor for her sister's salvation.

A few months after Kate's passing, Lillian and her husband planned a weekend trip to Cape Cod. They knew it would be their last visit to the ocean together. Her husband was terminally ill and had been told by his physician that he only had a few short months to live. The two hoped that this final adventure would leave them with some sweet memories.

Lillian had chosen a charming ocean-side inn that was considered the *best* in town. Most of the rooms had ocean views, which was a priority for Lillian and her husband. After checking in, the proprietress escorted the couple to their room. With great anticipation, the door swung open. Their eyes quickly scanned the room for their view of the water. There was none! How could that be? Lillian had booked the room specifically that way. The innkeeper explained that someone must have forgotten to write down the request for an ocean view when their reservation was taken. Unfortunately, there were no more seaside rooms left. Lillian confided that her husband was quite ill. Because they would have to spend most of their time inside, they needed a room with a view. Unable to accommodate their needs, the innkeeper suggested an inn down the road. She placed a call and secured a room with a view.

Lillian sadly packed their belongings in the car. There would be no overnight stay at the nicest inn in town. Lillian would have to let family members know of the change in plans. Hoping to cheer her up, Lillian's husband reminded her of the often-repeated belief that everything happens for a reason. Yet, when they arrived at their new lodging, it was a bit of a letdown. The inn had neither the charm nor the close proximity to town of the first one. Fortunately, the water views were much better.

A very jovial gentleman greeted them at the front desk. He asked if they were the Harts. They replied yes. He exclaimed, "Wonderful! We've been expecting you!" Lillian assumed that he had taken the call from the other innkeeper concerning their room. However, the man went on to say, "We received a call from your sister Kate, Mrs. Hart. She told us that you'd be staying with us for the weekend, and that I was to give you this message: 'Everything is okay and I'm doing well.'"

Relieved, astonished, and grateful, Lillian was able to spend her last Cape Cod weekend with her husband in the seaside inn that Kate had picked out. Her fears were allayed. Kate was okay. No need to worry anymore.

Nine months after she shared this story, Lillian passed on to be with her beloved husband, and sister, Kate. I miss our friendship and daily chats. I think of her often. Yet, in my heart, I know that just like Kate, Lillian is okay, too.

Keri Bodwell, a flight attendant, lives on Cape Cod with her husband and two children; she loves to travel and enjoys the woods and the beach very much. Keri's passions include gardening, home renovation, astrology, and color therapy.

Ninety-Nine

Brianne Duff

For as long as I can remember, my family and I have spent our summers at the ocean. All of my friends hung out at the beach or spent time on their boats. However, I knew that I wanted to become a nurse, so I worked at a local nursing home. One day, when I entered the nursing home, I heard Irish music playing down the hall. I immediately recognized the familiar tune because my grandparents were from Ireland, and my Irish grandfather sang to me often. Needing to find out where the music was coming from, I ventured down the hall around the corner and stopped outside the last room on the right.

All alone inside the room was a ninety-five-year-old gentleman, Walter O'Reilly. He was dressed very dapper with the few gray hairs on his head meticulously slicked back. The Irish music was playing loudly on his radio. With his *shillelagh* walking stick in hand, Walter danced an Irish step dance to the music. His incredible energy captivated me. For a while, I quietly watched this inspiring elderly gentleman enjoy the precious moments of life. Sensing my unannounced presence, Walter turned around, smiled a toothless grin, and invited me to come in.

We sat down, talked for a while, and soon became good friends; that was the beginning of me visiting him on a daily basis. The following summer, I didn't work at the nursing home, but I always made time in my busy schedule to visit my dear friend and take him out to lunch.

Walter and I shared August birthdays. A few years later, I decided to celebrate Walter's ninety-ninth birthday, this time by taking him out to dinner. Since he loved seafood, I chose an informal Gloucester restaurant well known for its fish. On that pleasant summer evening, we sat outside for dinner. Although Walter had no teeth, he ordered fried clams. I prayed he would not choke; I thought for sure that I would be doing the Heimlich maneuver before dinner was over. Fortunately, I didn't have to because Walter would pull out his pint-sized bottle of apricot brandy from his pocket, take a large swig, and wash the clams down.

Halfway through the meal, Walter started to cry. He sadly shared with me that his eldest son had passed away that week; he had just read about it in the newspaper. Walter was upset. Because none of his family had notified him, he had not been able to say goodbye or even attend the funeral. Ironically, the house across the street from where we were sitting had been his son's home. Walter cried a lot that day. At eighteen years old, my heart ached at the depth of his emotional pain and grief. Here was an elderly father intensely grieving the loss of his seventy-three-year-old son.

Following dinner, I took him to the beach house to visit my family. He kept our attention by telling stories and even enjoyed having a cigar with my dad. My family loved him, and to this day, they still speak of him. On that day, we nicknamed him "Ninety-Nine" in honor of his ninety-ninth birthday.

Over the next three years, I was away at college studying nursing. I continued to visit Ninety-Nine every summer. The summer after I graduated, I was employed as a nurse in Washington, DC. Missing the summer visits with my dear friend, I had been hoping to at least make it home by Labor Day. However, I spent my August birthday that year in Washington, DC.

As I drove home from work on my birthday, the strangest thing happened. I was thinking about Ninety-Nine and the birthdays we had shared in the past. Suddenly, all on its own, the car radio started to scan stations. Three times, it came back to an Irish music station. I couldn't figure out what was going on. But I had a strange feeling in the pit of my stomach. The next day, during a phone conversation with my mother, I shared my concern about Ninety-Nine. She became strangely silent; Mom did not respond to my comment, but instead she just wished me a happy belated birthday. I informed her that I would be home in October and would visit Ninety-Nine at that time.

Five weeks later, I returned home to visit my parents. Mom was at home when I got there; I told her that I couldn't wait to see Ninety-Nine. Tearfully, she shared that Ninety-Nine had died on my birthday—the same day that the Irish music had flicked on and off on my car radio. With tears in my eyes, I asked why she hadn't told me earlier. She couldn't tell me over the phone because Mom knew how connected I was to this dear man. Ninety-Nine passed away at the age of 103. I had started caring for him eight years earlier. The Celtic music had brought him into my life. Ninety-Nine left my life through the unexpected playing of Irish music on my car radio.

I am very grateful to have known Ninety-Nine. My birthday never passes without my remembering our extraordinary friendship. I laugh when I think back to being a teenager and zipping around town in my convertible with a one-hundred-year-old man sitting right next to me enjoying the ride. To this day, whenever my radio flickers to an Irish station, as it sometimes does, I know that Ninety-Nine is with me. He is simply letting me know that he is still in my life. I will remember Ninety-Nine forever.

MATERNAL SERENADE

Barbara Brien

I have worked as a staff nurse in a medical ICU for over nine years. Because patients in this type of unit are critically ill, they inevitably have a higher mortality rate than others. As a result, I've had many experiences with patients and their families at the end of life. I have become quite familiar with the reality of death and the emotions that accompany it. I've also learned that I have the unique opportunity to help make this process less painful for both patients and their families. Having done this many times, I was fortunate to be able to do this again with one family in particular who was facing the loss of a loved one.

While working the 3–11 shift, I was assigned a fifty-three-year-old man with schizophrenia who had been living in a group home since he was diagnosed at the young age of eighteen. Prior to the onset of his devastating mental illness, Billy had been a rising football star full of promise and personality. He had even earned a full four-year football scholarship to Syracuse University. Billy and his family were understandably crushed when he was no longer able to fulfill his life dreams. Following the death of their parents, his devoted sister, Mary, took over as guardian. Billy lived a much simpler life, working part-time in a grocery store. He even had a girlfriend who lived in the same group home.

In July 2005, Billy began experiencing back pain and went to his doctor for medical evaluation. The diagnostic testing showed a cancerous mass in Billy's lower back. Further testing revealed that the cancer had also metastasized, or spread, to his lungs and liver. By the time Billy had arrived in the medical ICU just a few weeks later, he was no able longer to breathe on his own, and he was on full ventilator support. Yet, Billy's doctors seemed encouraged. His lung biopsy report showed small cell carcinoma, which is normally quite responsive to chemotherapy. As Billy's guardian, Mary was faced with a huge responsibility to decide ultimately what would be best for Billy and whether or not to pursue aggressive chemotherapy. After much deliberation with the assistance of the health care team and her family, and careful consideration of what she felt her brother would want, Mary decided to "keep Billy comfortable" and not go forward with any further treatment.

Following the family meeting, I heard about Mary and her family's difficult decision to discontinue life support out of love for Billy. It was obvious that Mary, her brother, and her husband now needed much emotional support and kindness from me. I met them at Billy's bedside and made sure to provide an opportunity for them to talk. Mary reminisced tearfully about a picnic they had shared together just one week prior to Billy becoming sick and how grateful she was to have such a pleasant memory. They were all deeply saddened. I sat and quietly listened as they laughed and cried together about times gone by. When it was appropriate, I questioned about Billy's spiritual orientation. Then, I notified the hospital priest, who arrived shortly thereafter to pray with them.

Mary and her family had concerns about what to expect after we took Billy off the ventilator. I assured them that I would do everything possible to make sure Billy did not experience any pain or shortness of breath. I encouraged Billy's family to spend as much time as they needed with him, and then I began administering a continuous morphine drip through Billy's intravenous line. After a short time, his family told me they were ready and asked me to take Billy off the ventilator. At that point, they left, as they knew it would be too difficult to watch Billy take his last breaths. I reassured them that I would not let Billy die alone, and that I would continue to ensure that he was comfortable. Tearfully, they said their goodbyes and asked me to call them when he passed. I hugged them, offered my condolences, and they left.

Minutes later, while in my other patient's room, I noticed a change on the split screen monitor which simultaneously reports the vital signs on both my patients. Billy's side of the monitor had started to flash, letting me know that Billy's heart rate was dropping rapidly. I left quickly to be with him. I am often the only person in the room when a patient is dying, and I usually feel compelled to sing as he or she passes from this world. I find great comfort and spirituality in music, especially at the end of life, and I love to share that part of myself with my patients. During Billy's last minutes of breathing, I felt called to sing "Ave Maria." I stroked Billy's head, held his hand, and I sang the verses over and over again until the monitor let me know that his heart had finally stopped beating. Billy died a very peaceful death, just as I had promised.

I called Mary to deliver the sad news. I reassured her that I was with Billy the whole time. When I shared that I had felt moved to sing "Ave Maria" to him while he was passing, I heard her gasp on the end of the line. She was audibly weeping, and I questioned if she was all right. Through her tears, Mary told me that "Ave Maria" was their mom's favorite song. I replied that I didn't know why I had chosen that song. Mary responded, "I do." She went on to inform me that it was surely a message from their mom. Billy was finally reunited with their parents, and everything was going to be okay.

Barbara Brien, RN, wife of Gerry, mother of beautiful Mairead Diane and Kagan Beatrice, helped implement a family-centered MICU Palliative Care-Merging Cultures program at MGH in Boston. Her mission is to ensure quality of life for all patients.

BIRTHDAY SHOPPING

Lori Monaco

———

I will never forget the day I went shopping for my girlfriend's birthday present. After saying a quick prayer to find Susan something special, I found myself drawn to shop at Marshall's. As I looked around the store, I happened to notice a women's clothing rack filled with turtlenecks. Next, I heard a warm but formal male voice inwardly say, "Please buy that white turtleneck with the red hearts on it." I immediately knew it was the voice of my girlfriend's father, who had died years earlier. I did exactly as Susan's father instructed me. Happily, I left the store with her gift in hand.

Later that day, I felt prompted to enter a nearby gift shop. Before long, I found myself holding a Precious Moments musical water globe. Again, I heard Susan's father clearly state, "Please buy this for my daughter." I followed his instructions just as before. Leaving the store, I felt an inner peace, knowing I had honored this father's loving requests.

When my girlfriend opened her birthday gifts, she began to cry. Susan shared with me that her dad had bought her an identical white turtleneck with red hearts on it when she was younger. As a gifted singer and pianist, Susan also told me the Precious Moments musical globe played the same song that she had sung to him so many times over the years. When I told Susan how her father had actually helped me pick out her presents, she cried even harder. Susan sincerely thanked me for the meaningful gifts. I replied, "Please, don't thank me; thank your dad. He wants you to know he is around you, and that he loves you very much." Gifts can be such a gracious way for loved ones to express thoughtfulness and presence both in this world and the next.

Lori Monaco, wife of Peter and mother of Britney, Jordan, Evan, and Lindsey, is a professional tutor, editor, singer, songwriter, and intuitive who facilitates healing, growth, and transformation.

A Farewell Visit

Anne Bruno

⌐⤙

Gussy, a female patient in her eighties, lived in the nursing home where I worked. She had been diagnosed with dementia, but was fairly independent. Her being easily confused necessitated twenty-four-hour supervision. Gussy was pleasant, cooperative, and able to follow directions. Because she had difficulty processing communication, her responses were generally inappropriate. For instance, I might ask Gussy, "What would you like for breakfast today?" She would give a totally unrelated answer such as, "Yes, the sun is shining."

One morning, when I entered her room on routine rounds, Gussy said, "Don't bother me now...I'm talking to my husband." I looked around the room and saw no one. I knew her husband was a patient in a nearby nursing home. I was a little surprised at her statement, but took it in stride. It was typical for Gussy to make off-the-wall comments that didn't make sense. As she requested, I left her alone to be in the privacy of her own thoughts and went on to finish my morning rounds.

A few minutes later, the telephone rang. It was a call from the nursing home where Gussy's husband was a resident. A nurse informed me that Gussy's husband had died unexpectedly a short while before the call.

As I hung up the phone, I realized that Gussy was talking to her husband after all. I thought it was neat she was able to see him one last time. He must have been very important and made quite an impact to be able to bring her back to reality.

Gussy was an Old World Italian who had centered her entire life around her husband's happiness. That's what an Italian wife does...she makes her husband happy! This time it was her husband's turn to do something for Gussy. He came to pay a visit one last time, and in doing so, reached out to Gussy in a way no one else could.

SAFE ARRIVAL IN HEAVEN

Linda Lockwood

⌒

When I first met Rhodes Lockwood in 1992, he needed organizational help in his home. His wife, who had always taken care of their personal affairs, had died a year earlier, and Rhodes was finding it difficult to manage work and home on his own. A kind, mutual friend mentioned my name to him and suggested he give me a call. I was a good worker, organized, and available. I might be just what he needed. Following his friend's lead, Rhodes contacted me. We met the next day, and he hired me on the spot. Initially, we agreed that I would work for him two days a week. Shortly thereafter, he increased the time to three days weekly once he realized my capabilities.

From the moment I met Rhodes, I felt an instant connection. Although difficult to describe in words, something inside told me that this man was special. Little did I know how special he was, and that our chance meeting would eventually reshape the rest of our lives. Although he was seventy-four years old, Rhodes was amazingly energetic and youthful. Over the next year or so, we had the opportunity to have numerous conversations; I thoroughly enjoyed listening to his southern Virginian drawl. I deeply admired Rhodes, his work ethic, and his genuine concern for others. An example of that concern was clearly demonstrated in his role and commitment in bringing MET-CO to Wellesley, Massachusetts; this program bussed inner-city children to the suburbs to help provide them a better education.

Rhodes and I grew emotionally closer over the next two years, and in 1994, we were married. Not only was he a successful attorney, Rhodes was a consummate human being and a true gentleman. I was proud to be his wife. As healthy as Rhodes appeared on the outside, his looks were somewhat deceiving. Just four months after we married, he suffered a heart attack. Shortly thereafter, I watched him endure several major health challenges. Yet Rhodes never complained;

he was stoic and determined to live life to the fullest. And, for the time we shared together, he did. The two of us traveled often in the states and abroad. My husband never let on that he was sick or in pain. After an unexplained fall at home, he agreed to go for a check-up. Once the tests were completed, his doctor delivered the shocking news that Rhodes had nerve cancer in his right leg.

In spite of the diagnosis, Rhodes refused to let it slow him down. He still continued our daily walks with Simon, our black Cairn Terrier whom we both adored. With the development of further complications and lung cancer, his health plummeted. Within months, his prognosis was guarded. I hired nurses round-the-clock for our home to support him in every way I knew how.

Early in the morning on July 22, 1996, his night nurse awakened me to inform me that Rhodes was dying. I rushed downstairs to be with him. Tearfully, I took my husband's hand in mine, whispered farewell and watched my beloved Rhodes take his last breaths; it was 4:05 AM. Stunned, I struggled to collect my thoughts. I already missed him deeply.

The funeral home people came and left with Rhodes, and I found myself all alone in the house. Physically exhausted and emotionally spent, I forced myself to go upstairs to our bedroom. When I did, I was surprised to hear music playing from the radio on my side of the bed! That was odd. I hadn't set that radio alarm clock in weeks because Rhodes had been in the hospital. Then I remembered that every night just before we went to sleep, my husband would set the radio alarm for 4:30 AM the next morning. He had an odd habit of waking up early to eat breakfast and then returning to bed to sleep for a while longer. Since I had not set the alarm that morning, I knew Rhodes had sent me a clear sign. In an apropos way, he was letting me know he was all right and that he had safely arrived in heaven!

Although I was grateful that Rhodes was no longer suffering, our dog Simon and I ached for him in our lives. Simon's relationship with Rhodes predated mine, as the two of them had been together for fourteen years. Following his master's death, Simon's health rapidly declined and within five months he was blind, disoriented, and his hips were failing. I was forced to have him put to sleep. It was the hardest thing I have ever done but it does give me comfort to know that Rhodes, Simon, and my dad (who had died eight years earlier) are all together and safe in heaven.

Through the assistance of the Wellesley Scholarship Foundation and the help of several friends, I was able to establish the Rhodes G. Lockwood Scholarship in his memory, something that would have pleased my husband very much. Rhodes and I shared a wonderful love story. I wanted it to continue and don't understand why it ended so soon. However, a prayer that gives me solace and I strive to live by is, "God, grant me the serenity to accept the things I cannot change, courage to change the things I can, and the wisdom to know the difference."

Linda Lockwood carries Rhodes in her heart, along with her children, Justin and Amanda; son-in-law Bill; and grandson, William. A volunteer for the humane society, Linda finds reading true stories about individuals who overcome life's greatest obstacles provides much hope.

SISTERS

Nancy Connelly

———

Barbara was the fifth of six children and the third of four daughters.
She was thirty-nine years old when she died of breast cancer. We were
ten years apart in age; I was her oldest sister. When I left for college,
Barbara was only seven years old. As we grew older, the ten-year span
became muted and, as with all of my sisters, we became good friends,
sharing the most joyful and the most painful events in life.

Barbara was an athlete, a swimmer who was tall and strong, lean
and beautiful. In high school, she taught children swimming lessons.
During her late teens and early twenties, she swam competitively. I
still have all her trophies and ribbons.

My sister knew how beautiful she was, and she had no problem
letting others know it either. Looks were important to Barbara, and
she had plenty. Built nothing like her, our two other sisters and I were
envious of Barbara's gorgeous six-foot-tall, muscular body. It's ironic
that the most physically fit of the four of us would be taken down by
a cancer cell—something so small it was invisible to the naked eye.

Wonderfully creative, Barbara was a gifted painter and crafter able
to turn trash magically into treasure. She was also a gourmet cook who
treated all of us to magnificent holiday dinners and "come on over for
supper" affairs.

At the young age of thirty-six, Barbara was diagnosed with a very
aggressive form of breast cancer. The next three years were fought
with intelligence, dignity, and grit. Her medical course was stormy,
with failed chemotherapy treatment and after failed chemotherapy
treatment. A bone marrow transplant also failed. She experienced incredible stretches of high fevers, nausea, weight loss, and, of course,
baldness. Through it all, Barbara continued to offer encouraging
words such as, "Don't worry, I'll beat it. I'm better. I love you," and

"Okay, what's next?" My sister was always ready to give a hug and be hugged. When her physician told Barbara that she would most likely die within three weeks, my courageous sister invited all of her family to spend a week together to make lots of memories that would help sustain us in the time to come.

When Barbara realized that she would not survive her cancer, she asked me to spend time with her. As a sister who loved her dearly, I offered myself to Barbara in whatever capacity she needed—to be her sounding board, housekeeper, chauffeur, florist, but most of all, her friend. I promised Barbara I would take care of her and help her to die well.

As her disease progressed, I reduced my work hours so we could have one special day together each week to complete a wish list of things she hadn't yet tried. We went to day spas, Russian baths, the Ritz for tea, and on a spending spree on Newbury Street in Boston. When Barbara asked for one last trip to the Caribbean, I packed her up, along with her morphine pump, and we flew first class, completing another thing on her wish list. Barbara wanted to enjoy a week together and to soothe her aching bones in the warmth and beauty of St. Martin. My sister was prepared to die on that island, but God had other plans.

A few weeks before Barbara died, we were sitting in her living room together. I was living with her at this point, as she could barely manage to transfer herself from the hospital bed to her recliner chair. Barbara loved to sit in the recliner and spend the day gazing out through the window at the trees and birds. It was a cold, sunny February morning in 1997. We were sitting alone side by side; I was reading and Barbara was napping. When my sister awoke, I asked if she needed anything. Barbara smiled at me and very quietly asked with a startle in her voice, "Did you see that?"

"What did you see?"

"There they go," she said. "Look!" Even though I couldn't see anything, I asked what she saw. Barbara told me that three of the most beautiful women she had ever seen had just walked across the room by her chair and then went out the window. She continued saying, "And they *should* go out the window." Her voice was calm, as if seeing these women were a natural occurrence. When I asked who they were, Barbara told me she didn't know, but she thought they were women who went before her, women who would lead the way. Barbara never spoke of the vision or the women again ... I could feel her sadness ... I felt sure that her death was near.

Another vision shared by Barbara a day or two before she died gave me even more comfort. I recall this experience whenever I need an emotional hug. Barbara was now in bed all the time. She was having a difficult day due to the pain she was experiencing. No matter how hard I tried, I couldn't seem to bring her comfort. Barbara looked at me and said, "Nance, last night when I couldn't sleep and I hurt so bad, Nanny came and sat down right where you are ... and she said, 'Blackie (Nanny's nickname for Barbara because of her coal-black eyes), come with me and I'll take care of you.'" Barbara was so excited to see Nanny that she said, "I'm going to take her up on it, Nance. I'm tired of the pain. I need to go."

What brings me joy is the absolute trust Barbara had in her visions—that those women were her guides, and our Nanny, who had come to take her pain away and protect Barbara, still cares for her today. Barbara died on a cold, clear, starry Wednesday morning in February 1997. The room was so full of her presence I needed to open the window so her spirit could soar to the heavens. My heart is broken forever, but the joy I have woven into my grief is the memory of Barbara's faith and trust in her visions.

On the first anniversary of Barbara's death, I decided it was time to prepare a more permanent home for her ashes. At her request, they had resided in my home inside a hand-painted squash gourd with feathers on it that she had purchased on a reservation in Arizona. Barbara had the same kind of feather tattooed on her ankle the year before she died. My sister had chosen the gourd as the vessel in which to store her ashes, as she was a very down-to-earth kind of woman.

Barbara had two wishes regarding her ashes. The first was to have a portion of them buried in my garden. The second was to have the remaining ashes sprinkled in the sea at Cane Garden Bay on Tortola. I placed half of her ashes in the gourd. The rest were sealed in a brass urn that I placed on a rock in my garden, where it sits today.

Almost a year after her death, I was able to honor Barbara's second request to be scattered in the sea on Tortola. I flew down to Tortola with plans to rent a boat, sail out alone, release her ashes, and allow them to find their new Caribbean home. When I got there, the weather was beautiful but the seas were rough. It was so rough, in fact, that the locals considered taking a boat out dangerous and foolhardy. As each day passed, the ocean seemed to grow wilder, and my hopes of being able to accomplish my mission were dwindling. I felt restless and anxious, as her wishes weighed heavy on me. She needed a resting place, and I needed closure. I also needed to be able to keep the promise I had made Barbara to rest in a place that had always brought her peace, Cane Garden.

On the fourth day, I went to the dock and once again, the sea was pounding. I didn't see another soul or boat in sight. Then I noticed a young man standing next to a fishing boat tied to the dock. The boat was being repeatedly slammed up against the pier with each successive wave. I walked up to the man and asked if he would take me out in his boat. He politely told me I was crazy to want to go out on such a day. Then he asked why. I explained that I was there for Barbara and what I needed to do. He said he would do his best.

Due to the rough seas, it took him a while to motor the boat around to pick me up, but he persevered. We headed out to open sea where the waves wouldn't toss us around so much. On the ride out, we penetrated a heavy curtain of low-hanging clouds. On the other side of the clouds, it was beautiful, clear, and so bright that the sun hurt my eyes. We stopped at the point where the greenish color of the water transformed into a beautiful navy blue, which is only found in the Caribbean where the coral reef drops off to an impossible depth. The captain set the boat engines to idle; I went to the rear of the boat and started to pray. I prayed to Barbara for strength and grace to grieve with dignity, and to be able to share the love she'd given me with those who grieve painfully alone. I read a ritual out loud that I had prepared for Barbara, which included poems, a reading from Khalil Gibran, and a prayer from a Native American book of prayers.

Then, reluctantly, I sprinkled Barbara's ashes in those beautiful waters. They glittered, sparkled, and danced as I cried. The ashes formed a circle around our boat. I asked the captain to move the boat carefully so as not to disturb them. As we slowly motored away, I watched the circle of ashes dissolve and disappear. With the sun upon them, it looked as if the ashes were being lifted up out of the water with the rising clouds. They sparkled both in the water and above the water in a large swath for almost a minute until our boat was too far away to see them any longer.

Once the captain and I reached the shore, I sat alone for hours watching the spot where I had left Barbara's ashes, waiting for peace and hoping for closure or perhaps something that would bring me comfort. I wasn't sure what would make me feel better, but whatever it was, it surely wasn't coming. I needed to go, but at the same time, I didn't want to go. I stood up, stared one last time at the spot, knowing that I would never be back to this place that Barbara loved so much. I began walking through the sand up toward the road when Barbara clearly whispered in my ear. I heard her call my name once so realistically, I almost fell in the sand as I spun around to see her face. In that moment, I was so filled with her spirit and the sound of her voice that I couldn't bear to move for fear of losing the precious sound of the echo within my ears.

I miss Barbara. I can still feel her cheek upon my lips, the feeling of her hand in mine as we climbed the stairs together, the heaviness of her head upon my shoulder when we hugged. These poignant memories give me solace and strength, with the images of Tortola and the unforgettable sound of Barbara's voice calling my name.

Nancy Connelly, RN, a hospice nurse, has always been close with her five siblings. The nurturing, encouragement, and support of her partner, Ann, for forty years has enabled Nancy to continue in her important life work.

SYMPHONY OF THE HEART

Denise Kahn

The hospital in Athens was normally quiet, but today was different. The staff came to a standstill. Every nurse, doctor, and worker on the ward stopped what they were doing and listened. They couldn't understand what they were hearing. Each moved toward the sound—an incredibly sensual, booming, operatic voice that was coming from the farthest room down the hall. The singing was in Russian. What was happening? They were in Greece, not in Russia. This was a hospital, not an opera house. Intrigued, each and every one moved toward the room to look inside.

Their favorite patient, Louli, was lying in her bed, headset in her ears, Walkman on her chest, with a Moldavian aide holding her hand and sitting next to her. The aide, Lyuba, explained to the staff that she had just arrived for her shift and was listening to the Walkman when Louli asked for the headphones. The melodies playing brought Louli immediately back to her childhood days. Her mother, who was originally from Georgia (the former Soviet state), used to sing these songs to her. She also continued to converse with her in her native language. So, Louli, knowing both Russian and Georgian, among many other languages, immediately started singing along, and her dramatic soprano voice resonated throughout the halls of the hospital. The staff listened to the impromptu concert for over an hour to a woman they would never forget. Those words and sounds were to be Louli's last, as the cancerous tumor in her brain was unforgiving.

By the time I arrived from America, Louli could no longer speak, and her husband told me she was no longer coherent. I walked into her hospital room. It was filled with flowers, and a small icon of St. George lay next to the right side of her face on her pillow. I recognized the gold-painted wooden icon instantly. Louli never went anywhere without it.

Louli once told me that many years before, St. George had saved her life. Having just given birth to a baby girl in the hospital, Louli's heart had suddenly stopped. Despite the doctor's efforts to save her, Louli was pronounced dead. At that same moment, she experienced herself floating away and then drowning. She emerged from the water as a whale and swam to a beach where St. George waited for her with open arms. He talked to Louli and told her she was too important to leave just then. He also encouraged her to accept and understand the upcoming sacrifice. Moreover, St. George told her that the baby in her life would not be the one to whom she just gave birth. Louli did not fully understand all that he meant. But, she followed St. George's advice, and she made a choice to return to earth.

Although Louli survived, her baby did not. Yet, a couple of years later, I was born to her best friend, Dora. I leaned up against the hospital bed and took Louli's hand in mine. How I remembered her hands, her hugs, and every little detail of our lives together. She was my godmother, but to me, Louli was also a big sister, second mother, and best friend. Even in her deteriorated condition, she was still very beautiful.

Louli had always been a large, tall woman. In her case, however, it only added to her natural elegance, charisma, charm, humorous personality, and most of all, her selfless nature. I could still picture her walking into a room full of prominent personalities, everything from politicians, celebrities, artists, jet-setters, and Greek shipping magnates. What struck me most was that wherever she went, all these people—and there must have been hundreds—would stop to look at and listen to her, as her beauty, personality, and gentleness exuded from her. And they weren't wrong—she was always the life and joy of every party and get-together. Louli, in turn, loved them right back. Every once in a while, she would sing for them with her inimitable, remarkable operatic voice.

As I held her hand remembering all the wonderful times we shared, I gently spoke to her. To my astonishment, Louli turned her head and looked at me. She smiled and fluttered her eyelashes. Yes! She knew who I was, and I hugged her. She hugged me right back. I could feel her big, beautiful heart beating against my chest. Louli let me experience the symphony of her heart as I *felt* the most magnificent sonata in the world!

I had flown across the ocean to say my last goodbye, and I had planned to stay until the inevitable end. But Louli hung on, perhaps to stay with her beloved husband as long as she could. On the day my flight was scheduled to depart, Louli was still among us. How could I leave her? I couldn't. I decided to head back to the hospital instead of the airport.

Once I entered Louli's room, I softly caressed my godmother's cheek, remembering our shared fantastic symphony. Louli's eyes were open, staring at the ceiling. I gently held her hand; she managed a few last ounces of strength to squeeze back. Her beloved husband walked in and held her other hand. Their life together had been a devoted love story; after so many years, their mutual adoration had never once waned. With her last ounce of energy, Louli turned her head and looked at the man she adored. Never had I seen so much love and so many unspoken words as those uttered through the brilliance in her eyes. The devotion, care, adoration, and a lifetime of love came pouring through.

With one last little squeeze of my hand, Louli left us. I was devastated. I wanted to disappear myself; I wanted to become a cloud and fade into nothingness. Or better yet, I wanted to still be with her in whatever form she now took. In that moment, the only thing I knew for sure was that heaven was receiving the most perfect soul in the universe.

I went outside for some fresh air. I pondered the last few days. And then, it hit me—there were no sounds whatsoever! The busy Athenian boulevard was completely void of any traffic. How could that be possible? Athens is a city that never sleeps; it's busy twenty-four hours a day. There wasn't one single person on the street. I felt so alone.

Next to the hospital was a little flower shop. The door was open, and for some reason, I felt drawn to walk in. Again, no one was around. I was stunned by the magical smells of the flowers. My spirits immediately lifted. I looked around and discovered the most beautiful flowers I had ever seen; there were varieties that were completely foreign to me and absolutely exquisite in every way. I could only compare them to Louli.

Still alone in the store, a delightful upbeat song suddenly rang out. An American female vocalist, one I couldn't place, was singing "I Waited for You," a song I had never heard before or since. Of course, it was Louli! She had waited for me until I arrived in Athens, and she had waited once again that morning when I had decided to go to the hospital instead of the airport. My godmother had confirmed this for me through music.

I knew I needed to return to the hospital lounge where Louli's family members would be mourning. As I headed toward the doorway, I noticed the most magnificent orange rose lying on the floor in front of me. Since it wasn't there when I entered, and no one was in the store, I knew it was another gift from Louli. I picked it up, left some money on the counter, and walked out, rose in hand.

Later that afternoon, I went to Louli's home. Her husband was waiting for me with the veterinarian. He nodded to me and looked toward the corner. There lay her cat, Louli's most beloved pet. Frou-Frou was a big black-and-white cat with one of the most beautiful faces I have ever seen. She actually reminded me of Louli, with a kind of similar sweet look. What amazed me was that Louli had cancer in the brain, and her cat was also riddled with cancer throughout its body except the brain. I wondered if the cat in some way had taken on her mistress's ailment; animals tend to do that.

The cat's cancer was as advanced as Louli's. For the second time that day, another one of God's beings of light was being called to leave this earth. Frou-Frou let me hold her, and I felt her heart beating right next to mine. I once again felt the symphony of the heart. As we connected, this sweet little being began to purr her own miraculous little sonata, just as Louli had done. They had been so very close in life; now, in death, they were taking their next journey together. I had no doubt that the two would be welcomed with great love and serenaded with delightful music when they entered their glorious garden in the sky.

Louli's funeral was held two days later. I walked into a little flower shop next to the cemetery. It was filled with lovely red roses, lilies, and a multitude of other flowers, but none of them were right; I needed something really special. I wasn't sure what, but I would know it when I saw it. There it was—a glorious orange rose, half opened, just like the one next to the hospital. It was elegant, distinguished, and beautiful, just like Louli.

The cemetery in Athens is unique. Listed in the guidebooks as a site to see, everything from the little church, the walkways, the headstones and the walls are all made of marble. It is exquisite. Just by walking around, one can discover a great part of Greek history. Statues by famous sculptors adorn many of the graves, and many names of politicians, celebrities, and artists are prominent throughout.

I walked into the cemetery and headed to the viewing room, located to the left of the entrance and directly in front of the church. This is where Louli lay in her coffin. I walked up to have one last glimpse, but as I did, the workers were just closing the lid. It felt awkward to ask them to reopen it, but maybe it was Louli's wish that my last memory of her be the one we shared together. I let it go. I gently kissed the rose and placed it on top of her coffin. Others followed suit and laid their flowers and bouquets on top as well. People came and went, saying a prayer. For some reason, I couldn't concentrate on praying. All I could think was how wonderful she had been and that I wanted some alone time with her, which was impossible. It seemed every person Louli had ever known, even those who were ill and could hardly walk, were present. They had all made the extra effort to attend the service and honor Louli one last time.

After a little while, the pallbearers carried Louli's casket out of the viewing room. Everyone followed into the cemetery's little church. By the time we arrived, every flower and bouquet atop the casket had fallen off, except for my orange rose. It continued to lie there majestically. The traditional Greek funeral mass lasted about an hour, with several amazing eulogies offered. Afterward, everyone headed for the burial site. One might have thought a prime minister had passed away by the number of flowers and bouquets inside the church, at the graveside, and that were once again placed on top of her casket. No one had touched my orange rose. It lay there, even though I watched other flowers that were placed on top continue to fall off when they lowered Louli's coffin into the ground. Hundreds of flowers and wreaths from all over the world with lovely inscriptions written on their ribbons filled the surrounding area. One of the memorable inscriptions read *I can't imagine a world without you in it.*

Following the graveside ceremony, I was finally alone in front of the grave, just the two of us. As I stared at the rose on her casket, Louli's beautiful face suddenly appeared in a hazy cloud of orange, the same shade as the two stunning roses. Hovering above the coffin, Louli looked no more than thirty, in the prime of her life and beauty. She smiled at me as if I were still her little girl. Her smile always made my heart melt. That same smile made many women want to be her friend and prompted men to either want to continuously protect her or to immediately make passionate love to her. *Damn it, Louli,* I cursed, *why did you have to leave so soon? Do you have any idea how many of us need you?* Then, I heard her speak…

"Don't think like that, *agapi mou,* my love. It was my time to leave. I accomplished what I had to and tried to pave the way for others to progress. I had a wonderful and very full life. You all gave me so much love, and I only gave a fraction of it back. I had my share of success with my singing, my lovers, my friends, my animals, and of course, my darling husband. You were all so very special to me and still are. No matter what universe we find ourselves in, we will always be united by an unbreakable, unique bond. And you, my dearest little one, please continue with the goodness and wisdom you exude. Know that our hearts, yours and mine, will be forever one, for we are a symphony of the same heart."

I continued to stare at the coffin, but I only saw the orange rose, which had completely opened. It was in full bloom, in its exquisite prime, as I had just seen Louli. It was absolutely magnificent, as Louli had been. It reminded me of her beauty, external and, most especially, internal. I smiled the biggest smile I had in months. Anyone watching would have thought I was at a wedding instead of a funeral. I couldn't help thinking that, in her inimitable way, Louli was with me. She was pointing me toward a new beginning, not an end. My wish to connect with her had manifested. I knew in my heart that our sonatas would always continue.

6

Touch

HOW CAN THE TOUCH FROM a deceased loved one bring relief to a grieving individual? How can something nonphysical be physically felt? For the answers, just ask a bereaved individual who has received the miraculous gift of a comforting hug or kiss. Never underestimate the healing power of touch.

THE KISS GOODNIGHT

Vinette Silvers

My mother's presence was subtle but genuine as she gently comforted me one night. I was sitting in front of my computer struggling to write a poem about Momma. Never one to be short on words, I found this night to be different. I wondered how I could possibly find a way to express the magnitude of my love through the intense grief and pain I felt from her passing only days before.

I paused for a moment to talk with Momma to tell her how much I loved her and to ask for her guidance, just as I had done a thousand times before. She was certainly there with me, for the words suddenly came pouring out, as I quickly typed them onto the page. Then, my mother, Janet Rae Cecelia, decided to show me her playful and mischievous personality. While I was typing, Momma started changing the computer fonts and letter sizes and even made the curser dance all over the page. I felt so comforted in knowing she was there with me. I asked Momma to please continue to visit me and to show me signs whenever she was near.

After Grandmother Lena died, Momma would always find dimes, heavenly gifts from her mother letting her know she was near. So, just to be cute, I told Momma after she passed that she could send me some pennies down from heaven. Well, she did just that. I found pennies everywhere! They were almost any place imaginable—inside a shoe, high up on a pantry shelf, or even in the middle of a carpet I had just finished vacuuming. One penny even dropped down right in front of my feet out of *nowhere*. Momma's pennies arrived on almost a daily basis. They came even more frequently on the days I felt most blue. Sometimes, Grandma's dimes came along for the ride, too.

A year passed, and I felt it was finally time to grant my mother's wishes to spread her ashes in the majestic forests of northern California, alongside the ashes of my twin daughters, Isabella and Angelena. Due to premature birth, they had passed three and a half years before. I could not have imagined making this trip without my husband, Gregg, my daughter, Ella Angel, my best friend, Tiffany, and my mom's older sister, whom I consider my second momma, Auntie Lois (aka Auntie Lo).

Plans were made, and Auntie Lo flew in from Wisconsin. It was so wonderful to see her beautiful face, yet so bittersweet for both of us because Momma, Auntie Lo, and I had spent our whole lives together as three little peas in a pod. We were like the Three Musketeers. And now without my mother, we felt such great loss, emptiness, and sadness.

That first evening after Auntie Lo's arrival, the two of us decided to take a walk around my neighborhood to enjoy the summer warmth. Our conversation immediately turned to my mother and how we missed her so. As we walked along the paseos (pathways) talking about Momma, we noticed that each time we walked under a streetlight, the light would start to flicker, and then it would burn out. At first, Auntie Lo and I figured it was just a coincidence. Then, we had the sense that Momma was there with us, as we could feel her loving arms around us. By the time we reached home, a total of eleven streetlights had gone out during our walk!

It was pretty late, so Auntie Lo went to the guest room and started to get ready for bed. I was standing in the hallway outside her room talking to her about Momma when the hallway lights gradually began to dim. They got dimmer and dimmer until they went completely out. Then, they slowly turned back up again. Only the lights in the hallway were affected. In that moment, we both knew Momma's spirit was with us!

I leaned over to give Auntie a hug and a peck on the lips. As I kissed her goodnight, I couldn't shake the feeling that I had just kissed my mom! Dazed and astounded, I walked out of the room and started up the stairs when Auntie Lo said, "Good night, Vinette." She sounded exactly like Momma! I immediately responded with, "Good night,

Momma," without even thinking about it, and I walked upstairs to my bedroom.

Once upstairs, I froze. I suddenly realized what I had just said to my aunt; I was stunned! I ran back downstairs and asked, "Auntie, did you hear that? I just said, 'Goodnight, Momma!'"

"Yes, I did," Auntie Lo said. "I believe she is most certainly here with us!" This awareness rocked my world a bit, yet I was so very grateful for such a unique and beautiful experience.

A couple days later, five of us drove four and a half hours together to spread my mother's ashes. As we hiked through the forest past a beautiful waterfall, I could feel the spray on my face from the waterfall mixed with the tears welling up in my eyes. It wasn't supposed to be this way. Before she got sick with brain cancer, Momma and I had made plans for her to visit my twin daughters' memorial. Instead of bringing her with me for support, I was now preparing to spread her ashes.

At that moment, I prayed silently, "Momma, if you are here with me, as I believe in my heart you are, then please show me a rainbow." I could not believe my eyes; within seconds, there it was! The biggest, brightest rainbow I had ever seen and not just off in the distance. It was directly in front of me and in front of the boulder I was walking towards.

Excitedly, I yelled for my family to look. They stood in awe as I exclaimed, "I asked my mom to show me a rainbow, and she did it! She really did it!" My mother's spiritual presence continued to be felt throughout that trip. As sad as it was not having her physically there with us, I felt so comforted and blessed to have Momma caring for my babies.

Before my mother died, Auntie Lo asked her little sister if she had a plan to come back to visit after she passed; and, if so, what would she be? Momma replied, "A chickadee." Well, just before Auntie Lo returned home, the two of us decided to take a day trip to Catalina. It was a bright, sunny day, and we were waiting in line to get on the express boat. We were chatting about how much fun Momma and I had experienced on our last trip to Catalina, and how wonderful it would have been if she could have come along, too. Right then, a small bird (a blue chickadee) landed directly at our feet, pecking away at all the crumbs on the ground. Auntie Lo and I couldn't stop giggling about how the bird must have been my mother; it was tiny, cute, and loved to eat, just like Momma!

The evening before Auntie Lo's departure, we sat in her room and chatted. She was packing up her things while we talked, just like Momma did whenever she visited. Auntie Lo and I reminisced about the beautiful time we had just shared together and how my mother's spirit surely had accompanied us throughout the visit. When it was time to finally say goodnight, Momma swooped in and stole Auntie's kiss, just as she did on the first night. And, without hesitation, following Auntie's "Goodnight, Vinette" came my "Goodnight, Momma."

Vinette Cecelia Silvers, mother of Ella Angel, creates masterful, one-of-a-kind personalized collages. She dedicates her story to her beloved Gregg for his ongoing love and support, her magnificent Momma, and to her absolutely amazing Auntie Lo, who means the world to her.

A Memorable Hug

Mariflor Maulit-Uva

⎯⎯⎯⎯⎯

When I think about the death of my Uncle Danny, I think about the numerous people who came to his three-day wake and about the eighty cars that followed his hearse from the church to the cemetery. I remember the song "Danny Boy," sung so beautifully at his mass and how I had such difficulty speaking the words I had written to honor him in his eulogy. There was such silence as I stood in front of the altar. I could feel my eyes filling up with tears and my lips quivering. I knew those words by heart.

Uncle Danny touched so many lives and so many different people, from the very young to the very old. Many listening in the audience were members of his huge extended family, neighborhood friends, Filipino workers he had helped over the years, and individuals from the parish community. In the eulogy, I spoke about Uncle Danny's generosity and his tireless efforts to help his friends. I also mentioned his personal commitment to remember to do the things he enjoyed most. Not only was Uncle Danny known as an excellent cook, almost everyone in our community remembered his enthusiasm and deep love for fishing.

My uncle and I got to know one other quite well in the Philippines. His formal name is Reyorden Y. Maulit, but everyone called him Danny or Rey. Uncle Danny took care of my sister and me when our parents left to start a better life and future for us in the United States. I was five years old, and my sister, Maristelle, was three. Uncle Danny and Aunt Ester became our parents for a year and a half until we rejoined our own parents in New Jersey in June of 1976.

Because Uncle Danny worked a lot, we didn't get to see him much. But, when we did, it was always special. As a little girl, I remember him taking me to church on Sundays and then to the park to share a treat, such as shrimp chips; he would always allow me to bring something home for my sister. Afterwards, Uncle Danny would often turn on the record player, play his guitar, and sing along with the music. Singing with Uncle Danny while playing his guitar was a memorable pastime for our family.

Uncle Danny and Aunt Ester moved to the United States several years later. They lived with us in Jersey City until they had secured jobs and saved enough money to move out on their own. I fondly remember visiting them in their apartment, as well as my sister and I caring for our little cousin, Gabriel, whenever they visited us; frequent unannounced visits are common in our Filipino culture. Family gatherings are also important, and they were especially important to Uncle Danny. He rarely missed any of these traditional family affairs, even though he worked sixteen hours a day. Although my uncle may have been tired at our family gatherings, his smile was real, as he was always fully present for all of us.

Uncle Danny was chosen to be the godfather for my wedding. This is an honored role according to Filipino custom. The responsibilities include being a role model for married life, providing support, and taking over family matters in case of a tragedy. Uncle Danny felt privileged to fill this role in the multicultural wedding for my Italian husband and me. It meant a lot that he became my godfather, because it formalized his role in my life. It also proved to me Uncle Danny's intention of being a part of my life forever.

I remember the first time I heard the news that my uncle was very sick, possibly with pneumonia. Even though my mother told me that more testing was being done, I held on to the hope that he would overcome his illness. Two weeks later, I received the phone call from my parents telling me that Uncle Danny had lung cancer. I knew then my uncle was going to die.

On the night of Uncle Danny's death, my husband found me in our spare bedroom around midnight. I had fallen asleep on the guest bed while doing schoolwork. He had heard me crying hysterically, repeatedly yelling, "No, not now! No, not now!" My husband awakened me from what we both thought was a bad nightmare. Five hours later, the telephone rang. It was Mom calling to tell me that Uncle Danny had died four hours earlier, sometime after midnight, on July 16, 2003.

Since his death, I have had three separate dreams of Uncle Danny. The most memorable occurred approximately three months after he died. In the dream, I saw my uncle in the distance walking towards me in the midst of several other people. The dream took place in an academic setting and the other people in the dream seemed like students or faculty. Uncle Danny was happily walking towards me. He looked the same age as he did when he died, although he now appeared healthy and strong. Both Uncle Danny and I had great big smiles on our faces as we approached one another. I felt *so* excited! I longed to give my uncle a big, warm hug.

When I finally got to him, I hugged him for what seemed to be a very long embrace. His hug was so warm and so real, just like the hugs he had always given me throughout the years. Neither of us spoke a word. Then, he disappeared in my arms. Uncle Danny's hug in the dream gave me such a special feeling of being remembered by him. In my heart, I knew he still cared. Seeing him also reaffirmed my belief that my uncle was very happy and would always be near whenever I needed him.

On another occasion, I had a dream-like experience with him in a New Jersey park walking together, which we had done in the past. It felt so real that it is difficult to say whether it was an actual dream or not. I remember being in the park with Aunt Ester and my two little cousins, Gabriel and Joanne. My two children, Gabriel and Ian, were also with us. It was odd, though. I had the sense that Uncle Danny was with us. But in our conversations, we spoke of him in the past tense. I also remember my children playing in the playground while I sat and talked with Aunt Ester. I felt my uncle's presence so strongly that I question whether the time together was before or after his death. Nevertheless, the experience made me feel really close to Uncle

Danny. It also left me with the awareness that he longed to be with us as much as we longed to be with him.

The first two years after his death, whenever we visited our family in New Jersey, my boys would get sick with fevers. My parents claim that the fevers were due to Uncle Danny visiting them. Both Mom and Dad are quite superstitious. They believe that whenever a spirit visits, it affects the physical state of the living. This may be true, as the only symptoms the boys experienced during those trips were fevers, which resolved as soon as we arrived back home in Massachusetts.

It saddens me that my two sons will never get to know their Uncle Danny but I am reassured by the thought that he was with us in New Jersey, especially those first two years. Whether it is through his visits in dreamtime, his presence in New Jersey, or the warm, reassuring sensation that I feel whenever I visit his mausoleum, it is so comforting to know that my godfather is still watching over me.

Mariflor Maulit-Uva, Vice-President of Finance and Administration for Net Atlantic, volunteers for North Shore Women in Business, Beverly Kiwanis Club, and St. James Parish. Mariflor enjoys traveling, planning events, and learning; family time and quiet time are most important.

A Friend for Life

Elissa Al-Chokhachy

Ethel, a ninety-six-year-old woman with Alzheimer's, was bedridden. With the support of private round-the-clock nursing coverage, she was able to remain at home. Ethel slept twenty-four hours a day, except when awakened to be fed, bathed, changed, and repositioned. One morning, I arrived at 6 AM to find her sleeping comfortably. Since Ethel was not due to be awakened until 8 AM, I decided to take advantage of the time by meditating. I slipped off my shoes and stretched out my legs on the comfy white leather couch in the adjacent room. My lower back was resting up against the wide leather armrest; both my arms were at my side. Five minutes later, I felt an animal literally pounce on my belly! The weight seemed heavy enough to be either a large cat or a small dog.

I opened my eyes immediately and jumped to my feet with a start. I quickly scanned the room, but could not find an animal anywhere. How odd, I thought to myself; the night nurse didn't give me any instruction on what needed to be done for Ethel's pet. I searched upstairs and downstairs, yet still found nothing. No animal dish, animal food, or pet. I was somewhat troubled, as I didn't want an animal to go hungry on my behalf. The only thing I found was a 9 × 12 framed picture of two white Bichon dogs in the dining room.

The day passed, and I was perplexed. Not once did I see or hear an animal. Quite concerned, I questioned the nurse who had arrived to relieve me. She laughed and told me that although Ethel was very devoted to her two dogs, the last one had died about six years earlier; this nurse strongly reassured me that there were no animals in Ethel's home.

Coincidentally, inside my nursing bag, I happened to be carrying a new book that I had just purchased, *Talking to Heaven* by James Van Praagh. While Ethel slept, I read various accounts within its pages about communication with the other side. One story that caught my attention was particularly appropriate for me to read that day. The author described a deaf woman by the name of Susan who had come to see him with an interpreter. She was looking for information about a loved one.

During her session, James was able to accurately relay detailed information about Susan's house. He described her brown sofa under a window, which occasionally had a blanket on it. The author mentioned several pictures on a stand, some flowers on a shelf, and an orange rug with spots on it next to the front door. He went on to describe her refrigerator, which had many pictures of a dog on it. All of a sudden, James felt incredible love fill the room, and he spoke the name "Charlie." Susan broke down crying hysterically. It was only at that point in the encounter that she revealed the identity of Charlie as her hearing dog!

Susan confirmed that Charlie loved to sit on the couch all the time, and his favorite place was under the blanket. From time to time, he would claw on the orange carpet at the front door and pretend he was burying things. James went on to relay a message from Charlie that he loved Susan very much, and he still sleeps at the foot of her bed.

Because he had been in a lot of pain, Charlie was glad that she had him put down. He was now working from the other side to help get her another trained dog for the hearing impaired. The new dog would look like a white husky. Once the husky arrived, Charlie would make sure that the new dog knew what to do. Before the session ended, Charlie reassured Susan that she didn't have to worry. She would never be alone.

Up until this time, I had never entertained the idea of deceased animals staying around to help their masters. On that day, maybe I was stretched out in a favorite spot, and one of Ethel's Bichons got my attention. Her devoted companion just wanted me to know that pets live on, too, and he is still around, helping Ethel.

Mother's Hug

Hannah Marie

—◦—

I consider my mother a saint, as she was married to my self-centered father for over fifty years. A strong, creative, warm, and loving woman, Mother was a teacher by profession and also a teacher of the heart. We thoroughly enjoyed doing things together that either one of us thought was interesting. Mother loved all of her children more than anything. When it was my turn to become a mother, she helped me through the challenges that motherhood presented. It is safe to say that my wonderful mother will always be my oldest and closest friend. I have also been blessed with several dear girlfriends whom I adore and refer to as my "sisters in spirit."

My mother raised eight children and loved each of us for who we were and what she knew we could become. Upon the sudden death of her first child, an adult son, Mother was left with tremendous pain and suffered in ways only a parent can. Through it all, she always held on to the hope that, one day, she would see her eldest son again, along with her parents who had gone on many years before. The death of my brother was quite painful for all of us. Often, Mother and I would talk about the hope of forever, the eternities and the way that families could be together again after death. I would remind her that through the resurrection of Jesus Christ, we are able to be reunited with loved ones, family members and friends in a much better place—a place where there is no sickness, pain, or suffering—a place of knowledge, hope, truth, and love.

Several years after my brother's death, I faced the possibility of losing my own firstborn son, who had become quite ill. As a result of numerous operations and endless prayers to understand God's will, the will of our Father in Heaven, my son was able to survive and even grow into adulthood. Mom and I spent a lot of time together in those days. She was determined to get through the loss of her son; as a mother, I was trying to do the best I could to care for a child who had so many battles to fight. Through it all, Mother and I grew even closer. We gave strength to one another in so many ways. Needless to say, when Mother passed away from leukemia in 2002, the loss of her close contact and companionship felt huge.

I was with my mother at the time she passed. It was a sweet journey for her. I saw this in her eyes, as she returned to the eternal place we had talked about so many times before. With her two last breaths, my mother turned her head towards me and looked into my eyes. Without saying a word, I felt her thoughts ... *You see, I'm going now.* Mother's clear blue eyes spoke to me. Like the innocence of a small child witnessing the release and flight of a butterfly for the first time ever, my mother's eyes were wide with joy and her mouth open in awe for all that she was seeing. I know Mother's final breath wasn't really her last, for in that moment, she was taking a new breath. It would be her first breath on the other side where she would be joyfully reunited with loved ones who had gone on before her. In that moment, my mother's faith became knowledge. What a blessing to be with her at that time.

A few months later, I had a dream about my mother. I was standing in my driveway next to our carport. I remember seeing her standing in the circle of the driveway. Mother was young and healthy, and her skin was pink with color. I noticed there were several other people standing in the yard watching us, and I had the sense that they were loved ones, perhaps family members from generations long ago.

In the dream, I knew that Mother had died. But I also knew she was with me, and I wanted a hug. "Mom!" I exclaimed. We immediately embraced, and I felt Mother's hug so fully. She looked happy and well. Her hug felt exactly as I had remembered it. Then, I woke at 6:30 AM crying, because I was so happy to have one more hug from my mom. My husband, who was getting ready for work, heard me crying in my sleep. I shared my dream with him and how happy I felt. I was truly humbled with the gift I had received. Yet some part of me wondered why the Heavenly Father and my mom thought I needed an extra hug...

The very next morning, exactly twenty-four hours later, at 6:30 AM, I learned the reason why. My daughter, who was away at college, called me, crying hysterically. The police were with her. Someone had hurt my child, my beautiful child. I was two thousand miles away, and I couldn't get to her fast enough. I was devastated at such an atrocity.

In less than three hours, I was sitting on a plane on my way to help my daughter. I was trying so desperately to hold back my tears when I heard a small, quiet voice whisper, "I'm still here with you. You're not alone. Remember my hug... my love." It was Mother, still comforting me, still my ever-present strength. Even though she had passed from this world, my mother was there holding, comforting, supporting, and helping me through those difficult days, weeks, months, and years that followed. I know Mother will always be my strength for the rest of my life. And, one day, when it's my turn to pass through the veil and enter the next sweet world, Mother will be there to greet me with open arms, to give me a hug, and to welcome me home once again.

Hannah Marie is the proud mother of five children and has been happily married for over twenty-five years. When not caring for her own children as a stay-at-home mom, Hannah enjoys teaching preschoolers and helping students with special needs.

THE GIFT

Rami Al-Chokhachi

How does one begin to describe that which defies description? My father, Fattah Jabbir Al-Chokhachi, was my greatest influence. An immigrant from the Middle East in the 1950s, Dad came to the United States from a typical working class family. He knew education was his ticket to a better life.

Having begun his formal education in his home country of Iraq, Dad was given a college scholarship by the Iraqi government to study abroad at Ohio State University. Once there, he met my mother, a blonde, blue-eyed girl from Tennessee, and as they say, the rest is history. The two of them fell in love, eloped, and were married just a few months later on New Year's Day in 1959. Mom's parents were opposed to the marriage because they were certain this Arab was going to take their daughter away to some foreign land, never to be seen again. As fate would have it, they weren't too far from the truth.

In November of 1959, my brother, David, was born in Knoxville, Tennessee, and I followed nineteen months after that. At the time, my father was obligated to repay the Iraqi government for the education he had received in the states. So, in 1962, the four of us moved to Baghdad, Iraq. Little did we know that we would soon be living a life of luxury with Dad employed as an engineer by the Iraqi government. We were supplied with our own house, housekeepers, gardeners, vehicles, and even chauffeurs. Although I was too young to remember it, apparently we lived quite well. When I was three years old, things seemed to be going along smoothly until the government of Iraq was overthrown in 1964. The four of us had to literally flee the country back to the United States with nothing more than the clothes on our backs. Nevertheless, both my parents have repeatedly spoken fondly of those early days. And, had it not been for a strange twist of fate, we most probably would have continued to live in Iraq for the remainder of our days. It simply was not meant to be.

We returned to Knoxville, and as a family, started over. At the time, I only spoke Arabic, so my older brother served as my English translator wherever we went. Fortunately, Dad had been educated in the States and had little trouble finding work as a civil engineer. He continued to work for various engineering firms across the state until he finally settled in Memphis. I was in second grade at the time and, from then on, our family pretty much lived a typical American lifestyle. Then my younger sister was born. She was named Dunyah, which means "the universe" in Arabic. How perceptive of my father to give her such a name. Having already been blessed with his two sons, this daughter was his crowning glory.

In the late seventies, Dad eventually started his own engineering firm. Although I had originally hoped to become a lawyer, Dad's company was gaining steam. I decided to join him, as did my brother. With the three of us working full-time, Dad's business took off. His first two grandchildren were born, and Dad couldn't have been happier. Then the first Gulf War started. With Dad's family still living in Iraq, I literally had cousins fighting on both sides of the conflict. In some respects, it resembled a civil war within our own family. Although the cousins fighting on each side didn't know one another, I knew it. So did Dad. It bothered us both greatly.

The war came and went. Two more grandchildren were born, and Dad felt blessed in so many ways. Then, two days before Thanksgiving in 1999, Dad was diagnosed with stage three multiple myeloma, or in layman's terms, advanced bone cancer. He fought hard with aggressive radiation, chemotherapy, experimental therapy, and even a stem cell transplant. A deeply religious man, his faith never wavered. Dad's greatest joy came from being surrounded by the family that he loved, and, most especially, his grandchildren.

Christmas of the following year was to be our last Christmas with Dad. I was forty-one years old; I had never seen anyone die. My father had taught me how to live. Now, he would teach me his one final lesson on how to die with grace, honor, and dignity.

For the last week of his life, Dad was bedridden, and my brother and I kept vigil at his bedside. Our sister, who was caring for two small babies, remained in constant contact. We, along with our loving mother, were his caregivers. Our cousin, Elissa, from Massachusetts, was on her way with her daughter, and Dad knew it. He thought the world of Elissa. Being a hospice nurse, Dad knew that she would know how to help him, as well as the rest of the family.

Around 9 PM on the evening he died, the house was full of family. We had all taken turns at his bedside. It just so happened that I was sitting next to Dad holding his hand, telling him how much I loved him. I told him not to worry about anything and that my brother and I would take care of Mom; it was okay if he needed to go. Just then, Dad's breathing, which had been labored, stopped. I looked towards the foot of his bed to Elissa, who said, "Rami, you need to call your mother!" I called out to Mom, but there was so much going on that I didn't think she heard me. So, I called out again, this time with much more volume and emphasis. Everyone could tell by the tone of my voice what was happening, and they all came running. Instantly, the entire family surrounded Dad. The sound of wailing and audible prayers in his native language of Arabic was beyond belief. It was surreal. It was like a scene from a movie. It was as if my father's spirit was being lifted up by all of the sound. It went on for what seemed like an eternity.

In the midst of it all, I again looked towards the foot of the bed, and there stood Elissa. She had a sense of peace on her face which told me that Dad was going to be just fine. Elissa had so much more experience than me with this thing called death. And I knew she knew something I didn't. Over the years, my father had always told us that he had been given everything in life that he had ever wished for. As a child, he had always wanted to come to the United States, and he was able to do so. Dad had wished for a beautiful wife and family one day, and he had received those blessings. He had wanted to own his own business, and that came true, too. My father's final wish was to die with his family by his side and that wish was fulfilled, as well. What a blessed life my father lived. We should all be so lucky.

On February 23, 2003, Dad died an honorable and peaceful death. What an adjustment. As I write these words, six months have passed. On Father's Day, Elissa telephoned to offer me a gift. She asked if I would like to share an extraordinary experience that happened with Dad in a book that she was compiling. What a wonderful gift—an opportunity to pay tribute to the greatest man I have ever known. My father always treated others with the utmost respect and dignity; he looked down on no one. To me, that is the mark of a great man.

Three months after my father's death, I found myself still marking the twenty-third of each month in my mind with great reverence, reflecting on the many wonderful times we had shared. I had been thinking quite a lot about Dad and had been talking to him, as I still do. Even though I had never been much of a believer in supernatural things, I found myself asking my father to please send me some type of sign that he was all right. It was the night of May 23, 2003, and I had a dream that totally blew me away.

Even though I had experienced several ordinary dreams of my father after he had passed, this particular dream was remarkable and like no other dream I had ever had. In the dream, my brother and I were sitting at our two drawing tables at the family business working quietly and waiting for someone, although I wasn't quite sure who it might be. Suddenly, a very bright white light started to emanate from the hallway behind me. With a sense that someone was entering the room, I glanced over my right shoulder. Into our office walked Dad, nonchalantly, as if he didn't have a care in the world. His pace was much slower than normal, as if there was no hurry or urgency about anything. I couldn't believe my eyes. Dad looked incredibly healthy and was glancing around the room in a relaxed way. Both my brother and I were staring at him in amazement when David spoke up and said exactly what I was thinking. "Dad," he said incredulously, "*You look great!*"

Then, I noticed that the scar on the right side of my father's face from when he was a little child was completely gone. Dad turned to me and held out his right hand. I longingly held his hand in both of my hands and began to weep. I could *feel* the fullness of his hand in mine! I thought to myself how full and healthy his hand felt, unlike the way it was when he passed away. I remember touching the soft fabric sleeve that covered his arm. It felt like the softest cotton fabric anyone could ever imagine. And I could smell *his* smell! In fact, I noticed that all my senses were heightened. As I looked directly into Dad's eyes, he had the most indescribable peace emanating from them.

As I looked at my father, weeping at the joy of seeing him, Dad spoke. All he said was, "I have to go now." He withdrew his hand from mine, stepped back, and I pleaded, "Dad, come back again *soon!*" Then, my father stepped backwards and faded into a small ball of light, which burst into many different directions. I immediately awoke from the dream, but intentionally did not open my eyes for several moments. I wanted to savor every moment of what had just transpired, not wanting it to end. The dream occurred exactly three months to the day after Dad had died. I lay in my bed for well over an hour, replaying it over and over in my head. I never wanted to lose that feeling. I had been praying for a sign as to Dad's well-being, and I felt assured that my prayers had been answered.

When I told my wife, she cried, knowing it was so much more than a dream. I was so excited that I told everyone about it wherever I went. I wanted the world to know that my dad was really okay. I also shared the experience with Mike, one of my closest college buddies, who worked at the office with us. I was interested to hear what Mike would say, as he was extremely well read in spiritual matters. After listening intently to everything I shared, Mike looked me squarely in the eyes and said, "Rami, it sounds to me like you were blessed with a vision. A vision is a gift from God, and if so, you should be very thankful." The thought never crossed my mind. But, I also knew that Mike could be right. I have finally come to the conclusion that no matter what it was, somehow someone sent me the sign that I had been asking for. As a result, I now believe that my father is in a good place, and I no longer need to ask for a sign. I have already been given one.

I still miss Dad every day, more than I can possibly say. But I understand that life is a cycle, and the cycle continues. It is said that when a man teaches his son, he teaches his son's son. I truly believe that with all my heart. I believe my father raised me to be a good and honorable man, and that is why I have been blessed with minimal discipline problems with my own children. I hear other parents complain about their kids; fortunately, through the grace of God, I don't have those same problems with mine. I attribute those blessings directly to my own father's wisdom and honesty. My father's birthday is tomorrow, and this tribute is my gift to him. Dad, I'll see you again one day. I love you.

Rami F. Al-Chokhachi, partner at AFA Engineering, is the happily married father of Logan and Alyssa. He enjoys mountain biking, riding his Harley, and spending time with his wife, Julie, and his family.

A Comforting Presence

Susan Beetem

⁓

George Jeffrey Beetem was known as "Jeff" his entire life. Following his five-year battle with chronic lymphocytic leukemia, my fifty-year-old husband died in December 1997 surrounded by twenty family members and closest friends. Before he died, the two of us had made a pact. If there really was life after life, Jeff promised he would find a way to let me know. It just so happened that a few days after his memorial service, I was sitting in the living room with one of my closest friends, Linda, reminiscing about my husband. Our conversation began around dusk and, as the evening progressed, the living room naturally became darker. Unaffected by the dim light, we continued to talk, when I noticed something peculiar... an outline of Jeff in bright light had appeared on the wall behind Linda; I simply couldn't take my eyes off the image. Concerned, Linda noticed me staring at something and asked what was wrong.

As I started to describe what I was seeing, a second, identical image appeared on the wall behind me. Although the two images seemed to move a bit, they mostly stayed in the same spot on each wall. The two of us sat glued to our chairs watching him. No one spoke; time seemed to stand still. Then, he was gone. Jeff had come to visit us both. The moving images confirmed the existence of life after life.

Even more remarkable, a few nights following Jeff's memorial service, something awakened me in the middle of the night. I got up out of bed and walked to my bedroom door. At the top of the stairs, there stood Jeff looking out the clerestory windows! Appearing as a being of pure light, but quite recognizable, my husband turned and looked at me; our eyes met briefly. I wanted to say something, but no words would come out. Then, Jeff turned back to the windows, and I went back to bed. I wasn't frightened in any way; actually, I was comforted.

For the next six months, I had nightly encounters with Jeff. I usually woke up around 2 or 3 AM, and I would find Jeff standing at the top of the stairs looking out the window. He always turned to acknowledge me. I never spoke to him out loud; I didn't need to. During this time, the air in my home seemed to be consistently heavy and icy cold. Yet Jeff's nightly presence brought me reassurance and peace.

In June 1998, the kids and I went to visit my friend Nancy and her family in Southern California. One night, Nancy and I went to Los Angeles to see a psychic. Because I had never been to one before, I was extremely skeptical. I vowed to listen and say nothing, which I did. The evening was interesting. As Nancy and I were returning to our car, the psychic followed us out, telling me that there was someone who wanted to speak to me; his name began with the letter J. She asked if I'd recently lost someone. I nodded yes. The psychic said the person I had lost wanted me to know that he was there with me and would reveal information that only he and I would know.

The first thing the psychic told me was that Jeff wanted to remind me of how mad he would get whenever I left my wedding ring on the kitchen counter next to the sink while I was cleaning; he was sure that ring would end up down the drain. I was awestruck. That was absolutely true! Then, she asked if I had wooden stairs in my house. I responded yes. She said that he was saying something about standing at the top of the stairs every night, looking out the windows, and how it was one of his favorite spots in the house. I nearly fainted when she told me that! Then Jeff also apologized for being so difficult during the last year of his life when he was so sick and dying. He now knows how impossible he was—and he was!

After we returned to Nancy's home, I felt emotionally exhausted and spent. I climbed into the queen bed I was sharing with my thirteen-year-old daughter, who was sound asleep. As I reviewed everything that had transpired during that evening, I remembered that the psychic had told me I needed to talk out loud to Jeff. He couldn't read my mind.

I sat up on the edge of the bed and said, "Okay, Jeff, if you really are here, touch me." Suddenly, I felt an icy, cold grip on my left upper arm along with a buzzing and an electric-like shock that went up and down my body. Again, I said out loud, "I don't believe it—do it again!" Immediately, I felt another icy, cold grip on my left upper arm with the same buzzing and electric shock feeling go up and down my entire body. There was no denying it. *It was Jeff!* I cried with excitement and joy as my daughter slept peacefully next to me, unaware of what had just taken place.

The next day, we returned to Albuquerque. As I walked into our home, the first thing I noticed was that the air in the house felt light and warm. My husband had kept his promise.

A few years later, I was driving south on I-25 around one in the afternoon on my way to meet my daughter at the movies. I had just started to exit onto the San Mateo off-ramp. Then, the car in front of me hit sand, slammed on its brakes, and started to skid. Of course, I slammed on my brakes, and the person behind me slammed on his. All three cars were spinning out, and I was sure my car was going to end up over the side of the ramp down the cliff. Everything seemed to be going in slow motion; it was totally out of my control. Then, I felt Jeff's presence sitting next to me in the car. I couldn't physically see him, but I could feel his presence. I knew it was him; there was never a question about it.

Finally, my car stopped spinning, and so did the others. None of us hit anything. We were all safe. Then, each of us turned our car around in the right direction and continued down the off-ramp. As I drove away, I couldn't help but wonder if the other drivers had departed loved ones helping them in their cars, too.

Every once in a while, I still feel Jeff's presence. Sometimes it happens when I'm home. Other times it will be when I'm driving my car, and I suddenly feel his presence next to me. Whenever I feel Jeff near, I speak out loud to him. I tell him about everything he is missing regarding our children, how they are doing, and all their milestones. I don't get a response, but I know he is listening. Somehow, those conversations end up with me feeling reassured that Jeff hasn't missed a thing at all.

A LAST HUG FROM MOM

Carol Dullea

My mother, Betty Simpson, was a wonderful woman full of love, laughter, and life. When I think of her, I remember Mom's warm, loving smile. Even her voice seemed to have that same smile in it. Because Mom was a sentimental person, she cried easily whether she was happy or sad. It drove me nuts as a teenager. Now that I've grown older, I understand that Mom's tears were an outward expression of her incredibly huge heart. If I were to describe Mom in one word, it would be "love." She taught my three siblings and me to love God, our country, and each other. Most importantly, she taught us to love ourselves. It is by her remarkable example that we learned the true meaning of love.

Mom was also a worrier. She always wanted the best for all concerned. Because of that, she worried about everyone and everything. A perfect example of her caring and compassionate nature was an episode that occurred during the late '80s, which my siblings and I have laughed about for years. For noise and safety reasons, the residents of Sluice Pond, a small pond next to our home, were trying to prevent avid boaters who lived on the pond from using jet skis. One day, a young man knocked at our door and asked Mom to sign a petition banning the jet skis from Sluice Pond. Mom became quite upset, thinking that the "Jetskis" were an immigrant family who were being discriminated against. How could he ask such a thing?! This was typical of Mom's ongoing love and concern for others. The Jetskis story was only one of the many cute, but dumb things Mom would think and do. In fact, there were so many that my siblings and I coined such events as "doing a Betty." Now, occasionally when one of us "does a Betty," we laugh and lovingly reminisce about how much Mom would have enjoyed it.

About eighteen months prior to her death, Mom was diagnosed with breast cancer. She had a lumpectomy, radiation treatment, and chemotherapy. Mom seemed to be doing fine, but a few months later, she complained about abdominal pain that seemed to be worsening. Because she believed the chemotherapy was causing her stomach pains, Mom was planning on discontinuing the treatment. However, two weeks later, she was admitted to the hospital for bowel surgery. The doctors told us afterwards that Mom was seriously ill with colon cancer. For the next six days, she remained on a respirator in the ICU. Our family members visited often. Through our tears and grief, we rallied to be a support for Mom, Dad, and each other.

Every evening before I left the hospital, I would tell Mom how much I loved her, and I would give her a kiss goodbye. I remember longing to hear my mother's voice just one more time. Less than a week later, my father, siblings, and I met with her doctors and discussed quality-of-life issues for Mom. Unanimously, we decided that Mom would want to be taken off the respirator. After the meeting, we went to her hospital room and formed a circle around the bed as the respiratory therapist removed Mom's breathing tube. Two minutes later, Mom died peacefully while we were praying.

My own grieving process was just as one might expect. There were tears, some guilt, and of course, the inevitable "Why me?" Overall, I thought I handled it pretty well. However, when I least expected it, I would start to cry. Afterwards, I would feel better and move on. These moments occurred less and less as weeks passed.

Then, one gloomy afternoon on my way home from work, I found myself thinking about Mom for the first time in quite a while. By the time I arrived home, I was very sad and missed her terribly; I felt so alone. I lay down on my bed to take my usual late afternoon nap and then burst into tears, sobbing like a broken-hearted child. Then, all of a sudden, a wonderful feeling came over me. I felt enveloped, as if someone were giving me the most loving hug imaginable! It brought me right back to the times when Mom hugged me as a little child. Initially, I was startled. Then I relaxed, stopped sobbing, and allowed the most incredible feeling to take over. It was almost like being wrapped in a warm, snuggly blanket. Without a doubt, it was the most wonderful, loving, and peaceful feeling I have ever had in my life. Not only did it make me feel good enough to stop crying, it actually made me smile!

This nurturing experience lasted only a few minutes, but it is something I will never forget. On that extremely difficult day, I truly believe Mom hugged me one last time. In my heart of hearts, I knew my mom was at peace. She was just making sure I was all right. Thanks to Mom, the great news is that I am.

Carol Dullea is an administrative assistant in the Emergency Department of NSMC Union Hospital. She enjoys spending time with her family, traveling, NASCAR, and volunteering for the New England Organ Bank and as support staff chair of the New Hampshire Gay Men's Chorus.

7

A Sense of Presence

Ever felt an angel's breath in the gentle breeze?
A teardrop in the falling rain?
Hear a whisper amongst the rustle of leaves?
Or been kissed by a lone snowflake?
Nature is an angel's favorite hiding place.

—CARRIE LATET

THE GIFT OF PRESENCE IS one of the greatest gifts that can be given. Caring, compassion, and physical presence can mean the world to the dying and the bereaved. After someone has passed, bereaved individuals often have a sense that their deceased loved ones are still around. Sometimes, this sense is conveyed through a heightened connection to nature. Other times, presence is experienced through an energetic recognition of the individual. These unexpected visits provide solace, hope, and reassurance.

Gifts from Big Daddy

Phillip G. Crabtree, Jr.

———

Until I was seven years old, my grandfather, Corbin Meriwether, and I shared what would be considered a typical grandfather-grandson relationship. However, the year I turned seven was when everything changed for both of us. In that year, my parents divorced and my grandmother, whom we lovingly referred to as Little Momma, died of cancer. As a result, both my grandfather (or "Big Daddy," as I called him) and I were left with huge, empty voids in our lives.

Shortly after that, Big Daddy became more involved in everything I did. He was the father figure that I very much needed, and I became the son he never had. From then on, we were the best of friends. Some of our favorite pastimes were hiking, bird watching, and visiting wildlife refuges. During those times, I loved to sit back, relax, and listen to Big Daddy tell so many wonderful stories. Whenever we were together, the troubles of the world seemed small.

In 1979, when I was nine, Big Daddy took me on a vacation. Together, we toured the Caribbean Islands. We had a great time. While I was there, he bought me a white T-shirt that I liked. The front of the t-shirt had a picture of a yellow duck cartoon caricature wearing oversized sunglasses. In one lens of the glasses there was an image of Martinique, and in the other lens, the island of St. Martin. In twelve months or so, I outgrew the t-shirt, but held on to it for a long time, not wanting to part with it because of its sentimental value.

In 1990, I was twenty years old when Big Daddy passed away. It was such a difficult loss. In an effort to be strong for my mother and family, I suppressed my grief and held things in for quite a while. After several months, I felt disconnected from the carefree spirit I had as a child. I knew that in order to reclaim this precious part of myself, I had to face the reality of my grandfather's death. I began to revisit some of our favorite places. Reliving these memories helped to restore the little boy inside my heart. The carefree spirit that was once missing now returned with an even deeper love and respect for Big Daddy, his wisdom, and his teachings.

Several years later, I went to work in Nashville as a musician. Music and guitars had become a big part of my life. I decided to put my Caribbean duck T-shirt to good use. Instead of using an ordinary cloth to polish my guitars, I used the T-shirt from Big Daddy. The shirt served more as a talisman for me of my grandfather than a polishing cloth. It was like having a small, special reminder of Big Daddy with me always.

As I approached my thirtieth birthday, I was feeling pretty down. After noticing the first signs of aging and admittedly falling short of where I wanted to be in my life, several special people had also recently died. I was feeling pretty alone until one memorable evening…

I had just returned home from music rehearsal and went to my room as I always did to clean my guitar. I took out my Gibson Les Paul standard and old T-shirt from the guitar case to polish the guitar before putting it away. What was unusual about that night was that when I picked up the t-shirt, for some reason, my mind flooded with memories of Big Daddy. Since I cleaned my guitars fairly often and had been using the cloth for years, it was unusual for me to think of my grandfather every time I used it. However, that evening, I had lots of memories of Big Daddy. I finished polishing the guitar. Then, I put it away.

I was getting ready to turn in for the night when out of the corner of my eye, I noticed a tiny, fluffy, brilliant white feather, no bigger than a thumbnail, in the middle of my bedroom floor. As I picked it up, I was totally captivated by the feeling and presence of Big Daddy! He spoke to me, acknowledging that I had been hurting inside for quite a while. Big Daddy let me know that he was with me and always had been. He told me that life is about living now, not in the past or the future. And, one day, we would be together again. Something profound stirred inside me. I felt incredibly uplifted! For the moment, all of my troubles seemed small. Later that night, I searched all through my room to see if the feather could have come from something I owned, but nothing was found except the pleasant memory of my grandfather.

From that day on, thanks to Big Daddy, I have learned to view things not so much with my eyes, but rather to listen and feel things more with my heart. For a while, the feather served as a daily reminder of the teachings I received that night from my grandfather. I have since given the feather to my mom; I knew it would lift her spirits even more than mine. I have retired the t-shirt; it has served its purpose well. Although Big Daddy's presence was quite brief that evening, its impact will be with me for a lifetime ... all because of the tiniest, white angel of a feather ... one of the many loving gifts I received from my grandfather.

Phillip G. Crabtree, Jr. restores and repairs vintage stringed instruments for the Gibson Guitar Corporation in Hermitage, Tennessee. As he did with Big Daddy, he still enjoys being in nature, watching classic movies, and most importantly, seeking God's word, heart, and blessings.

I Am Always With You

Dana Peters-Ventrillo

———

My Italian mother died at sixty-five years old. She was a beautiful woman with big blue eyes and a smile that never stopped. Known for her delicious eggplant parmesan and homemade apple pies, my mother was the best cook. Everyone loved her. She was the type of person who would give her last dollar to anyone who needed it. One time, while she was hospitalized, my mother actually crocheted a sweater set and an afghan for a pregnant nurse caring for her. She made sure to complete all of them before she left the hospital because she didn't know how much time she had left.

To my mother, her children and grandchildren were her life; she lived for them. When diagnosed with colon cancer that spread to her liver, my mother fought hard for her life with chemotherapy, but it destroyed her. She couldn't do it anymore, and we brought her home to die.

Since her death, I always see my mother in my dreams. In one powerful dreamlike experience, she came to visit me. I opened the door at my sister's house, and there she was. I was surprised to see her. We hugged and kissed. My mother told me that she had come to talk to me. She said, "You have to stop being so sad and worrying about me. I am very happy, and I am always around you. All you need to do is call me. I am and always will be here for you." I started to cry, because I was so happy to hold her in my arms and touch her. Then I woke up. For over an hour, I could still smell her body and feel her presence. I know my mother loves me. She will always be my guardian angel.

Dana Peters-Ventrillo, LPN, wife, mother, and grandmother, was inspired to become a hospice nurse by her mother's visit. Thankful for her mother in her life, Dana happily shares this awareness with her Merrimack Valley Hospice patients and their families.

The Rainbow Follows the Storm

Joan M. Lunn

Steve and I were high-school sweethearts. Deeply in love, we were inseparable. For years, Steve was active in DeMolay, and I was a member of the International Order of the Rainbow for Girls, and both met in the same building. During Tuesday night Rainbow meetings, I would secretly leave a love note for him underneath a designated candleholder. On Wednesday evenings during DeMolay, Steve would retrieve the hidden love note I had written.

While we were in college, Steve enlisted in the ROTC. By doing so, he would become an officer in the Army, and I could follow him. The choice to enlist was obvious; we wanted to stay together. Following our graduations from college, Steve and I were married. Each time Steve received a military assignment, we would be blessed with a beautiful rainbow, our symbol of hope letting us know that everything would be okay.

Probably the most significant rainbow we received involved Steve's Vietnam deployment. Like most of his friends, he had received orders to depart for an unspecified location there. A few months later, as Steve's ship sailed into the port of Guam, an auspicious rainbow appeared and actually followed his ship into the harbor. Steve took a picture of the rainbow and sent it home to me. I felt reassured that, one day, all would be right with our world. We were among the lucky ones; Steve came home safely. My husband and I were able to purchase a home and raise two sons together. Throughout the years, lots of rainbow blessings came and went for all of us.

Then, during a routine physical in 1987, a small lump was discovered on Steve's prostate gland. A biopsy confirmed prostate cancer. For the next nine years, surgery, blood tests, radiation, chemotherapy, and checkups became a way of life. Despite his battle with cancer,

Steve continued to work, play, travel, and carry on as normal a life as possible.

His health deteriorated and Steve became bedbound, requiring home care. It became obvious he was not going to bounce back. On the morning before Father's Day, Steve was not responsive. Later that day, he died quietly in the arms of our son, surrounded by those he loved. No one could ask for anything more. Steve's long, painful ordeal was finally over.

I telephoned one of my husband's fraternity brothers to notify him of Steve's death. Bob's response was, "What a wonderful Father's Day gift. God gave him rest." I held on to that thought, which brought me such comfort after our thirty-four years of marriage.

Since his passing, Steve sends me rainbows on a regular basis. The rainbows are my husband's way of letting me know changes are taking place, all is well, and most certainly, life continues on. In March of 2000, I was driving along the highway when I saw the brightest rainbow I had ever seen. I called a former Rainbow friend to tell her my husband was sending me a message, letting me know everything would be okay. The next day, I took a flight to visit my bright, social, and active ninety-two-year-old mother in Florida. Once there, I soon discovered that she had peacefully died in her own bed overlooking the Gulf of Mexico. Our family released a large bouquet of balloons on the evening before her funeral. The next morning, we awoke to another rainbow.

Over the years, I have felt Steve's presence with me. There is no doubt that my husband helps me find my way. He did this for me when he was alive on this earth, and he continues to do it for me now. If I misplace something, I simply stop and ask him for help; then, I find the lost item within minutes. The same is true with front-row parking spaces. Steve helps me find them, even on the busiest of shopping days.

As time goes on, I dream of my husband more and more often. Because there is usually a rainbow in these dreams, I know Steve is sending me our sign to let me know all is well. The faith instilled by my parents has kept me strong through everything that has happened. I know that if I hold firmly on to the hand of faith, the rainbow will follow the storm, and all in my life will be well.

Joan Morgan Lunn is a retired speech and language pathologist and mother of two grown sons. She enjoys reading, traveling, and doing church work, although her most special time is spent with her grandchildren.

TIME TO MOVE ON

Jane Potter

⌒

Born into a family of modest means, my husband, Calvin Richard Potter, was the third of five siblings and the first to graduate from high school. At that time, the world was in a state of political unrest, as World War II had already begun in Europe. Cal, like so many other young men, felt compelled to join the war effort. The Army, Navy, and Marines all had rejected him due to a heart irregularity from a childhood case of rheumatic fever. Knowing his deep desire to serve in the armed forces, a family physician friend provided medication for Cal to take twenty minutes before his U.S. Naval Reserve entrance physical. Cal took the medicine as directed, intentionally not disclosing his childhood history of rheumatic fever. Although the examining physician detected a heart irregularity, the doctor assumed it due to situational anxiety and approved Cal's assignment into the U.S. Maritime Service. At the age of twenty, Cal reported for duty.

An officer and ensign in the USNR, Cal's main responsibilities as a radio operator consisted of sending and receiving Morse code messages in addition to making sure every radio shift was covered. I rarely saw him, as his ship would be at sea for long stretches at a time. Cal wanted me to marry him on one of his weekend leaves, but my parents, particularly my father, preferred that I wait.

Along with many other locations, Cal's ship, the *A. Mitchell Palmer*, patrolled the Mediterranean Sea. Once the Mediterranean was secured, it regularly visited the port in Southampton, England. It also participated in the D-Day Armada on June 6, 1944. Although Cal himself did not go ashore in Normandy on D-day, his ship, along with many others, provided ammunition, medical supplies, equipment, and necessary provisions for all the troops who did. The war ensued, with hundreds of thousands of soldiers and civilians losing their lives. The Germans surrendered on May 8, 1945. With the dropping of an atomic bomb in Hiroshima, Japan, on August 6, 1945, and a second bomb in Nagasaki, Japan, three days later, the war came to an abrupt halt on September 1, 1945.

With the war ending, on his next trip home, Cal and I were married. He served on active duty for three more months until his official discharge from the service. Soon afterward, when his mother needed a coal delivery and the local heating company needed a driver, Cal offered to help. The fuel company immediately hired him. Before long, he was involved in the mechanism of operating their retail business. Eventually, we built our own home and had five children: three boys and two girls.

When Cal was in his mid-forties, his circulation began to fail in his legs. My husband eventually needed a below-the-left-knee amputation. Fortunately, Cal adapted well to the surgery and the prosthesis. Because of his serious cardiovascular condition, he finally made significant lifestyle changes needed during the last fifteen years of his life.

On the night before my husband died, Cal and I were excited about our plans to take our children out to dinner the next day to celebrate their birthdays. We went to bed as usual. Perhaps sensing something, the two cats snuggled up unusually close to Cal just before we went to sleep. A little while later Cal awakened me, asking if I would get him an extra blanket. In all of our years of marriage, he had never requested one before. I was the one who was usually chilly. I got up, covered my husband with a blanket, and then we both went back to sleep.

I woke up a second time to Cal's heavy breathing. Then, I heard him strap on his prosthesis. The next thing I heard was a thud. I turned on the light to find Cal laying on the floor; my husband was dying right in front of me. I quickly called the ambulance and started CPR. When the ambulance arrived, the EMTs were unsuccessful in their efforts to revive him. My husband was gone.

His sudden dying was such a shock for all of us. We buried Cal's ashes in the family plot above his mother's remains and next to our grandson, Andrew. I still don't know how we got through it all, but we did.

Friends and family were so supportive. Yet once they had all left, I felt so isolated. I often found myself searching for Cal. I would discover myself up in the attic or down in the cellar looking for him. It was confusing to me. Intellectually, I knew he had passed, but I could feel his presence. I would have to repeatedly tell myself, "Cal is not here," but I still felt his presence.

About six or seven years after Cal died, I was lying in my bed asleep. The house alarm system was set, when around 3:30 AM, I heard the lock in my front door click. In the old days, whenever Cal worked late, he always stopped by our bedroom to let me know he was home. We would briefly exchange a few words. Then, he would go out to the kitchen for a snack. On this particular night upon hearing the door lock turn, I sat up in bed expecting Cal to come in. However, my husband walked right past our bedroom, turned right, and went down the hallway.

Fully dressed in his ensign uniform wearing his long, black officer's overcoat, Cal was young again, around the same age and in the same health as when we married. He was wearing his black Merchant Marine winter hat with the visor that had a gold braid across the front. It seemed strange, though, for him to be wearing a hat inside our home. Cal proceeded to walk out through the center living room window, originally designed by us when we built the house to be converted into a front door one day. He walked with his distinctive gait and familiar, casual slouch, as my husband was never one to stand straight as an arrow.

When I awoke, I questioned what I had just seen, especially since Cal had been dead for several years. Yet, I was still in a state of knowing that Cal had just visited me. It was real. I got up and walked around the house; I still could feel his presence. In Cal's own way, he was telling me to stop mourning him and to let him go on to his next life's adventure, whatever or wherever that might be. It was also time for me to get on with my own life.

Cal's visit definitely helped me to move through my grief. Despite his death, I had continued to long for my husband, wishing he could be with me. Life had moved on, but I really hadn't. Cal's visit helped me go forward once again. He was right. It was time to move on, and I am glad I did.

Jane Potter, EdM, a mother, grandmother, and great-grandmother, coordinates the Elderly Outreach Program, Health and Education Services, Inc., Beverly, MA. Always ready for another adventure, Jane has an adventuresome spirit and enjoys traveling the world.

8

Dreams

*Six weeks after his death, my father appeared
to me in a dream … It was an unforgettable experience,
and it forced me for the first time to think about life after death.*
—CARL JUNG

DREAMTIME IS A PLACE WHERE we are able to work through the issues of life. While we sleep, we often find ourselves subconsciously addressing personal concerns and stressors. For those who remember their dreams, this can be an important place for communication when we least expect it and need it most. Communication comes in a variety of forms. It can be visual, auditory, tactile, or any combination of the three. Within this realm, loved ones who have passed are able to bring us valuable information, help and guidance. They often appear much happier, more peaceful, and in younger and healthier bodies. In dreamtime, our deceased loved ones can also provide an opportunity for a renewed connection, much-needed clarity, the resolution of conflict, and one more chance to say goodbye.

A Comforting Call

Lorraine Angel

⌐∼⌐

Uncle Alec was my favorite uncle, a very jovial Irishman of medium height with a permanent grin on his face. My uncle was a talented storyteller and took great pleasure in passing on his knowledge, especially to children. When growing up in County Down, twelve miles due east of Belfast in Northern Ireland, he always included me in the family vacations with Aunt Edna and their three children.

As a family, we spent summers together in a rented thatched cottage by the sea and Mourne Mountains. Uncle Alec would take all the children for long walks every day. Together, we visited the Dundrum castle ruins and walked along the various beaches and sand hills searching for shellfish, wild strawberries, and crab apples. He was our very own Pied Piper. We would follow along behind him as he taught my cousins and me about the things we encountered in our travels. We learned about the different species of birds, flowers, butterflies, and various aspects of nature and history in that unspoiled part of Ireland. One of our favorite pastimes involved digging for cockles. We loved to take these tiny clams home so we could cook and serve them with vinegar and pepper as an afternoon treat.

In July 1975, Uncle Alec was hospitalized with terminal cancer. It was evident he didn't have long to live, which was hard on all of us. It sounds crazy, but I knew the moment he died! I was finishing work at the office, preparing to leave. While putting on my coat, there was a loud crash behind me. The wire basket, which had been on my desk, had fallen onto the floor. The basket held my work tasks for the next day, and the papers scattered everywhere. I was puzzled. How could that have happened? I was standing twelve feet away from the basket, and no one was near the desk. In fact, I was the last person in the office. I looked up at the wall clock. It was 5:30 PM. At that very moment, I thought about Uncle Alec.

Shortly after I arrived home, the telephone rang. My cousin was calling to tell me his father, Uncle Alec, had died that afternoon at 5:30 PM. After explaining to my cousin what had happened in my office at that exact time, we thought it all a bit strange.

Approximately two years later, I had an upsetting dream one night. In the dream, I decided to phone Aunt Edna, Uncle Alec's widow. I recall seeing a small, unfamiliar living room with a soft, light-colored couch, chairs, and a table with a phone on it. I had the sense that this was the place where Aunt Edna lived. The room looked like an apartment, yet for as long as I had known Aunt Edna, she had always lived in a lovely home. I noticed there were no windows of any kind. I was glad to know Aunt Edna would be safe and secure from any intruders, since she lived alone.

I picked up my phone and dialed her number. The phone rang several times. Then, much to my surprise, I heard an organ playing the most beautiful sacred music, such as one would hear in a church or in a famous cathedral. I wondered if I was listening to an answering machine. In those days, answering machines were quite rare, and very few people could afford them. It made me laugh. Uncle Alec and Aunt Edna were always ahead of the rest of us when it came to the latest innovations. I remembered thinking, "There they go again!"

Suddenly, the music stopped, and I heard Uncle Alec's voice on the other end of the line. He questioned, "Is that you, Lorraine?" I replied it was. In a very reassuring way, Uncle Alec said, "Don't worry. Everything's going to be all right." Then the phone went silent. I awoke with such a start. The experience was so real that it took me a few seconds to realize that it was just a dream, even though it seemed so vivid. Then it hit me that Uncle Alec was dead, and I burst into tears. A little while later, I thought about the dream but quickly dismissed it.

A couple months later, my father unexpectedly became very weak and disoriented. My mother and I brought him to the emergency room in an ambulance for evaluation. We were at a loss as to the reason for his sudden decline in health. For years, Dad had been treated for severe stomach pains with several medications. While in the emergency room, we were informed that Dad could be terminally ill with cancer of the lungs and brain.

My father was admitted, and we braced ourselves for the worst. The final test results arrived with no sign of cancer at all. We were all elated. It turned out Dad was suffering from a near-fatal reaction to all the drugs he had been prescribed for his stomach problem. Since he wasn't receiving those medications during this hospital stay, Dad quickly recovered. It was only then that I remembered the dream and my uncle's message.

Uncle Alec and my father had been the closest of friends for more than forty years. He had been my dad's best friend and brother-in-law. My dear Uncle Alec had come to offer me solace. He wanted to let me know in advance that, no matter what it might look like, Dad would be all right. Uncle Alec was right: Dad recovered just fine. Even though many years have passed, I still clearly recall the beautiful music and my uncle's voice reassuring me that everything would be all right.

Lorraine Angel, a wife, mother, and retired office manager, was born in Bangor, County Down, Northern Ireland. A resident of Massachusetts, Lorraine enjoys reading, gardening, bird watching, and especially traveling home to visit her family in Northern Ireland.

MY PRAYERS WERE ANSWERED

Patrick Gadsby

———

Love for a grandparent is one of the most special relationships any child can have in his or her lifetime. I believe the same is true for the grandparent. I remember gazing into my Pop Pop's eyes as a child and feeling a warm, indescribable love that never ends. Through a broken heart and contrite spirit, I lovingly share this story of my grandfather's eternal love.

Born in 1913, Alfred Doron was the eldest of three children raised in Philadelphia, Pennsylvania. His family endured the hardship of the Depression. Despite a world filled with war and rumors of war, Alfred grew up to be a fine young man. At thirty-seven years old, he met and married beautiful Dorothea Ellison; they raised five daughters together. My mom, Cheryl Lea, was the youngest.

As a boy, I remember traveling to visit Pop Pop; the trip seemed to take hours. I can still see the warm and inviting two-story, white-shingled house. An old rock fence guarded its front with tulips blooming nearby. The backyard was filled with beautiful pink, red, and yellow roses, and exquisite red and white rosebushes adorned the side door. Because Pop Pop loved his flowers, he reminded us often that the roses were his substitute grandchildren when we were not around.

As soon as we arrived at Pop Pop's, I would run out of the car into the house through the side door and straight into his arms. Pop Pop showered me with absolutely the best hugs and kisses ever. In the kitchen, he would reach up into the cabinet and get me some orange slice gumdrops from the clear, round glass jar with the red lid on it. He always kept a variety of candy and cookies around, but Pop Pop knew I loved the orange slice gumdrops the best.

Over the years, the love that Pop Pop and I shared continued to grow. As a young teenager, I visited him even more often. I helped Pop Pop with the yard work, and in turn, he took me deep-sea fishing.

Those times fishing side by side were some of the best times of my life. When I was just fifteen years old, my Pop Pop passed away. The world I knew changed forever. On the day we spread his ashes over the place he loved so much, I prayed for comfort for my family, all the while blaming God for the huge loss I was facing. It was to be my last prayer for some time. Whatever faith I possessed seemed to vanish into the abyss of grief and despair.

My life at that time seemed to take a course of its own. In the winter of 1996, I joined the Navy, which proved to be far more difficult than I ever anticipated. Serving my country demanded a great deal of sacrifice. My job required me to be far away from home. Because of eighty-hour work weeks, I often neglected my relationships with others. Transfers occurred regularly and friendships would end almost as quickly as they began. Also, it seemed virtually impossible to find a girlfriend strong enough to endure the commitment I had made to my country. I began to believe that marriage was no longer an option while serving in the Navy. In order to protect myself from future disappointments, I emotionally distanced myself from others.

My service onboard a Navy submarine consisted of six-month deployments overseas, often not seeing the light of day for months at a time. I felt alienated from my family and my country. Feeling all alone for the first time in my life, my faith in love and life was dwindling. A year and a half later with nowhere to turn, I sought refuge in the bottle. Filled with despair one evening, I asked God to forgive me for turning away from him. I desired my heart to be healed; the pain was too great for me to handle alone. Needing direction in my life, I asked God to guide and comfort me in my loneliness. In that moment, the burden I held was miraculously lifted, yet I was not prepared for what happened next.

That night, I had a dream. I saw myself kneeling in my bedroom in total silence. The room was so quiet that I didn't want to risk breaking the silence, not even with my own breath. In the corner of the room was a comforting white light, as bright as the sun about to break the horizon, that surrounded a figure I could not readily discern. The individual was dressed in a long, white flowing robe, and I noticed that the person's feet were not touching the floor.

Calmly, without the slightest bit of fear, I moved closer, and I immediately recognized the person as my Pop Pop! He was about fifty years younger. His gray hair was now dark brown, and his eyes, which were filled with more light than color, were warm and loving. My heart was filled with so much love that tears of joy rolled down my cheeks!

Pop Pop spoke to me softly, saying, "Your prayers are heard, and you will find what your heart desires most at the end of the journey." Pop Pop smiled at me in the same way he always had. Once again, I felt the warmth of his smile consume me. I quickly looked around the room to get my bearings. When I looked back, Pop Pop was gone. In a moment, his absence was replaced with a feeling that can only be described as the eternal love a grandfather has for his grandson. I was so grateful for what Pop Pop had done for me. When I awoke, I discovered my absent faith had returned.

The days to follow were filled with a renewed sense of hope and promise. *Your prayers are heard, and you will find what your heart desires most at the end of the journey.* Taking heed of my Pop Pop's words led me to Carrie Anne, the greatest gift I could have ever received. We fell head over heels in love and were married within the year. From the moment we saw one another, the emptiness in each of our hearts disappeared. Carrie Anne and I found strength in one another that we never knew existed. We discovered an everlasting love that will bind us together forever.

Carrie Anne and I have been married for several years and are blessed to be the parents of two beautiful girls, Emily Anne and Melody Rose. As I look at my wife and daughters, I now realize that Pop Pop not only brought us together, he also brought me the gospel to understand the journey. The unconditional love shared with my family has helped me regain faith in my Heavenly Father. Thankfully, through church scripture, community, and family, I recognized that trying to drink away problems does not solve them. The Church of Jesus Christ of Latter-Day Saints teachings have helped me better comprehend my Pop Pop's visit.

I have since visited Pop Pop's old homestead. The house now lies empty. The white shingles are faded. The stone fence that once guarded the home is now crumbling. The lawn is overgrown and needs tending. Even the paint is peeling off the yellow garage. When I walked around to the backyard, I discovered that Pop Pop's roses were still blooming; their beauty was overwhelming. I smiled. Even in spirit, my Pop Pop's love continues on, as it blossoms in all of his "grandchildren," in my heart, and in the hearts of all those who love him.

Patrick Gadsby resides with his family in South Carolina. Employed at a power utility company, Patrick is very much enjoying being in one place with roots, surrounded by family.

In His Own Way

Pam Koehler

———

Roland Gagnon was a son, brother, father, husband, friend, and grandfather. He started working at the age of seven to help support his family; he was one of six children. Because Dad joined the service at the age of seventeen, he was not able to graduate from high school, even though he was intelligent. Self-taught in so many ways, my father loved to read and search out answers to many of life's questions.

As a husband and father of four, he gave enormous amounts of himself to his children, grandchildren, and especially to his wife. Although he did not readily show his emotions, we realized years later that he always had a warm heart; he just never allowed us to see it. Dad and Mom fully enjoyed their retirement together. Happy and healthy, they traveled all over the world. Five weeks after their last trip to Italy, my father died suddenly from a heart attack.

Following Dad's death, I was deeply troubled. I questioned God as to why it had to happen so quickly and without warning. I was five months pregnant, and I wanted Dad to be able to meet my third child, his eighth grandchild. Ironically, I had just purchased theater dinner tickets for my parents as Christmas gifts two days before his death. So, instead of Dad taking Mom to the show, I brought her. We did our best under the sad circumstances.

Five days after the theater dinner date, I had my first dream of Dad. In the dream, Mom and I were standing in the crowded theater lobby waiting for the show to begin. Behind Mom was Dad dressed in his black slacks, burgundy suede suit coat, crisp white shirt, and black patterned tie, the same outfit we had buried him in. I was shocked to see him. "Dad! Why aren't you here with Mom?" I asked. "You're supposed to be the one taking her to the show, not me!"

Dad had the most serene, peaceful look on his face, an expression I had never seen prior to his death. With a very simple yet calming smile, Dad relayed to me that he was in eternal peace. He was happier than he had ever been and wanted me to know he was doing just fine. With Mom never realizing that he was standing right behind her, I awoke in tears, absolutely astounded at what had just happened. Excitedly, I telephoned everyone in our family. Dad had visited me! I wanted them to know that he was all right. My siblings were not as enthusiastic, but Mom was deeply moved and wanted to know every detail.

A year later, my father appeared to me yet a second time. In the dream, I was standing near a riverbank well known in town for kayaking, speaking with a few people I knew. Someone gently grasped the fingertips of my right hand. I looked over, and it was Dad. He was dressed as before, with the same serene expression on his face. Dad looked at me and softly said, "Come with me." No one noticed that my father was there, nor did they respond when the two of us left. Holding my hand, Dad led me to some steep granite steps a few hundred feet away. He motioned for me to walk down a few steps so that I was looking up at him. "Dad," I asked, "why does this keep happening to me? Why do you keep appearing in my dreams? I want you to do this for Mom. She needs to see and know what you've allowed me to see and know."

In response, Dad calmly and peacefully replied, "In my way and in my time, I will let your mother know that I am doing fine...I don't think she is ready just now. But, I want to reassure you that I have never been more at peace. I am happy, and I am doing just fine." Again, I woke up with tears gently rolling down my face. Feeling more at ease, I decided to keep the dream to myself.

On the day that would have been my parents' fiftieth wedding anniversary, I drove my mother to the cemetery to visit Dad's grave. After spending time there, my mother began to talk about some of the things they had done together and the huge void she had felt since his passing. I told Mom that although I understood the grief associated with losing a parent, I could not relate to the pain of losing a spouse. I suggested that she might consider a support group for bereaved spouses. In that moment, Mom confided, "I have something strange to tell you..."

Apparently three months earlier, Mom had traveled to Key West, Florida. While walking alongside a marina and reflecting on the last time she had been there with Dad, a strange feeling came over her as if someone were watching. Mom quickly turned around and saw a man who so much resembled my father that she actually called out, "Roland!" As soon as she did, she realized that it couldn't possibly have been Dad...

While Mom was relaying the story, I couldn't help but remember my father's words in the second dream. *In my way and in my time, I will let your mother know that I am doing fine.* I immediately shared the dream and reassured Mom that no matter where she was, Dad would always be by her side. Mom agreed that the man's striking resemblance was a gift from Dad. He was letting her know that he would always be with her until they were reunited in heaven once again.

My mother was so thankful I shared that dream. I am so grateful that I had the opportunity to do so. Since then, I haven't had another dream of Dad, and I am honestly all right with that. I know that Dad is truly happy, serene, and at peace.

Pam Koehler, happily married to Jeff, is the mother of three wonderful children, Zachary, Hannah, and Joshua. Employed in real estate, she feels especially fortunate to have her family close and the comfort and enjoyment of friends.

GRAMS

Patti Alden

⌒

We called her Grams, but her real name was Stella. She had sparkling light blue eyes that smiled back, a chuckle of a laugh, and the tiniest of feet. When I was growing up, I often wondered how Grams balanced herself so well on those little feet. My grandmother had lived in the same house all her life from the time she was a young child. She was never sure of her exact date of birth because the doctor who delivered her was drunk on the day she entered this world. I'll always remember that her favorite place to eat lunch was the Blue Bonnet in Hadley, Massachusetts, and she always kept a bottle of cream soda under her kitchen sink.

One day in the spring of 1996, Grams became quite ill with pneumonia. I was almost five months pregnant with my first child when my father called the family to the hospital to say our goodbyes. In a quiet moment alone with Grams, I sat on the right side of her bed and whispered stories in her ear. I reminded my grandmother of the fun times we'd had together and reassured her that I would never forget her. Using a Doppler stethoscope I found next to her bed, I located my baby's heartbeat. I then shared with Grams the rhythmic sounds of the new life growing inside of me. I asked Grams to please watch over my baby; the squeeze of her right hand in mine clearly told me she understood. Somehow, saying goodbye to Grams while giving life helped put the circle of life in perspective for me. I felt blessed for the time I had on earth with this very special person, as well as blessed for the opportunity to say goodbye and share that special moment with her. When Grams died, I celebrated her life more than I mourned her death.

Grams was buried on a sunny day with a cool breeze. A small group of family and friends stood in a circle around the gravesite. Feeling a chill, I walked back to the car to get my sweater. When I returned, I was unable to re-enter the circle. Just then, an elderly man wearing a brown tweed derby hat leaned over to me and said, "Do you hear that mockingbird? That's your grandmother." I turned left and tilted my head to listen to its beautiful song. When I turned back, the gentleman was gone. I never saw that man in the brown derby hat again.

Five months later, I gave birth to a beautiful girl named Amelya Rose, who was blessed to have her own special guardian angel, Grams. Shortly after her birth, Amelya was diagnosed with asthma and prescribed a variety of medications. For months, I spent most nights trying to rock Amelya to sleep, sometimes for hours at a time. After numerous sleepless nights with no improvement in my daughter's health, my hopes for a solution began to wear thin. In the quiet of the night, I began praying and asking Grams for guidance, sensing she was close by.

One night, after praying for my grandmother's help, I had a wonderful dream where Grams and I met in an old white farmhouse for a cup of tea. As we sat across the kitchen table from each other, I told Grams how good it was to see her again. She looked exactly as I remembered her, with her eyes as bright and blue as the sky. I listened intently as Grams gave me advice about how I could help improve my baby's health. When she finished, Grams stood up to say goodbye. In a panic, I asked how I was going to remember what she told me once I awakened from the dream. Grams responded simply, "Don't worry, you will understand." Then I awoke, startled by the feeling of my body falling back onto my bed.

Amelya's health remained unchanged for several months, yet *I* was changed. I worried much less. The time I had spent with Grams in that old farmhouse felt so real to me. I was thankful for the peace in knowing that, in time, everything would be okay.

One day while visiting my home, my mother asked if she could bring my cat, Cassidy, temporarily to her house. Mom thought perhaps the cat was the root of Amelya's health problems, so she took Cassidy home with her the next day. Sure enough, within two weeks, Amelya's respiratory problems completely cleared up. Although my husband and I had originally wanted our baby to be tested for possible allergies, the pediatrician advised against it since any allergy testing under the age of three would be inaccurate. Yet, unbeknownst to any of us, Amelya was allergic to cats. Fortunately, once Cassidy was out of the house, Amelya's respiratory symptoms disappeared. Grams was right: I *did* finally understand the problem. Our daughter will be forever blessed with her special guardian angel.

Patti Alden, co-owner of a gourmet food market in North Conway, New Hampshire, enjoys outdoor sports with her husband and children. Early in her youth, Patti discovered that messages and guidance can come through dreams with those who have passed.

A NIGHT OF REMEMBERING

Laura Settle

⎯⎯⎯⎯

I celebrated the end of my high school career with friends at my senior prom on May 12, 2006. I had a fun-filled evening with so many wonderful memories, but the next morning, I was hit with some sad news. My poppi, Umberto Tomassone, had died on his ninetieth birthday, the night of my prom. An overwhelming sadness fell over me, especially because I had been out partying when he passed.

Poppi grew up in Cranston, Rhode Island, with his Italian immigrant parents. They traveled to Ellis Island by boat to enter the United States. He was very wise and often told me stories of WWII and about hand-painting planes for the war. As I grew older, I realized I had inherited Poppi's artistic side, since I've always enjoyed drawing, painting, and various forms of arts and crafts.

My poppi was an outdoorsman. He loved to fish and camp, and I accompanied him on many of his trips. When I found out he'd passed away, I was upset because I wanted him to see me graduate from high school. Education was very important to Poppi. He loved to learn and also loved to teach me new things. Although we grew apart as I got older, we were the best of friends, and I always looked up to him.

On April 25, 2007, Westfield State College held its annual Light the Night ceremony. It is a program sponsored by the Department of Residential Life to remember those individuals who have truly made a difference in our lives. Each year, hundreds of students write messages on paper bags in honor of loved ones. Votive candles are placed inside the bags, after which they are taken outside during the evening, lined up alphabetically, and lit. I decided to honor Poppi that night and wrote his name and mine on one of the bags. I'll never forget the rows of memorial candles that lit the campus walkways. It was truly breathtaking to see so many loved ones remembered.

Surprisingly, Poppi came to me in a dream later that night. In the dream, I was driving my car when I received a frantic phone call from my mother. She was yelling, "Hurry, hurry! Poppi is sick. He might not make it. Come quick!" I rushed to get there, and when I found him, he was lying on a sidewalk. I held him in my arms. Poppi was skinny and brittle and unable to stand. I cried, telling him I wasn't going to let him go. Poppi only looked into my eyes and gave me a reassuring smile.

The next thing I knew, he was sitting over a large, dark hole on a metal beam. Poppi easily straddled the beam, as though he were a young child. I stood on the road next to him, and we talked happily for a short while. Suddenly, my eyes opened, and I found myself awake in my dorm room bed. My eyes were damp with tears. All day long, I felt at peace as I replayed the dream of Poppi in my head. I was so comforted to see how happy he was, and that his mannerisms were those of a young man. The dream uplifted me; I was happy to know he was okay.

The only other dream I had of Poppi was about five months after he passed. Always one to take naps, my poppi was sleeping on his bed, as usual. I was little, maybe five or six years old in the dream. I jumped up on the bed, and then he moved. I cried, "Oh Poppi! I thought you were dead!" He answered in a gentle voice, "I'm not dead, Laura. I'm right here." Then Poppi hugged me, and I *felt* his warm embrace! I woke up feeling so happy. Poppi had let me know he was all right and would always be with me.

It's been almost a year since Poppi left us. I think of him every day. Sometimes, when I'm outside, I can feel him in the wind as it blows through my hair and brushes my cheek. I can hear his voice in the birds that sing. Rather than mourning his passing, we celebrate his life. Thank you, Poppi, for everything. I love you.

Laura Settle is studying environmental science at Westfield State College, where she enjoys outdoor sports, drawing, painting, and crafts. Spending time with family and doing fun things with friends are most important to Laura.

A Surprising Goodbye

Irene M. Tomkinson

One day, my friend Alice called to ask for a favor. Would I accompany her to the hospital? Her dear friend, George, a young man in his forties, was dying of cancer, and she needed moral support. I had only casually met George at a couple of Alice's parties. Even though George was just one of the people in the crowd to me, I agreed to go. I was a trained social worker and was happy to help in whatever way I could.

Alice picked me up shortly thereafter, and together we drove to the hospital. For about a half-hour while Alice visited, I sat outside George's room. My chair was across the hall, and I was just barely able to see that George was unresponsive and probably in a coma. However, I never entered his room. I intentionally gave Alice the space and time she needed to say her goodbyes. I was glad to be there for her.

Two nights later, I had a dream. George and I were both in rowboats, and his boat was approaching mine. I remember how peaceful it all was and how incredibly safe I felt. George waved to me, the slow friendly wave that boaters usually exchange who don't know one other on the open sea. As his boat sailed past mine, our eyes connected. We held the glance the entire time. Then George waved one last time, as if to say, "See ya."

I thought to myself, "Hey, what are *you* doing in *my* dream?" Then, I waved back with my right hand to say, "See ya, buddy." I awoke from the dream, rather surprised at what had happened. I looked over at my bedside clock. It was 4:10 AM. "Hmm...," I thought to myself. I rolled over and went back to sleep.

The next morning, the phone rang. It was Alice, calling to say that George had died during the night at 4:10 AM. I realized it was the exact same time that I awoke from my dream. I felt tingles of recognition run through my whole body as I thought of its significance. I excitedly told Alice what had happened, and it was clear that George had come to say goodbye. I'm not sure why George came to visit me instead of Alice. I only know that he did.

Irene Tomkinson, MSW, co-founded Pathways to Personal Growth in North Hampton, New Hampshire, with her husband, David. She is the author of Not Like My Mother: Becoming a Sane Parent After Growing Up in a Crazy Family.

Transition

Linda Scott

⟋⟍

When I was twenty-four, my fifty-year-old mother was diagnosed with lung cancer. It was hard to believe because Mom was always the strongest and most vibrant person I had ever known. I later discovered that the average life expectancy for individuals with her type of cancer was four months, so the fact that Mom survived two years was probably a tribute to her health and indomitable spirit.

I lived in another city but spoke with her frequently on the phone. I also traveled home as much as possible to help out. When I sensed her condition was worsening, I quickly went home to be with her. When I arrived, Mom appeared gaunt except for a swollen belly that looked as though she were pregnant. My mother could barely speak; whenever she breathed, only one side of her chest moved. Dad was sick with a cold. Because he didn't want to make her sicker, he asked if I could stay with her that night, which I did. It was such a long night because she cried out in pain often. It hurt my heart to hear her; I felt so helpless.

The next day, Mom looked at me and told me something was wrong. Dad, my brother, and I followed her ambulance to the hospital, where they worked on her in the emergency room for quite some time. Mom died shortly thereafter. Although I didn't know how we were going to live without her wisdom at the center of our family, I felt a sense of relief for an end to the terrible suffering she had endured.

Later that day, I remembered a dream I'd had the night before while sleeping next to Mom in her bed. The dream was a complete contrast to the stark experience of pain and unpleasantness surrounding my mother's death. In the dream, I was one of several people dressing a young woman in her bridal gown. The bride was standing in the center of my parents' double bed in our home in the Philippines. I never saw the face of the bride; I was simply at her feet, arranging the hem of her beautiful, floor-length, pristine white gown. I also had the sense that several other brides were being readied in other rooms. Then, someone came to the door and told us, "It is time. Your bride is next." I had the sense of sending my bride off with so much love and care.

I often find myself reliving the moments of suffering that led up to my mother's death. Whenever I do, my uplifting dream comes back to remind me that the terrible death I witnessed was not the real and true experience for Mom. Regardless of what the physical body may manifest, transitioning from this life to the one beyond is a sacred and holy passage only to be undertaken with great reverence and joy. I will be forever grateful for the gift of the beautiful dream that I experienced.

Linda Scott, PhD, MAc, enjoys teaching courses ranging from Introductory Psychology to Mind-Body Medicine at Hood College. With a small private practice in acupuncture, she and her husband live in a historic town in Maryland with their cat, Zen.

Forgiveness from Dad

Kerry Kidger

My dad, Gerald O'Brien, was a wonderful, kind, and gentle man. He was born in London, England, but was raised in Ireland near the Shannon River. He married my mum who was raised in the nearby County Kerry area. As the story goes, the two married, had five children, and moved to America in 1963. As their youngest child, I was Daddy's little girl. Sadly, after forty-five years of marriage, my parents broke up, as my dad had an eye for the ladies. My mum took this horribly, as did all five of her adult children. Approximately one year later, Dad and Mum became platonic friends. I secretly hoped they would get back together, since they were both in their early sixties.

The second year after their split, my dad was finally allowed to attend Mum's Christmas celebration. He visited my family and me afterwards. I asked him, "Dad, tell me the truth. Are you and Mum getting back together?" He replied, "I will always love your mum. But things have changed, and I am happy with my friend Jean. You would like her…" My Irish temper reared its ugly head, and I said despicable things to my father that day. I asked him to leave my house and to never visit or contact me again. My parting words were, "The next time I see you, you will be six feet under!" Then I slammed my front door behind him.

Four months passed. While at work one day, I received a telephone call from my husband. My father had died of a massive heart attack on April 21, 1991. His death hit me like a ton of bricks. Being from Europe, we had no family here. I also had never experienced a death close to me. I most probably would have either drank myself to death or been institutionalized had the following events not taken place.

Three days after we buried my dad, I cried myself to sleep on the couch. During my awake-but-dreamy state, Dad appeared right next to me, looking down at me. I felt so overjoyed by his presence. I told him how sorry I was for what I had said. He reassured me, saying, "Love, I know. Don't worry. I do love you, and I know you always loved me." Dad kept telling me everything would be okay now and not to worry. Then, he was gone, just as quickly as he came. I cried so hard from losing him all over again that I actually woke myself up; it was all so real. I sat on the couch for a long time, reliving each moment of this experience. Dad's visit lifted the huge burden of guilt I had been carrying. Filled with his love and a sense of peace, I felt great. Excitedly, I shared this story with every member of my family.

Two weeks later, I found out I was pregnant. Because I now had to take care of the two of us, the surprise pregnancy helped me work through my grief. Following an ultrasound, the doctors told me I was having a boy. He was due on December 28, 1992. My husband and I decided to name him Gerald O'Brien Kidger, after my father. Even though all of my family members had names that began with the letter K, it was important for me to honor my dad's memory.

On December 20, around 3 AM, Dad visited me a second time. I could feel so much love and warmth from his presence. I was delighted. Once again, Dad reassured me that everything was going to be okay and not to worry. I told him that I was having a little boy, and our son would be his namesake. Dad corrected me and told me I was having a little girl. She would be born on the twenty-first, the same date my father died. I should name her Shannon. Amidst my tears, Dad continued to tell me that it would be okay and not to worry; then he was gone. My crying woke my husband up, and I shared what had happened. My husband assured me it was only a dream; I wasn't due until the following week, and we were going to have a boy. When I called Mum in the morning to tell her what had happened, she gasped in disbelief. Apparently, Dad had wanted to name me Shannon after the county he had grown up in. But because she had won that battle, I was named Kerry after her county instead. Amazingly, only Mum and Dad knew this information. The story spread like wildfire throughout our family.

That same afternoon around five, I went into labor. My husband and two sisters came to the delivery room to be with me. Seven hours later, on December 21 at 12:01 AM, I delivered a baby girl, just as Dad had foretold. When the doctor surprisingly announced, "It's a girl," we all started crying. Then, he asked us what her name would be. My husband looked at me and then to the doctor. In a tear-filled voice, he said, "Shannon O'Brien Kidger." Of course, we all started crying again. My family and I are often asked why her name starts with an S instead of K like the rest of us. We respond by saying that S is because Shannon is special. And she is. In a sense, her birth saved my life.

Many years have passed, and Dad continues to visit me during the most trying times of my life. On one particularly difficult time, Dad appeared in my dream. I was riding a bike through a field. It was so great to see him! I could feel our shared love, and I felt so peaceful and happy. Dad took me inside a building that had rooms with wooden beams, a flagstone path, and a bedroom with a dog named Bonzo lying on the bed. Dad and I went outside down a rocky path alongside the water's edge. We talked as we walked side by side. Lovingly, my dad reassured me again that everything was going to be okay. When it was time to leave, I told him I wanted to stay. Dad said simply, "Not now."

I cried as we walked toward the field; Dad kept telling me that he loved me. When I turned around to look at him, he was gone. I felt empty. When I opened my eyes, I found myself lying in my bed. I smiled because Dad, my guardian angel, had come to make me feel better again. I knew he would always be there to reassure me and to help me believe that life does continue on the other side.

Up until this point, Mum was not a believer in any of these things. When I called her to tell her about Dad's visit, she was shocked. Mum told me that the house I described from my dream was Dad's childhood home in Ireland. Bonzo was the dog that Dad had as a young boy. Mum said it was impossible for me to know about the beach and all of it, since she had only been there twice herself when she was young. On that day, Dad helped my mum to believe. I am very blessed to have had these visits from my dad.

Kerry Kidger, wife and mother of three grown children, was born in London, England. She has spent most of her life in the USA. Kerry enjoys her family, friends, long walks, and training her two German shepherds when the kids aren't around.

BUMPS IN THE ROAD

Wendy Bonner Spicer

I met Mike at AAU basketball tryouts. Little did I know that making his team and playing for him would be the opportunity of a lifetime. Very outspoken and cheerful, Mike had the charm to strike up a conversation with just about anyone. He had a unique way of motivating his basketball teams; I loved his personality from the start. My coach guided me through all the bumps in the road of my teenage years. When he died, I felt lost without him.

Mike was the wisest person I have ever known. With an understanding of the world and the people who lived in it, he had a passion for coaching girl's basketball. Even his smallest actions offered great insight to his players. I closely observed everything he did, because I knew the more I understood Mike, the better I would understand life.

While I was in middle school, my mother became ill and emotionally unavailable. We became distant when she moved away in order to regain her health. With Mom unable to care for my sisters and me, I became very dependent on my father. I hid my pain, frustration, and sadness behind my constant "game face" and extroverted personality; but Mike saw right through me. He shared a personal tragedy to help me understand my reaction to my mother's illness. My coach encouraged me to confront my feelings of anger and abandonment by teaching me that these feelings are normal. I also learned that my mother never intended to hurt me by leaving. My coach provided constant love and support for me; Mike became the second parent figure I desperately needed.

Car rides to AAU basketball tournaments were my favorite times with Mike; it seemed like we had all the time in the world to tell stories, laugh, and discuss the challenges of life. During these road trips, Mike taught me the importance of working through difficult situations in life. He also taught me to be more patient with myself. Not everything can be solved in a matter of minutes, and complicated issues take more time to mend. As he coached me in basketball, Mike coached me in life. With thoughtful intention, he forced me to discover the answers for myself.

Mike and I shared a love for all sports. During my sophomore year in college, I was named an All-American selection in field hockey. On that same day, Mike was diagnosed with a rare form of cancer. When he shared his diagnosis with me, I did not understand the severity of his condition. Many people battle cancer and survive; I wholeheartedly believed that Mike would do the same. I simply could not imagine life without him. Less than two months after his diagnosis, Mike called to tell me that he was being moved into hospice care. After hearing this news, I collapsed on the floor of my dorm room and cried; I knew there was no remedy for my heartache. My heart and my mind felt as if they were going in different directions. I could not accept the fact that he was dying.

I was able to spend the last three days of his life by his bedside. During that time, I met many of his old friends, athletes, and members of his family. Loved ones traveled from up and down the East Coast to say their final goodbyes. Some had not seen Mike in years. It was as if some sort of magnetic force was drawing them back; he made such an impact on so many.

Mike died one week after his admission into the hospice home. In the moments before he died, I sat with him and held his hand. I fought off my tears, because I knew my coach would not rest peacefully if he worried about me. Mike pointed to the small duffel bag at the foot of his bed and asked me if it was packed and ready to go. He also asked if I had packed a videotape of my most recent basketball game so that he could watch it. His bag, along with the videotape, was sitting at the foot of the bed. This was Mike's way of saying goodbye; he was ready to die. I gripped his hand tightly, and I promised my coach that I would work around this bump in the road, just as he had taught me. I am still working on that to this day.

It has been several years since Mike passed away, but I still feel his presence daily, especially when I step onto the basketball court. After Mike died, I longed to see him in my dreams so that I could hear his voice and feel his love. But, I knew I would have to be patient, just as Mike had taught me. Once I released some of my grief, my coach finally appeared to me in a dream.

My dream took place on a warm spring day. It felt enjoyably quick, the same way a delicious ice cream cone seems to disappear in an instant on a hot summer day. The grass was a beautiful, bright green, and the sunlight was reflecting off the sidewalk. The air felt crystal clear. At first, no one was around me as I stood on the sidewalk with my eyes looking down at the ground. Then, I slowly lifted my eyes, and a familiar figure came into focus. Mike was standing about a hundred feet away, beaming his unique and constant smile right at me.

Patiently, Mike waited for me to take the first step towards him. Then, we walked swiftly towards each other. Mike appeared relaxed and steady while I felt completely helpless. We stood face to face; my mouth moved soundlessly as I choked on my words. The dream felt so real, and he seemed so alive. As he did whenever I was upset, my coach placed one hand on each of my shoulders; Mike reassured me that I would be okay. Yet being okay had little meaning for me in that moment. Did okay mean that the pain I had been feeling from losing him would eventually subside? Did it mean that I would no longer cry myself to sleep at night?

Even though I could not fully comprehend what Mike meant, his reassurance soothed me. As usual, his words were comforting. Somehow, I knew that I would be okay moving on without him. Tension released from my body. I smiled. As soon as I did, the dream ended; it seemed to vaporize along with Mike's comforting presence, the warm temperature, and lovely scenery. Also, when I awoke, I discovered that some of the grief and pain I had been experiencing had subsided.

It's been six years since Mike passed away. His impact on my life remains unchanged. The knowledge, the life lessons, and the memories we shared still continues to comfort me. I still miss Mike dearly. But, bumps in the road are a part of life; my coach taught me that. This one is just going to take a little extra time.

Wendy Bonner Spicer teaches biology and coaches at the Flint Hill School in Oakton, Virginia. A newlywed, Wendy has three fun-loving sisters—Julie, Lindsay, and Marnie—and two adorable dogs.

A Chance to Say Goodbye

Danielle Pelletier

When Memere died, I felt empty and depressed. I missed her terribly. I was fifteen years old, and this was my first experience with death. I found myself surrounded by my family's pain as well as my own. It felt awkward, because none of us knew what to say to each other. Nothing anyone said or did could make me feel better.

I loved my memere (grandmother). She was such a caring and compassionate woman. Ever since I was a little girl, my mother's family would gather at her house every Sunday after mass. Memere would always have homemade soup and fresh bread from the bakery ready to be served. We would eat together, and afterwards, she would pop a movie into the VCR for me while the family visited. I felt cared for, well loved, and as comfortable as if I were in my own home.

Memere was essentially a single mom from the time that Pepere became ill. He required long-term care at the Veteran's Hospital where my grandfather remained until his death. Even though she was forced to parent alone, Memere demonstrated an amazing ability to keep all eight of her children in line throughout the years that followed. Despite the challenges she faced, my memere was always in a good mood. Even though she had a heart condition, nothing could dampen her spirit. She believed that when God was ready to take her, He would, and she wasn't going to waste any time worrying about it.

After having lived for years with my aunt, uncle, and cousins, Memere made the decision to move into an elderly apartment complex. My other grandparents, who lived in the same facility, checked in on her frequently, because we were worried about her living alone. Shortly after moving there, Memere was rushed to the hospital for a heart problem, and thankfully, she survived. Memere insisted that she was still capable of living on her own. Following a second hospitalization for congestive heart failure, Memere finally agreed to move to the Brook House, an assisted-living home for elderly women; Memere loved it.

My grandmother made so many new friends that whenever we called, that's all she talked about. She was able to come and go at will. Yet, on one of her outings, Memere fell. My aunt took her to the hospital, this time for a broken nose and a swollen eye. From then on, Memere seemed to take life at a much slower pace. She rarely left the facility other than her visits to the hospital, which became more frequent.

Her last day at the Brook House was a sad one. Memere was once again rushed to the hospital. She spent almost a month there, and we visited every day. Memere was always upbeat, as if everything was going to be okay. At the end of that extended hospital stay, her doctors decided that Memere could no longer live at the Brook House; she would have to move to a nursing home. Memere did not want to go. Vividly, I remember Memere telling my mother she wouldn't last a week in a nursing home. But, when given no other option, Memere held her head up high, put her feet on the ground and made the best of it. She finally made the decision that if this is where God wanted her to be, it was okay with her.

After moving to the nursing home, Memere started to get involved in a lot of different activities. She even signed up for a lunch trip to Pier 4, a famous seafood restaurant in Boston about an hour away from the facility. In her usual fashion, Memere was trying to make the best of it. To her, it was all that mattered.

The night before she passed away, my parents took her out to dinner. The next morning, Memere died unexpectedly at the nursing home. Memere had always taught me that everything has a purpose or meaning. Perhaps her eldest son's visit at the time of her death was a confirmation of what she had been talking about. I will never forget that day. Mom, Dad, and I had just attended my friend's church graduation. Afterwards, everyone was invited to go to a party at her house. Before leaving for the party, Mom suggested that we stop at home first. We walked into the house, and Mom went downstairs to check the messages on the answering machine. As she did, inexplicably, I felt my stomach begin to sink. Then, I got a huge lump in my throat. Suddenly, I heard a scream. I ran downstairs to find my mom lying on the floor crying in pain, unable to take in what had just happened. Memere had died. I felt helpless. I stood there in shock unable to do anything. I couldn't believe what I was hearing. The next two days were a blur.

I had never attended a wake and had no idea of what to expect. That night, before leaving for the funeral home, I wrote my memere a letter. I told her that I loved her and that I never had a chance to say goodbye. After tucking the note inside my pocketbook, I left for the wake with my parents.

The funeral parlor was filled with flowers. Lying there in her casket, she didn't look like the memere I had known all my life. I started to cry. I knelt down in front of her, said a prayer, and placed the note I had written right next to her inside the casket. The waiting room was filled with tearful faces everywhere I looked. Memere was an amazing person. It was obvious she was treasured by many.

I had never attended a funeral. The people singing together and the priest talking about how Memere was now in God's hands seemed like a dream; it didn't feel real at all. I never imagined that I would feel the amount of pain and sorrow I did. Even though everyone kept reassuring me I would be okay, I couldn't stop crying. All the numerous hugs that they gave me didn't help. It felt like a piece of my heart was missing.

A few weeks after the funeral, I had the most wonderful dream. It was a warm June night. I had gone to bed early, even though I didn't have to get up for school the next day. I remember the dream perfectly. My whole family was at my house for a party. All my aunts, uncles, and cousins from my mom's side of the family were there.

We were all sitting inside the first floor den laughing and joking around. Through the doorway of the den, I happened to notice

Memere coming down the stairs. Wearing the familiar green cotton dress she often wore, my memere was headed outside. Memere looked happy and healthy, just like she did before she got sick. As she walked through the doorway onto the porch, Memere waved goodbye to all of us and headed towards the outside porch door.

I quickly ran to catch up to her. As I looked through the screen of the front door, I was able to see her one last time. Memere was standing on the porch, holding the outside door halfway open. She had a big smile on her face, just like she always did. Memere waved goodbye to me. As she did, she looked directly into my eyes, exactly in the way she had done so many times when I was a little child. Then, she turned around and walked away. In the past, her eyes had always comforted me. This time, I stood there silently crying with tears running down my face. No one else seemed to notice. I was so sad. I knew that she was gone, and I would never see her again.

Amazingly, when I awoke from the dream, I woke up smiling! I felt complete happiness that Memere had read my letter and had actually come back to say goodbye! Memere wanted me to know that she was okay and happy where she is. She brought me two parting gifts, which I never thought were possible—an opportunity to see her one more time, and a chance to say goodbye, which I desperately needed to do. As a result, I have been able to finally come to terms with saying goodbye to my memere. I now know in my heart that she will never forget her loving family or me. Thank you so much for coming, Memere. I love you!

Danielle Pelletier received her bachelor's degree in business from Salem State College. Danielle would like to dedicate her story to her memere, Theresa Bedard, for the undying love and affection she shared with all her children and grandchildren.

COMFORTING REASSURANCE

Marianne Withington

My husband, Cricket Withington, was by far the finest person I have ever known. An attorney well respected in the field, he truly cared about his clients and always went above and beyond the call of duty. Also, as a captain in the U.S. Army, he served for one year in Vietnam as an advisor to the Vietnamese people. My husband adored his children, his family, and his friends. He loved life. I was very proud to be his wife. We spent over twenty wonderful and fun-filled years together. However, our time together was cut short when he succumbed to renal cancer in June 2007.

Following his death, I went through a very bad time, partly because I could not get the final images of Cricket's struggle out of my mind. It plagued me for weeks. I only wish I could have done more for him. Desperate for some sort of sign, I begged Cricket and God for almost two months to please let me know that he was all right. Nothing happened.

One day, I encountered a problem with my new car that Cricket had helped me purchase. For some reason, the keyless ignition wasn't working; the car was dead. I telephoned the local dealership, who told me that the key could have lost its programming. I should try the spare key, and if not, the car would need to be towed. Cricket was the only one who knew where the spare key was stored!

I was an hour away from home with two friends. Tearfully, I telephoned Cricket's cousin who lived next door. Would he please go inside my home and search for the key? For the next half-hour, I guided him over the phone to all the places I thought Cricket might have stored the key. No luck. Frustrated, I hung up the phone, as we were leaving for the hotel to get an early start for the race the next morning. Emotionally stressed, I prepared myself to have the car towed the next day.

That night, Cricket came to me in a dream. Wearing his usual shirt and jeans, he looked healthy, just like he did before he got sick. Confused, I asked him, "How can you be here?" Cricket answered, "I am always here." Then, he walked over to the bar in our kitchen where I noticed a brown wicker basket. Just then, I awoke and immediately sat upright in the hotel bed. It was 5:30 AM. One friend was already in the shower. As soon as she came out, I told her about the dream of Cricket and where I thought the car key was located. Two and a half hours later, I telephoned Cricket's cousin with a second request to please check my home. Only this time, would he please check for a brown wicker basket in the kitchen? Sure enough, the key was there in the basket! Problem solved. This was the sign I had been praying for!

Two days later, I woke up very early in the morning. I was feeling extremely sad and missing Cricket terribly. I pleaded with him to please send me another sign. I needed to know if he was happy with the way I had been living my life since he left. I had been trying so hard, but it was so difficult for me going forward without him. I fell back asleep. A short while later when I woke up, I immediately reminded myself that I needed to set the alarm for 7 for work that day. Then, I heard Cricket's voice clearly say, "The alarm is already set." And it was! I told my husband how much I missed him. Then the strangest thing happened. I actually felt a heavy weight on the bed next to me, and I felt someone kissing me. I don't know whether I was half asleep or fully awake, but it happened.

Amazed and grateful, I knew Cricket was all right, and that he approved of the path I was taking. What a blessing! My husband's presence reassured and deeply comforted me. There was no need to carry the anguish anymore. Thanks to Cricket, I now finally have peace.

Marianne Withington lives in Plymouth, MA. She is a music instructor, an actress, and an avid runner who has run in many marathons, including the Boston Marathon.

GRANDPA'S GOODBYE

Karen Thwing

Grandpa was special. He had a great mind, loved to read books, and was very knowledgeable about current events. His favorite baseball team was the Red Sox, and he loved to watch them on TV. A generous and loving person, Grandpa made sure all of his grandchildren received wonderful gifts for birthdays and holidays. And oh, could he dance! I enjoyed slow dancing with him so much. It felt like I was floating on air as we moved across the dance floor! He was always the perfect gentleman.

Grandpa was never quite the same after Grammy died. He loved Grammy deeply and spoke often about how much he missed her. When Grandpa became ill, he never complained about being sick; however, he talked frequently about dying. Ready to be reunited with his beloved, Grandpa died from complications following vascular surgery.

Hours before he died, my grandpa came to me in a dream. In the dream, he was lying in a hospital bed with a bright white light shining down upon him that illuminated his face. He looked so peaceful. Grandpa turned to me and said, "I'm ready to go now." I awoke shortly thereafter with an inner knowing that Grandpa had died. On that morning, I received word that my grandpa had passed on to a place I believe to be wonderful. He had come to say goodbye. Grandpa let my family and I know that his suffering was over. He would be all right; he was with his beloved wife, and he was finally at peace.

Karen Thwing, RN, has worked for ten years as a nurse on a medical floor at Brigham and Women's Hospital. She and her husband, Mike, enjoy their active twin sons, Ben and Will, and their beautiful daughter, Emerson.

Farewell for Now

Goldyn Blanco

It's been eight years since my mother died. Our special moments were filled with laughter, love, and joy. My mother gave me life, sheltered me, and filled me with her love. When I look back at my childhood, I smile, as I remember riding in the car with her on those beautiful, sunny days in Los Angeles. My mother would be driving my big sister, little brother, and me, and the car windows would be wide open; her hair would be blowing in the breeze. Thoroughly enjoying the moment, she would lovingly smile at all three of us. She was calm, understanding, sincere, and always helpful. I wanted to grow up and be just like her.

Mami died on the day before her thirty-third birthday from cancer of the stomach; I was eleven years old. I never had a chance to say goodbye. I was too young to know what to say, to feel or even how to react; I did not understand the impact of her loss. All I knew is that she wasn't coming back, and I wasn't a little girl any longer; I was a suffering young woman left behind.

The week following her death, my father moved all of us to live with his parents. My grandparents, as well as our family, welcomed us with open arms and so much love. Yet, dramatic changes took place in my young life. Once my older sister moved out, I was left to do the things for Dad and my little brother that my mother used to do for all of us. I never realized how quickly those precious, carefree days of youth would disappear.

Two weeks after she passed away, my mother came to me in a dream. In the dream, I saw her standing outside our home in Los Angeles. It was a warm, sunny day, and she was wearing a long, white flowing dress. My mother looked *beautiful*...she had come back! I felt enormous relief to see her.

As we walked down the street together, Mami explained that she had to leave; she would not be able to come back. She bent over and gave me a kiss and a hug. As my mother held me tightly, she told me everything was going to be okay and that one day, I would understand why life was physically separating us and why I wouldn't be able to see her again. Even though she wouldn't be there with me physically, my mother would always guide me and I would never be alone. I stood motionless with tears running down my cheeks; I could not believe she was leaving.

I watched her cross the road all alone. She had a brilliant, golden glow that surrounded her entire body. Gradually, she started to disappear. Then she turned around and waved goodbye to me. I waved back, with tears in my eyes. I looked up at the sky, thinking that maybe everything would be fine in the end. Life went on, and I was not alone. My empty soul slowly filled with a soothing and loving warmth. Then I woke up. I immediately started to cry. Looking back on it, I think she came to say farewell, at least for now, since I didn't have a chance to say goodbye to her when she was alive.

Mami, in the eight years since you've been gone, I have learned that life is about moving on; it is up to me to make the most out of every moment in my life. Because you taught me the true meaning and value of love, I share that love every day with my family, friends, and all those around me. I know you believed in me and that I would achieve many things in life; I am working hard to realize the dreams you held for me. And, even though my light was dimmed when you died, it is getting brighter each and every day. I love you, Mami. Thank you for everything. I know I will see you again.

Goldyn Blanco, a criminal justice student, juggles school and a full-time job. She is grateful for God's abundant blessings and the continued support from her family. Her father, siblings, and nephews are the absolute key to Goldyn's happiness.

Saying Goodbye to My Dad

Eleanor Casey

It's been over forty years since my father died. I was eleven years old, and my sister Helen was eight. On that evening, Mom was working as a cashier, and Dad was home in charge of us. While we were all watching television around 8 PM, Dad got up from the couch, walked toward the dining room, and mentioned that he was feeling lousy. Dad told us that he needed to go upstairs and lie down. As it neared 8:30, Helen and I knew it was time for our cat, Mimi, to take her medicine. Dad was the only one who could give it, so we proceeded upstairs to wake him up.

As Helen and I entered his darkened bedroom, we softly called out, "Dad, Mimi needs her pill." No response from Dad. We went over and tapped Dad on the shoulder. Still nothing. By that time, the two of us were getting a little scared. My younger sister, who loved to frighten me, started talking about monsters, especially the one I feared most, the werewolf. Well, that was all that I needed. I ran out of the bedroom as fast as I could, followed by my little sister!

After going back in and trying unsuccessfully to awaken him, we went downstairs to tell Nana and Uncle Charlie. This led to a whirl-wind of confusing events: Mom coming home crying, Nana throwing herself over her son's body, the family physician declaring him deceased, my older sister and brother arriving crying in anguish, and the priest giving Dad the last rites. At the end of that long, sad evening, I was sent to my uncle's house to stay for a few days. I was not allowed to go to my father's wake or funeral. It took me a while to get over Dad's death. To make matters worse, our cat, Mimi, was put to sleep right afterwards. Mom told me Mimi was sent to a farm, but I knew she was just telling me that so I wouldn't feel so bad. I soon lost my appetite; developed tunnel vision, which lasted for months; and experienced debilitating depression.

My father always loved to play the harmonica for us. I can still hear one of the songs, "Sally's in the Kitchen with Dinah," that he used to play. After he died, our family looked everywhere for his harmonica. It was nowhere to be found. It was so sad not having Dad or his music in our home any longer. Not only that, I never got to say goodbye to my dad.

A year later, I had a dream one night. I remember being at a wake with flowers all around, and I could hear someone playing the harmonica in the background. People were talking to me in the dream, but I don't remember who they were or what they were saying. I also wasn't aware whose wake I was attending.

When I awoke, I had a strong urgency to search for something, but I wasn't sure for what. I asked my more intuitive sister Helen to help me. We looked everywhere. Finally, our search led us to the closet in the dining room, where lots of clean clothes were stacked inside the ironing closet. The two of us started searching through the pile of clothes. There, wrapped up with all of the clothing, was Dad's harmonica! We couldn't believe it. After all that time, the missing harmonica had finally been found. My sister and I will never forget that day.

I have always been a skeptic about God's existence. Whatever the dream and subsequent harmonica discovery might have meant, it resulted in giving me a strong sense of closure in regard to my father's death. Every time I return to that memory, I feel contentment and peace.

Eleanor Casey, wife and mother of Alexandra and Rebecca, resides in a seaside Boston town with her husband, John. Eleanor teaches math, tutors at a local community college, and enjoys family, friends, camping, volunteering with a conservation group, and traveling.

A FAMILY AFFAIR

Lori Monaco

⟋⟍

Uncle Dave, known as David Wolfe to the rest of the world, was my dearest uncle. Without a father figure in my life, Uncle Dave became a father and a loving grandfather for all of us. A slim 5'10" man with curly brown hair and laughing brown eyes, he was the best storyteller and one of the most incredible listeners I have ever known. From when I was a little girl all the way to becoming a grown woman and mother, Uncle Dave was there for me. Even though he lived out of state, he made sure to ask about the books I was reading, my academic achievements, and my marital woes. He even knew the grade and activities of all four of my children.

On the night he passed from a fatal brain tumor, Uncle Dave came to me in a dream. He appeared vibrant and healthy, with his hair no longer gray, clearly a younger version of himself but still very wise. My uncle spoke of some prior events that had occurred in our family, and he offered reassurance of his continued love and tender care for me. However, Uncle Dave also admonished me about a relationship of which I had not been able to let go. Divorced for almost five years, I had been involved in an on-again, off-again relationship with a sweet guy. He was a good guy, but not the right guy for me. Uncle Dave said, "Someone is coming into your life. Cut off this relationship that is going nowhere, and make room for a wonderful man!"

Unfortunately, I didn't listen to him. So two months later, he returned to me in another dream. This time, Uncle Dave firmly said, "You're not listening to me. It is time to make room. Enough is enough!" Uncle Dave rarely spoke to me in this tone, and I felt ashamed that I had not followed his wise counsel. I promptly ended the relationship that was going nowhere.

Within a few short weeks, I met a lovely, faithful man full of integrity, named Peter. However, I was distressed. Peter's Sicilian Catholic parents did not want him involved with a Jewish divorcée with four children. Who could blame them? My ex-husband's parents, also Sicilian Catholic, had been unhappy with my religious background for years. Was I going from the frying pan into the fire?

One day, I was wandering along a New England beach, intensely meditating and praying about the situation. Suddenly, my grandmother on my mother's side began to communicate with me internally. She had passed away when I was five years old. My Jewish grandmother shared some family secrets regarding her daughter (my aunt) who had married a *goyim* (non-Jewish) man. My grandmother confided that she'd been extremely unhappy with my aunt's marriage. In fact, she didn't speak to my aunt for quite some time. I had never heard this story before. My grandmother, having learned a tough lesson from her own experience, urged me not to judge Peter for his background or his parents. She said, "He is a good man, and you will have a good life together. It's the heart of the man, not his religion or ethnicity, that counts."

As soon I reached home, I telephoned Mom, and I asked if my aunt had married a gentile. I also asked if my grandmother had disowned her for a while. My mother was silent on the other end of the line. Then she said, "How would you know this? This is a family secret." I quickly changed the subject. Shortly thereafter, I accepted Peter's proposal of marriage.

Every once in a while, I still have dreams of Uncle Dave. I feel him near, especially when I'm going through challenging times. I recently visited his grave, and once again, Uncle Dave shared many things about my family and me. I will love him forever. I am extremely grateful for his guidance in helping me make room for my dearly beloved husband. Peter and I have been very happily married for over five years. Thanks to Uncle Dave, I am a more fulfilled woman, wife, and mother.

A Day of Remembrance

Archford Bandera

⌒

Grandma lived in the rural town of Mudzi, Zimbabwe; we lived about ten minutes north in the capitol of Harare in Chitungwiza. Other than school vacations while I was growing up, I never had a chance to talk with her in depth, because Grandma lived in a different area than my family. Grandpa died when I was very young. After his death, Grandma took turns living with each of her six sons. When I was seventeen, it was my dad's turn, and Grandma came to stay with us. That's when I bonded with her. In the past, I had always been one of her grandkids. Now, I had a chance to really get to know her.

During this time, I learned that my grandmother loved cucumbers. Each time I had a little money, I would stop to buy cucumbers for Grandma and make her cucumber salad. She really loved that. On my eighteenth birthday, September 11, 2000, I had planned on spending time with Grandma after school. When someone turns eighteen in our culture, that person is considered an adult. Elders talk to the person about adulthood, welcome him or her into the adult world, and give the new adult a blessing. That's why I wanted to see Grandma for my eighteenth birthday. I wanted Grandma to officially welcome me into adulthood.

As soon as I got home from school on my birthday, I learned that Grandma was in the hospital, and she died shortly thereafter. Why did this have to happen on my eighteenth birthday? Her death took me by surprise, not only because it was my birthday, but also because I was in the process of finally really getting to know her. It was very unfortunate. My grandma was such a nice lady. She would always tell us stories, and she was one of those grandmas who loved to spoil her grandchildren, especially by giving us extra privileges. That was one of the things I really liked about her.

In Zimbabwe when someone dies, the funeral starts from the moment the person dies until the day he or she is buried. For three days, our huge extended family, friends, neighbors, and church members mourned her loss. During this time, I was so worried about Grandma. She had left us so unexpectedly. Why did she have to die?

On the night Grandma was buried, I had a dream about her. Grandma looked so happy and healthy. She also looked much younger. Grandma was eighty years old when she died, but in the dream, she looked middle aged, maybe in her fifties. Even in her eighties, Grandma had always looked young for her age, but in the dream she looked even more youthful. Grandma was sharing stories with my cousins and me, and then gave us all some advice. Afterward, Grandma and I went for a walk together. She told me, "Everything is going to be fine. You need to stop worrying."

I woke up and couldn't believe that I'd just dreamt of Grandma. I told my other grandmother what happened, and she told me the same thing. She said, "It's okay. These things happen. Your grandma chose to visit you after her death. There is a reason why. Probably, since it was your birthday, that's the reason why." People die when their time has come, but for some reason, I just didn't believe that it was really Grandma's time. After the dream, I realized that Grandma had really gone to a safe place somewhere. She was happy and was looking down on all of us. I also realized that Grandma wants us to continue to be good, to live our lives, and to be safe. Seeing Grandma helped me to come back to my senses. After this dream, I was somewhat back to normal, but I didn't feel completely whole for quite some time.

When someone dies in our family, we usually place the tombstone on the grave on the one-year anniversary of his or her death. That's what we did for Grandma. However, we also honored the tradition from the Mudzi area where she had been raised, close to the Mozambique border. Our family and a few close friends gathered together for a ritual called "Bringing Back the Spirit of the Person." This ritual is done to cleanse the spirit. Also, it calms the spirit down to prevent bad things from happening to the living. It also neutralizes any witchcraft that may have been done before or afterwards to the deceased person, so that no one will turn against one another. On the day we gathered to honor Grandma in this way was the same day that the events of 9/11 changed the world. Our family supported one another through the enormous losses of both. Once again, my birthday was filled with sadness instead of joy. For the next few years, people were fearful that other bad things were going to happen on that day. Thankfully, they didn't.

In Zimbabwe, the eighteenth and twenty-first birthdays are considered the most important birthdays. Even though my parents had planned a celebration for my eighteenth, nothing happened, and understandably so, because Grandma died. When someone turns twenty-one, the individual is presented with a "Key to the World" representing his or her official entry into adulthood. When I turned twenty-one, I was living in the United States. My mom mailed me a Key to the World she had mounted on a wooden plaque. I really love it! It is hanging on the wall in my apartment. I decided to spend my twenty-first birthday with my friends in Kentucky. Once there, my friends reassured me that bad things were not going to happen. They also suggested that we should go to a party together that night. It turned out that the party was really for me. When we walked in, everyone started singing "Happy Birthday," and they even had a twenty-first-birthday cake for me too.

Having my birthday on September 11 has not been the easiest, with Grandma dying and the events of 9/11 that happened the following year. When my mother gave birth to me, God knew that my birthday would be special. Certainly, no one can forget this day; it is an important day. With things finally now getting back to normal again, I'm getting back to loving my birthday.

Archford Bandera, a native of Zimbabwe, is studying business administration at North Shore Community College. Active in student government and community outreach, Archie has volunteered his efforts in New Orleans, Girl's Incorporated, and My Brother's Table.

STILL WATCHING OVER US

Phyllis Standi

My husband died suddenly more than seventeen years ago. A wonderful husband and father, Tim's passing was a shock to all of us. Until seven years ago, his presence had been noticeably absent in my life, until early one morning around 3:30 when I heard a terrible crash outside. A girl driving home late that night had smashed into my son's old, reliable car parked on the side of the road. Fortunately, although her car was totaled, she didn't suffer a scratch. We waited outside for most of the night until the tow trucks finally arrived. The accident occurred at the exact time that Tim had died.

Three hours later, my sister called to tell me about a dream that her husband, Doug, just had involving Tim. In the dream, Doug's office was in the huge pine tree in front of my house (don't laugh). He was coming out of the tree when he saw Tim pacing on the sidewalk back and forth. Doug said, "Hi, Tim. What are you doing here?" Tim explained that he was just outside watching over things. He was also very anxious to get into the house, but couldn't. Doug looked at him and said, "Life sure is short, isn't it, Tim?"

"Life's not as fast here as it is up there," Tim said, as he looked up at the sky. With that, Doug woke up, unable to shake the feeling that Tim was very worried about my house. The dream seemed so real that my brother-in-law woke his wife up at 3:30 AM to tell her about it. When my sister telephoned me, she was quite surprised to hear about the accident that had happened at exactly the same time that morning outside my home.

All day, I kept thinking about the dream, "If Tim wants to get into the house, then why doesn't he just come in?" It was late in August and starting to get a little cold outside. That afternoon, I was sitting in my home with all the windows wide open; I was freezing. Normally, I would have closed the windows and turned the furnace on.

However, for some reason, I kept the windows open that day and even that night when I went to bed. This was highly unusual for me, as I had become quite frugal as a widow.

The next morning, I decided to turn up the thermostat, but nothing happened when I adjusted the dial. That was another unusual thing. Normally, I would have never noticed that the furnace didn't go on. Throughout our twenty-five years of marriage, Tim would get so upset with me because I was never aware of sounds in the house, such as water pumps or furnaces running. Yet, Doug's dream about Tim made me unusually cautious, concerned about all the things that could be wrong in my house or with my family. I decided to go down to the cellar and check out the situation. When I did, I heard the sound of dripping water. The water was coming from my furnace!

I telephoned the furnace man, who came right over to assess the problem. Apparently, when my house's new chimney had been installed a month earlier, debris had fallen in and blocked the chimney opening. The blockage caused a safety mechanism malfunction, which in turn created a buildup of condensation. Had I shut the windows, turned on the furnace, and gone to bed as usual, we might not have woken up in the morning. When I think about why Tim didn't come to me in a dream, it was probably because he thought I would not have paid any more attention to him in death regarding those matters than I did in life. He was probably right. Now, my family, friends, and I have such a good feeling knowing that Tim is watching over us.

One other thing recently happened; it is only the second time that anything has occurred involving Tim and our family. My husband loved children, and they loved him. He especially enjoyed playing with our baby niece, Ana. Tim would walk up to Ana and put his index finger out; she would put hers out, and they would touch. Nothing more than that, but Ana loved it. She did it every time they saw one another. Ana was ten months old when Tim died.

My sister and her family have a lakefront home with a long dock. A few months ago, she was sharing how much she regretted Tim not being able to see her girls growing up. She was especially disappointed that he had never met her daughter, Maggie, who was born two years after his death. A few weeks after that discussion, Tim visited my sister in a dream. In the dream, she was sitting at the end of the dock with her two girls. As Tim walked towards them, my sister said, "Hi, Tim. How are you?" Smiling, he replied, "Fine." Then, he walked over to Maggie and held out his right index finger. She did the same, and they touched! My sister woke up afterwards with such a happy feeling.

Shortly after that, my sister held a birthday party for Maggie. Since family holidays and special occasions are usually spent at our parents' home, it was the first time that my eighteen-month-old grandson, Timothy, had visited her home. My sister and I were talking in the kitchen when Timothy walked up to her. She looked down and said, "Hi, Timothy."

With that, Timothy put out his right index finger, smiled at the two of us, and walked off; my sister had not yet told me about her dream. When I think back on all of these events, it makes me smile. I am so comforted to know that Tim is still in our lives. He is watching over us, and he's been able to meet his sweet little niece and namesake after all.

Phyllis Standi, a folk artist, founded a charitable organization to benefit the working poor and families unable to be helped through the usual human services systems. Phyllis creates art for friends and family and makes sure to spend time with her grandchildren.

It Will Happen

Dianna Fisher

My grandmother, Elizabeth "Bessie" Murray, was born in 1896 in Cavan County, Ireland. Awakened by a rooster, each morning she was up at 6 AM to perform her chores of turning the turnips, digging the potatoes, chasing the chickens into the pen, and driving the cows home from the field with a stick. Once the daily chores were completed, Bessie, the third oldest of nine children at home, would play with her younger siblings in the fields, chasing rabbits and picking wildflowers. At dusk, they would happily trek home to their mother's homemade Irish stew. Before entering her home, Bessie would stand outside, just for the opportunity to breathe in the delicious aromas that seeped through the cracks of the old wooden door. In the evening after clearing the dishes, she would sit with her mother next to the fire and knit or sew. As Bessie grew older, she slowly became discontented with life on the farm. She dreamed of traveling to places described by her two older sisters, Rose and Mary, in their letters from America. Her father wanted her to marry an Irish farmer, yet Bessie longed for much more. She pleaded for her father's permission until he finally acquiesced. At the tender age of eighteen, Bessie set sail for America with thirty pounds in her pocket from her father.

Her ten-day journey began in October 1915. Little did Bessie know that she would never see her parents again. During her first two days on the boat, she became sick from the rocking motion, food, and the crowded conditions. Bessie traveled in the belly of the boat and relied upon her dreams of America to sustain her through her voyage. Fortunately, time passed quickly. During the day, her kinsman would gather to dance and sing, but the nights were long and lonely for Bessie. For comfort, she would clutch a piece of sod that she had taken from the farm on the day of her departure, and she would reminisce about days gone by with her family. As the day of her arrival approached, her one thought was, "All I have to do is walk off this ship, and I am in America." And, as she started slowly down the gangplank, Bessie broke into a run when she spotted her sister, Rose, whom she had not seen in six years.

Bessie lived with her two sisters until she found employment at Lynn Hospital. It was only after saving enough money to bring her younger sister to America that Bessie finally allowed herself to relax and enjoy her new life. They enjoyed going to dances together and going to the arcade at Revere Beach. There, she eventually met her future husband, John Noone. They married and went on to have seven children. Once her family had grown, Bessie returned to Ireland. It had been thirty-two years since she left. Sadly, both her parents had died years before. Bessie visited friends and other family members, but realized America had become her home. Even though she visited Ireland only one more time after that, she always kept her little piece of sodden earth from the homeland.

My grandmother's life was filled with simple pleasures and happiness. However, at the age of seventy-three, she lost her oldest son and was grief stricken. Soon after, her husband John developed cancer; he was in and out of the hospital frequently. On the day he died, Bessie was sitting by his bed holding his hand. He turned to her and said, "Thank you for a beautiful life." He closed his eyes and slipped away. Her husband's death hit her hard. My grandmother considered her marriage the single most important event in her life.

Nanny was not an overly demonstrative person in her outward expressions of love, but I always knew she loved me through little things she did. She attended every recital or play I ever participated in and was present for my graduations. My grandmother was very proud of my accomplishments and was incredibly proud when I became employed as a nurse at Lynn Hospital. Nanny was a woman who was available to her children but never demanding of them.

One of the few times that she told me she loved me was when she was dying. I recall that November day in 1990 when I received the call at work. Nanny had just been rushed to the emergency room with a heart attack. I ran down to the emergency room to see her. I peeked behind the curtains and saw her breathing was labored. She looked so frail; all the color in her cheeks was gone. Happy to see me, she asked if I could bring her a cup of tea—that was all she needed to feel better. As an experienced nurse, I realized that Nanny would die shortly unless she was placed on a ventilator to help her breathe. I felt such sadness at the thought of losing my grandmother. I needed to leave her for a few moments and told her that I would see her later. Nanny said goodbye. When I reassured her that I would be right back, she said, "No, Dianna. This is goodbye." Shortly after that, Nanny was transferred to the coronary care unit and placed on a ventilator for a few days.

I visited her daily to help comfort her. One Sunday morning when I was getting ready to leave the CCU, I told her that I loved her. She turned to me and said, "I love you, too." Then, she fell asleep. As she lay there sleeping, I whispered in her left ear, "Nanny, please intercede on my behalf when you get to heaven so Michael and I can have a baby." I knew in my heart that Nanny would help us if she could. I was with her on the day she died. Nanny was surrounded by her family and knew she was well loved by all.

While alive, Nanny would often ask me when I was going to have a family. Sadly, I would have to explain that even though I wanted a family, it wasn't my choice that I had no children yet. Nanny repeatedly reassured me and told me not to worry; it would happen. After she died, I continued to pray to Nanny to please intercede on my behalf for a child.

Three years into our marriage and still childless, we were referred to a fertility specialist in Boston. This whole process became frustrating and incredibly time-consuming. Every time we went through a cycle, and I didn't become pregnant, I would incessantly wonder if I had done too much or not enough. Five years later, as we finally came to terms with the possibility that we might never have children, we stopped trying,

Then on a cold winter's night in 1996, Nanny came to me in a dream. In the dream, I was wearing her old flannel nightgown and was sitting in a lawn chair holding a chubby little baby in my lap. Nanny was standing in front of the baby and me. She was wearing her favorite blue sweater resting on her shoulders, buttoned at the top only. My grandmother leaned forward and wagged her right index finger back and forth in front of the baby's face, trying to make him or her laugh. Nanny had a big smile on her face, and I was joyfully laughing in the dream. I awoke, fully expecting Nanny would still be with me. The time with her was so incredibly vivid. I felt her presence so strongly. Suddenly, in that moment, I realized that the next time my husband and I embarked on the infertility roller coaster ride, we would be victorious. I had such a sense of calm and confidence. When I started up the treatments again, both my physician and the social worker commented on the noticeable change in me. I knew in my heart Nanny had come to reassure me things would work out.

Sure enough, I became pregnant after our first in vitro fertilization cycle. I delivered a healthy baby girl in February 1998, whom we named Rachel Elizabeth, after my grandmother. Then, just two and a half years later, I conceived a second time. When I saw the chubby face of our newborn son, I realized that he was the child in the dream with Nanny. Little did I know it at the time, but my grandmother was telling me I would be blessed not just with one child, but two.

There is not a day that goes by that I don't think of Nanny or thank her for coming to me. I have never had another dream so clear or vivid of her, but I truly believe Nanny came to deliver the message, "Don't worry, Dianna, *it will happen*." And it did!

Dianna Fisher, RN, wife of Michael and mother of Rachel and Christopher, works as a Union Hospital case manager and a Salem State College clinical instructor. She likes to golf, garden, and read, but she mostly spends time with her family.

9

Angels

For every soul, there is a guardian watching it.
—THE KORAN

HAVE YOU EVER BEEN TOUCHED by an angel? Has your life been transformed as a result? Angels come in a variety of forms. Some have wings, and others appear in human form. They come as helpers, teachers, and healers. Their impact is profound and their gifts are many. Whether it is through their heavenly songs, their encouraging presence, or the angelic intercession on our behalf, remember to give thanks for angel blessings.

Daryl's Angels

Candice M. Sanderson

My husband, Daryl Sanderson, was an ambitious, energetic, and wonderful man. He loved life, and he lived it to the fullest in his short thirty-five years on this earth. A building contractor by profession, my husband was president of the West Kentucky Homebuilders Association when he became terminally ill with cancer.

Daryl was always laughing; he had the most beautiful smile. I think it was his smile that first captured my heart. Daryl especially cherished our precious little daughter, Cassie, who had just turned four years old when he succumbed to melanoma. This vicious form of skin cancer metastasized throughout his body and into his brain.

During the last week of his life, Daryl was hospitalized at Lourdes Hospital in my hometown of Paducah, Kentucky. I spent my days and nights at his side, sleeping on a cot next to him so that he would never be alone. About every four or five hours, I would slip out of his room so I could stretch my legs and grab a cup of coffee. I took my breaks in the ICU waiting room because of its close proximity to Daryl's room and its overabundance of coffee. I usually spent five to ten minutes drinking coffee and mindlessly working on one of the puzzles scattered throughout the room before returning to Daryl's side.

On September 2, 1987, I took my usual break in the waiting room. After almost a week of this routine, I knew all the regular visitors to the ICU. When I walked though the waiting room doors that morning, I immediately noticed two "newcomers." I'm certain they weren't visiting a new patient, for there had been no new admissions that day. Nonetheless, there they were … waiting, simply waiting … sitting and casually talking with each other. The two men had their chairs positioned side by side facing a large picture window overlooking the city as they sat and waited. But, I wondered, for what? Waiting for whom?

Both men looked serene, peaceful, and quite out of place for an ICU waiting room, where most visitors were anxious and stressed.

As I began piecing a puzzle together, I couldn't help but overhear their conversation. One man told the other that he had once seen an angel on a busy street corner in Cincinnati. He said the angel was right in front of him, flew straight up, right over the traffic and into the sky. I'll never forget what he said next. His exact words were, "Funny thing about it, though. The angel had wings on his feet!" I immediately froze. I looked up and stared at these men. Although the comment certainly astounded me, the other gentleman graciously accepted his friend's story with a kindhearted, casual nod. Then they were silent, content to sit and continue their vigil of waiting.

A few minutes later, I returned to Daryl's room. The chaplain of the hospital entered, and I asked him to pray for a peaceful death for Daryl. My husband was comatose, and there was nothing more that could be done medically.

Father Dillard closed his eyes and began to pray. The prayer he offered was so beautiful. As I stood there holding Father Dillard's hand, standing at Daryl's bedside, I felt a sense of profound peace and calm, which I had never experienced before in my life. Then, I heard Father Dillard call for the "angels with winged feet" to carry Daryl home.

My eyes flew open. What? Did I hear him right? Never in my life had I heard of angels with wings on their feet. Yet, within a matter of minutes, I had heard about these angels *twice*! I sensed that I was in the midst of a transcendent experience that was incomprehensible. I knew in my heart that the angels with winged feet would, indeed, carry my husband home. A short time later, Daryl peacefully departed from this life.

I kept this very personal experience in my heart for the longest time, not able to share it with anyone without shedding tears. Several years later, I decided to tell one of my sisters, Eleanore, the story. As a missionary, she travels to third-world countries to spread the word of God. Eleanore exclaimed, "Candie, don't you know? Those men were the angels sent to carry him home!" She explained that angels can manifest themselves as human beings upon the earth. She also reminded me of the Bible verse "Be not forgetful to entertain strangers; for thereby, some have entertained angels unaware." (Hebrews 13:2)

Now, I realize why those "men" were just sitting and waiting in that ICU waiting room on that memorable day back in 1987. They were waiting for my husband... waiting to carry my beloved Daryl on the wings of angels to his heavenly home.

An Angel in Uniform

Richard M. Wainwright

It was the middle of May 1996. I was physically, emotionally, and psychologically at the lowest point in my life. I felt so overwhelmed. My beloved wife, D'Ann, had died of cancer. As a devoted husband, I felt I had failed in my efforts to find a cure. Furthermore, I was now responsible for caring and making decisions for my mother-in-law, Nina, whose health was failing. I needed a short break, so I decided to head to our Florida time-share at Eagle's Nest on Marco Island. My boys would look after Nina.

As I was driving through Rhode Island, I kept replaying the last eight months of my life over and over again. Somewhere on Route 95 south, for the first time in my life, I emotionally lost it. I moaned and I cried. Tears eliminated my vision and I did not know or care where I was, or even whether I lived or died. I totally forgot my responsibilities to other loved ones. D'Ann's loss, along with Nina's immediate and constant caring, had pushed me beyond my psychological strength.

My head hit the steering wheel, and my foot flattened the gas pedal. Moments or minutes went by. Flashing bubble lights and a siren brought me back to reality. I looked at the speedometer. I had gone from sixty-five miles per hour to ninety-three miles per hour. I slowed down and turned off the highway as the Rhode Island state trooper pulled in behind me.

When he got to the window of my car, I was still sobbing. The officer didn't yell at me; he gently asked what was wrong. The dam broke. I told him everything that had happened and how I felt. He listened patiently, was sympathetic, but eventually said he still had to give me a ticket. However, he recommended I write a letter to the police department when I sent in the ticket, explaining the circumstances. Then, Officer Smuts, wearing badge #40, handed me my ticket.

He instructed me to wait a few minutes to be sure I was all right. I followed his advice and was back on the road five minutes later. Less than a half-mile away was a sweeping turn that probably would have ended my life and possibly the lives of others, had I careened over the edge. I more or less held it together for the rest of the trip south. When I got to Marco Island, I wrote the letter, mailed the ticket, and forgot about it.

When I returned home two weeks later, I called the Rhode Island State Police, as I wanted to write Officer Smuts to thank him for saving my life. Inexplicably, I was told there was no Officer Smuts on the force, and all badge numbers had four digits instead of two. Nine months later, I got a letter from a Rhode Island judge dismissing the ticket.

Since the passing of my beloved wife, I have been on an incredible spiritual journey. Through the pain and the despair, I have been blessed with several amazing and wonderful experiences, such as the one with Officer Smuts, which have changed my life. From a skeptical, despairing agnostic, I have become a firm believer in the hereafter, so much so that I felt the need to share my experiences in the book *Closer Than We Imagine*. Hopefully, through sharing our journey, D'Ann and I will be able to bring comfort and hope to those who have been physically separated from loved ones. All the events that have unfolded since D'Ann's passing have provided more than sufficient evidence that spiritual life is never-ending. We will see our loved ones again.

Richard M. Wainwright, award-winning author of ten inspirational young people's books, wrote Closer Than We Imagine *following several amazing spiritual events with his deceased wife, D'Ann. He and his wife, Judy, divide their year between Scituate, Massachusetts, and Palm Coast, Florida.*

SOMEBODY'S ANGEL

Teresa Delaney

⁓

In June of 1981, I traveled to Canada with a group of classmates. At the time, I was about nine weeks pregnant. Aside from missing every delicious French breakfast and several early excursions due to morning sickness, I was having a great time. Of course, the advantage of sleeping late was being able to stay out late.

One evening, my friend Pam and I went exploring through the old section of Montreal. There were several street musicians and sidewalk vendors selling all sorts of jewelry, clothing, and art. The feel of the city was enchanting. We decided to venture a little farther into the more modern section of town.

Pam and I had walked toward the stadium and were headed back to our hotel when we stopped at an intersection. The four-lane highway was deserted, but we waited for the "walk" sign before attempting to cross. After a few minutes, the sign appeared, and I stepped out onto the highway. Suddenly, I heard the roar of an engine coming from the left. I looked up to see a car racing down the hill toward me, with apparently no intention of slowing down or stopping for the light. I was paralyzed. I couldn't move. Then, I felt a hand grab my right shoulder and pull me out of the way to safety. The car sped by, the driver never sparing us a glance.

Standing on the sidewalk, stunned from the experience and still trying to catch my breath, I turned and thanked Pam for pulling me out of the way and for saving my life. Pam stared at me for a long moment. "I never touched you," she said. "I couldn't get to you, or even scream."

"You didn't touch me? You didn't grab my shoulder?" I questioned.

"No, I swear."

The two of us stood on that sidewalk for what seemed like an eternity, each trying to comprehend what had just happened. *Somebody* pulled me out of the street. Maybe it was my guardian angel or the guardian angel of my unborn son. Or, perhaps it was the angel of the person who was driving the car. But one thing is certain: on that day, someone intervened on my behalf and on the behalf of my baby. I know it was an angel.

Teresa Delaney, charter member of the Smoky Mountain Romance Writers, enjoys all types of books. When she is not reading or writing, Teresa enjoys traveling through beautiful mountain scenery on her motorcycle, which keeps her guardian angel very busy.

A Kind Messenger

Marie Thomas

My husband John died in the summer of 1998. He was a sensitive and loving man, hardworking and quiet. For more than two years, John fought cancer that had metastasized to his bones. I cared for him at home throughout his illness. After my husband died, I needed to know that he was okay. I had done so much for John for so long. In fact, my whole life had revolved around his care. Shifting my concern away from him was difficult, but it was important for me to refocus because of our three children. At first, I prayed a lot to get through those empty nights without John. Especially during the nights, I would find myself praying for a sign to let me know he was all right.

A few nights after he passed away, I had a dream. I awoke in the dream and found myself lying in a bed; the location felt familiar, although I did not recognize the place. Lying next to me in the bed was a handsome fellow with light brown hair who appeared to be in his mid-thirties. Wearing blue hospital scrubs, the man had his head propped up in his hand on the pillow. He had been watching me while I slept.

I was startled! I asked the man who he was. Very kindly, the man told me that he used to work with hospice helping people pass over. However, he didn't do that anymore. I sensed his gentle, loving almost angelic presence. "I am here to tell you," he said, "that John wanted you to know he is very far away and resting deeply. He was exhausted after all he'd been through." I felt overwhelming relief and gratitude, and was filled with a sense of peace. If it were possible, I wanted to stay in that experience for days. I found myself soothed and comforted by the messenger and the message.

When I awoke the next morning, I felt amazingly refreshed! It was the first time in days I had awoken feeling peaceful, relieved, and at ease. I am so grateful for that kind messenger who visited me while I slept!

Marie Thomas and her three children created a memorial garden in the backyard for her husband after he died. The children, who are now grown, healthy adults, will always treasure the experiences shared with their dad.

Eric's Angel

Deborah Brent

In mid-September of 1982, I entered the ninth month of my second pregnancy. Everything had gone along fairly routinely up until the last four weeks of the third trimester. By October 5, I had been in labor three times, and my precious baby showed no signs of wanting to leave my body. That evening, I was hospitalized. My obstetrician examined me and discussed our options. After some deliberation, the decision was made that he would induce labor the next morning. However, the doctor also talked about all the things that could go wrong—just what a pregnant mom needs to hear when she's as big as a whale. My baby's life was threatened, and there was a chance he might not survive. I was scared for my baby and for me.

I lay there praying to God in the darkened room. My prayers were answered when, all of a sudden, my deceased Grandmother Mawsy appeared next to me in a hospital bed. She was wearing the same black dress we had buried her in four years earlier. I could actually see the small, multicolored rectangles, which looked like tiny stained glass windows on her dress. Her hair was fixed up prettily, just the way she liked it. Grandmother Mawsy was wearing her glasses and had *real* teeth. From the time I was a little girl, my grandmother's smile was usually a toothless one. She hated wearing false teeth and only wore her dentures in public. And, surprisingly, she was happy. Grandmother Mawsy was not noted for a happy or a bubbly personality.

In the vision, there was another person wearing a white robe standing at the head of her bed, as if ready to push the bed somewhere. Grandmother Mawsy didn't reach out to touch me, and I didn't try to touch her. She simply told me that I would be fine, my baby would be fine, and not to worry. Then, just as quickly as she appeared, the vision ended, and she was gone. The nurses had not given me any drugs. I was not asleep, so it couldn't have been a dream.

The next morning, as planned, the doctors induced my labor with pitocin. Although the contractions were strong and regular throughout the day, my baby's head finally coned, and then wedged in the birth canal. This was a life-threatening problem. At 6 PM, the decision was made to do an emergency C-section. Fortunately, we both came through it fine.

Today, that baby is my six-foot, twenty-four-year-old son, Eric. He is working two jobs and attending auto body school. My husband and I are proud of him. Grandmother Mawsy was right... everything turned out fine.

Deborah Brent, mother, grandmother, and genealogist, is an eighth-generation East Tennessean. A former Family History Director for the Church of Jesus Christ of Latter-Day Saints, she is a member of Romance Writers of America and the Smoky Mountain Romance Writers.

My Guardian Angel

Joan Meese

For more than a year, I regularly visited my eighty-four-year-old hospice patient, Mame. I felt privileged to have the time to develop a deep level of intimacy with this spunky lady whose amazingly positive attitude was present even on the gloomiest of days! Often, I would ask Mame where she got her positive attitude from. Was she born with it? Or did she develop it over the course of her life? Each time I asked, Mame just smiled mischievously, as though she was unwilling to reveal her deep secret.

For Mame's eighty-fifth birthday, I brought her a balloon with the inscription, "Don't count the years! Just enjoy the glow!" These words described her perfectly. On that birthday, Mame was *so* happy that she literally beamed with joy. "I'm still here!" she declared proudly. "They told me I'd be gone. But, I'm still here!" Over the next three months, her condition gradually deteriorated. Mame seemed to hang on at the end much longer than her family expected. When she finally died, I went out to make the pronouncement visit. It took about an hour and a half, and then I left.

On my way back to the office, I was driving down Route 1. It was a grey, misty day, and I was feeling sad. I had grown accustomed to my regular visits with Mame. Just two and a half hours earlier, she had gone to God; I was missing her. I was driving slower than normal because of the slick weather conditions. Without any warning, the driver of a car heading in my direction on the other side of the yellow line suddenly cut in front of me! Failing to use his turn signal, he left me no time to react. In that moment, I was convinced I was going to die.

Time seemed to slow down, as my life flashed before my eyes. Instantly, I realized that Mame was in the car with me. Although she was not physically there, I felt her presence. I looked up and asked, "Mame, what on earth are you doing here? Are we going to heaven together?" Before the impact of the collision, my last memory was the sensation of Mame's reassuring arms around me.

The ambulance and fire department had difficulty removing me from the wreckage. I was brought by ambulance to the hospital. Based on the damage done to my vehicle, I should have been much worse off. With only a few bumps and bruises, I was a very fortunate young lady. I knew it was because Mame had been with me. Without a doubt, Mame saved my life. She was my guardian angel.

Over the years, I have given my automobiles names. In the past, I have traditionally named them all Betsy. However, since the accident, I now affectionately call my cars Mame, in honor of my guardian angel.

Joan Meese, RN, hospice nurse, learned from her parents that dying at home and death are natural processes. All the chapters in Joan's life, including marrying her husband, Jim, have been directed by her God, a power greater than herself.

QUEEN OF THE CASTLE

Patricia Margaret Nelson

My mother, Mary Elizabeth O'Hara, was born in Salem, Massachusetts, under the astrological sign of Leo. As the queen of her castle,
she ruled my father, brother, and me with an iron fist. Her wonderful
rock gardens were her pride and joy. They were filled with different
kinds of flowers, shrubs, and rocks she had collected from around
the world. An accomplished artist, Mother painted water scenes and
flowers. It was tragic when she could no longer see well enough to
paint, and when her arthritic fingers refused to properly guide the
brush along the canvas. She was also incredibly intuitive, but refused
to acknowledge her intuitive gift until she was in her late seventies. I,
too, am blessed with the same gift of intuition. On the day I shared
this with Mother, she told me about an experience she had napping
one afternoon. Her deceased parents had come to her in a dream, and
when she awoke, my grandmother, in her favorite polka-dotted dress,
was standing next to her, smiling.

Life was difficult growing up because Mother had a drinking problem. When I was fourteen years old, she joined Alcoholics Anonymous
and became a recovering alcoholic. She sponsored many women over
the next twenty years, accepting wholeheartedly her new purpose in
life.

At the age of seventy-nine, Mother became quite ill and was referred to hospice. My husband and I cared for her up until the time
of her death. Our time together was precious as we got to know her
through the eyes of the women she had helped in AA. I was amazed
to learn about all the wonderful deeds she had done for so many.

The last summer of her life was a beautiful and loving time. We
would sit and recall all the times we had worked together in her garden, as well as the happier memories we had shared. We were very
fortunate that our family was able to come together one last time that

summer. Mother was able to finally make amends with her son, whom she had not seen for over twenty years, as well as with a former husband, who still loved her but had long since remarried.

Much too soon, the time came when the "Queen" took to her bed. At that time, she passed reign of her castle to me. Mother had done everything she needed to do, and she was now ready to go see God. Along with praying, crying, and laughing together, we talked about her approaching transition, which helped the two of us find peace.

One afternoon, about a week before Mother died, my brother and I were talking in the kitchen when we heard a loud knock at the front door. I answered the door to find a nice-looking, elderly gentleman. He introduced himself as Dick and told us that he had heard our mother was ill. Dick visited with Mother for about an hour. Afterward, he thanked us profusely for allowing the visit. Before he left, Dick told us how wonderful Mother was and about all the good she had done for the AA program. During their visit together, my brother and I laughed like two school kids at how funny it was for us to be chaperoning our mother with her male visitor.

Later that evening when a female friend of my mother's telephoned to see how she was doing, I shared about Dick's visit. A little while later, I mentioned the friend's phone call to Mother, as well as Dick's visit, because she sometimes had trouble remembering things. When I told my eighty-year-old mother about Dick's visit earlier that day, Mother was shocked. She sat straight up in bed and informed me in a strong, confident voice that the gentleman visitor I had just described had been dead for many years!

Thinking my mother must have been confused, I telephoned one of her friends a little while later to discuss what had happened. When I did, her friend corroborated Mother's story and told me that Dick had indeed died quite a few years earlier. Dick had been a close friend of Mother's. He was also the individual she had worked with in order to bring AA programs to the state and county jails in Massachusetts.

When he died, my mother and many others were devastated at the loss of such a great man.

The only possible explanation I can come up with for that memorable afternoon is that an angelic friend came to visit and prepare my mother for the final journey she was about to take. And, when the day arrived that my mother passed from this world to the other, I was able to smile through my tears and whisper, "Until I see you again, I love you, Mom."

Patricia Margaret Nelson, LPN, wife, mother, grandmother, and great-grandmother, is a published poet in the Who's Who of Poetry. She has received the Outstanding Achievement Award in Poetry and the Choice Editor's Award, and has served as United States Ambassador of Poetry.

Papa's Bringing Me the Moon

Brigitte Perreault

⌒

Papa was a kind, decent, and gentle man. Thin in stature and 5'10" tall, he was initially employed as an auto mechanic. Later, he became a warehouse manager for an electric supply company. He worked hard his entire life. Yet despite his best efforts, he always seemed to be going uphill, never quite reaching the top. My father was extremely generous at heart and although he may not have been wealthy in the material sense, he was a man who would readily give the shirt off his back to someone in need.

Deeply devoted to his wife and seven children, Papa was my rock. Yet growing up was difficult for us; Mom struggled with many health problems, including dementia. She became quite ill the same year Papa retired from his job. At a time when life was supposed to be getting easier, things became increasingly difficult.

As a dedicated husband, Papa lovingly cared for her at home a lot longer than most people could have. Whenever Mom did weird, quirky things, my siblings and I would look at each other and chuckle; Papa would shrug his shoulders and smile, saying, "That's my baby!" Eventually the day came when the situation at home was no longer manageable. With great reluctance and a heavy heart, my father was forced to admit my mother into a nursing home, where he visited her daily. So Papa wouldn't be alone, my husband and I sold our house and moved with our two children back to my childhood home.

Although Papa loved all his grandchildren and great-grandchildren, he developed a special bond with my third child, Allison. I am so grateful that Papa was there when she came into the world. From the moment she was born, Papa was hooked. He constantly took pictures of her, always tried to make her laugh, and loved to rock Allison to sleep. Early on, his little granddaughter became fascinated with the moon, and each of us took turns taking her outside every night to see it.

Allison was almost two years old when we found out Papa had bladder cancer; his condition was terminal. The news was devastating for all of us. When we got home from the doctor's office, I cried uncontrollably while my father comforted me. Papa did not shed a tear for himself; if he did, it was in private. He remained as strong as he could, and continued to visit my mother until it was no longer possible. Papa gave me specific instructions about whom he wanted his personal belongings to be given to once he was gone. One day, we were joking together and reminiscing about some of Mom's quirky habits, as well as some of her favorite belongings. My father asked, "Do you remember that necklace your mother always used to wear, the one with the moon?" At that moment, a look of realization and joy came over his face. He declared happily, "I know who's getting that!" It struck me as funny that it hadn't occurred to either of us that Allison shared her love of the moon with my mother.

Papa's wish to remain home with hospice care was made possible through the loving help of family and friends. Inevitably, Papa's health declined, and his condition worsened to the point that he was no longer able to speak. Around that same time, Allison, who had always been a sound sleeper, began waking up at night. Whining, she would say, "Mommy, turn off the heat. I can't sleep!" I was puzzled because the temperature in her room was the same as in every other room in the house. On one night when I went to shut the radiator off in her bedroom, Alison protested, "No, that's not the heat!" Frustrated, I said, "Then tell me where the heat is and I'll shut it off." Allison pointed at the ceiling. Later, I told my husband that I believed "the heat" was a sign that the end was near for Papa.

The next morning, Allison began to talk about "the heat" again. I listened, even though I desperately wanted to ask more questions. I was afraid that if I interrupted, my little daughter would stop talking about it completely. Allison told me that there was an angel in the heat. Tears filled my eyes as I tried to maintain my composure. Wondering if Papa's angel could be his own mom coming for him, I later asked him if he had seen her yet. Although he couldn't speak, that day, Papa nodded "yes."

After that, we picked Mom up from the nursing home and brought her home to see Papa one last time. When we wheeled her over to his bed, this woman, who had been completely bedridden and devoid of any expression for years, actually let out a cry. My family and I were all moved and bewildered. That was the only outward emotional expression she made that day, but it was plenty for all of us. Although Papa was not conscious during her visit, his facial expression changed while she was there. He smiled slightly, and seemed to be trying so hard to open his eyes. I truly believe Papa knew she was there.

That same night, after my mother was returned to the nursing home, my family and I gathered around Papa to spend time with him. My niece took Allison outside to see the moon, as usual. While they were looking at it, Allison announced very matter-of-factly, "Papa's going to bring me the moon on Sunday."

Two days later, Allison woke up crying. She was complaining of the heat again. It was early Sunday morning. Then, my sister came into the room. I told her what had just happened with Allison. "That's not what woke me," Landra replied. "I heard the garage door shut." We decided to check the garage, and the garage door was locked! That door was the same door Papa used whenever he entered or exited the house. Could it have been that Landra heard Papa leave?

We anxiously went to check Papa. His still-warm body confirmed that Papa had passed away only minutes before, just as we had suspected. Our family gathered around him; I held Allison as she gave her grandfather a last kiss goodbye. On that Sunday, Allison inherited Mom's moon necklace, as foretold.

Occasionally, Allison still speaks of the angel in the heat that took Papa that night. I believe my daughter continues to see Papa. Once in a while, she catches me off guard and mentions her papa's name or something he did. Papa's death was one of the most beautiful experiences of my life. Although I miss him more than I could have ever imagined, I am extremely grateful that he was at home with us when he died.

Mom passed away the following February, less than a year after Papa left us. Because Mom had been the one who was always so ill over the years, we had assumed she would be the first to go. Looking back, however, it only makes sense that Papa crossed over first so he could welcome his baby home.

Brigitte Perreault, wife of Gary and blessed with three beautiful children—Jaimee, Cameron, and Allison—is a middle school teacher who loves working with children. Brigitte enjoys reading, writing, and especially spending time with her family.

10

Near-Death Experiences

*Heaven comes to people and their loved ones
when they are dying. It is not uncommon for angels
to appear when people are on the edge of death,
and people who have had near-death experiences
often describe feelings of indescribable peace.*
—GARY KINNAMAN

THOSE WHO SURVIVE CLINICAL DEATH find their lives changed forever; the experience of God's infinite love, peace, and light is transformative. Some describe memorable reunions with loved ones who have died. Others report seeing spiritual teachers, beings of light, angels, and the presence of a Higher Power. Amazingly, any fears of death and dying vanish. Although each person's experience is unique, one common thread is the profound, overwhelming presence of God's love.

The Other Side

Elissa Al-Chokhachy

My uncle, Ralph Weedon, was a Presbyterian minister. Married to my gracious and loving Aunt Radine for over forty-two years, he was the beloved father of two and the proud grandfather of four. Uncle Ralph was a calm, quiet, and kindhearted man. His gentle, loving presence and soft-spoken nature have always held a special place in my heart.

Years ago, I had planned a trip to visit my aunt and uncle in Louisville, Kentucky, for the first time. However, two weeks prior to my visit, Aunt Radine called to tell me that my uncle needed emergency open-heart surgery. With my ticket already in hand, I told her I was glad to come to provide whatever support might be needed.

Uncle Ralph made it through the quadruple bypass fine but experienced several post-operative complications. After being rushed to the operating room for a second round of open-heart surgery, he developed pneumonia and became septic with a staph infection. Finally, a third round of cardiac surgery was needed to clean out the infection.

When I arrived, Uncle Ralph was unresponsive. Most of my time was spent at his bedside in the CCU or in the adjacent waiting room supporting my aunt and family. The doctors told Aunt Radine her husband had less than a 50 percent chance of survival. Thanks to his excellent medical care, the grace of God, and a multitude of prayers, Uncle Ralph was able to overcome the multiple medical challenges that he faced.

The following June, I attended a Brenton family reunion in Tulsa, Oklahoma. It was great to see everyone and to meet so many extended family members for the first time. The highlight of my trip was seeing Uncle Ralph alive, healthy, and well. Significantly thinner, he had lost over forty pounds. Yet, my uncle appeared bright, alert, and so pleased to be there in his own quiet, unassuming way.

Late one evening, Uncle Ralph and I were chatting in the recreation hall and then walked back together to our lodging. Once there, the two of us sat on the front step of one of the little cottages and conversed for quite a while on that warm summer night. At one point, Uncle Ralph turned to me, looked me straight in the eye, and quietly said, "You know, Elissa. I went to the other side."

"You did?" I asked, amazed at what he had just confided to me. Uncle Ralph looked so peaceful and calm as he continued. "Yes, I did, last year, when I was so sick in the hospital." He paused. Very quietly, he said, "I went to the edge of the River Jordan. Archangel Gabriel met me there. He told me if I crossed, I would not be able to return. It was up to me... I didn't cross the river."

At the time, I sat silent, as I respectfully tried to take in the depth and breadth of what my uncle had just told me about life beyond. He had experienced it firsthand. I'll never forget that night. Although I don't know the significance of the River Jordan, I learned many years later that the Archangel Gabriel is also referred to as the Archangel of Resurrection.

In a recent conversation with my aunt to wish her a happy eightieth birthday, I shared with her again what Uncle Ralph had told me in Tulsa. Aunt Radine said, "Oh yes, Elissa. He shared it with quite a number of people over the years." During his near-death experience, Uncle Ralph had witnessed the most intense and brightest light he had ever seen in his whole life. He had also experienced the most warm and welcoming feeling and a peace that was almost indescribable.

Aunt Radine went on to tell me in the eight years that followed Uncle's Ralph's experience that she had witnessed a significant change in her husband. Even though he was a man of faith and had preached to hundreds over the years about eternal life, some part of him was afraid to die. Yet all that changed when Uncle Ralph went to the other side; he was no longer afraid to die anymore.

When my Uncle Ralph passed from this world, he had a peaceful crossing; Aunt Radine was at his side. Uncle Ralph, thanks for your kindness and thanks for your love. I'll see you on the other side.

GOING HOME

Patricia Margaret Nelson

In my fifty-seven years on this earth, I have needed major surgery eleven times. My most recent surgeries were due to a condition I was born with called Arnold Chiari's Malformation. This cranial bone malformation restricts the normal flow of cerebral spinal fluid in my head. As a result of increased intracranial pressure and impaired cerebellum functioning, my cognitive memory, depth perception, fine motor function, and my ability to walk and talk have all been affected.

Growing up, I made countless trips to the doctors for vague, nondescript symptoms. Nothing was ever found, and I was repeatedly sent home with my complaints dismissed. Despite the lack of answers and the multiple challenges I faced on a regular basis, I was forced to keep going forward. For years, I was plagued with horrendous headaches, especially when I coughed, laughed, or sneezed, along with the sensation of a wide band tightly gripping my head.

Then, at fifty years old, a car accident left me riddled with severe head pain, unrelieved by months of continuous physical therapy. Extensive neurological testing finally revealed the Chiari malformation in my head. My symptoms continued to worsen, and five different surgical procedures were performed. When I woke up in the ICU after the cranial cervical spinal fusion, a physician's assistant had just stopped by. "Boy, am I happy to see you!" Denise said. "You sure caused a lot of worry!"

"Why would I cause you any worry?" I asked, confused. Denise explained I had been asleep for three days after the surgery, and that everyone was extremely relieved I had woken up. I told her that I had dreamt during the surgery, something that had not happened before. When I started to describe the dream, a funny expression came across Denise's face. I continued anyway. "It felt like I was dancing on a cloud or something," I told her. "Very freely, I was just floating, almost in slow motion. In the dream, I looked down at my left arm; then, I said to myself, 'Look what they've done to my arm! It doesn't move! Now what?'"

Surprised at what I had just shared, Denise said, "Patty, it wasn't a dream; it actually happened. During the surgery, eighty percent of your cerebral cortex stopped functioning. Afterward, when we tried to remove your endotrachial tube, you went sour on us; you *stopped* breathing! You have been on life support for the last three days; we almost lost you." During that conversation with Denise, I only shared part of what I remembered during the surgery. The entire experience was quite phenomenal. Some people talk about a big white light. Well, it's true. While I was under the anesthesia, I actually saw the light. It was very, very bright, almost misty in nature, and all-encompassing. My entire being was engulfed in the light. It was white, and it was warm. And, I could smell a sweet, fragrant aroma of roses and other flowers, as sweet as the nectar of a lilac.

I also heard beautiful music. It sounded as if the angels were singing inside the Chapter House of the Wells Cathedral with absolutely perfect, magnificent musical acoustics. The arrangement sounded very similar to Handel's *Messiah* being sung by a choir of angels. Everything was filled with love, warmth, and comfort; it felt so much like home. Experiencing the light, music, and aromas was like being bathed on a beach by warm sunshine and caressed by the ocean breeze on a beautiful summer's day. It was such a relaxing, happy, and peaceful feeling. There wasn't one ounce of fear in my body.

Somehow, I had a sense of where I needed to go, and I wasn't the least bit afraid. I stepped through the light into a tunnel. The tunnel was very well-lit and bright, bright, bright. There were so many bright lights that I felt almost as if there were hundreds of cars inside the tunnel with me, all with their high beams on. I felt my body moving very quickly through the tunnel in the direction of the white light, and I had the sense that the tunnel was just wide enough for my body to fit. As I traveled, I felt the breeze on my face and heard a whooshing sound from my rapid movement. I also heard the beautiful sound of angel voices singing all around. Every once in a while, when I looked toward the sides of the tunnel, I was able to see the faces and wings of cherubs. For as fast as I was traveling, it seemed to take a long time to get to wherever I was going. Finally, when I reached the end of the tunnel, the lovely angelic music that I had been hearing stopped.

In the distance, I could see a large mountain in front of me. The pine trees and small rolling hills appeared much closer. The landscape looked so much like a beautiful Canadian countryside setting. The whole panorama almost reminded me of heaven on earth, or should I say, a more perfect earth in heaven.

Just in front of the pine trees, I could see the shadow of my mother-in-law, Verna, who died at the age of ninety-six. As her image became clearer, I could tell Verna appeared much younger. At the time she died, my mother-in-law's hair was pure white with a little black streak on top; she wore glasses for as long as I can remember. The younger Verna appeared to be in her thirties or forties. Her thick, brown hair was curly; it was pulled back in a small ponytail on top of her head and cascaded down her back. Verna was not wearing any glasses, and there wasn't one wrinkle on her skin! My mother-in-law looked very young and very much at peace. Enthusiastically waving her left hand at me from about twenty feet away, Verna looked so very happy. It felt great to know that she was excited to see me.

Then I heard a male voice gently tell me that I was only there to visit. I had to go back because the work that had been planned for me to do was not yet finished. I felt sad that I had to leave this mystical temple of love. Completely engulfed in the present moment, I hadn't thought of my loved ones back home. There was so much love all around me! I was thoroughly enjoying the beautiful blue sky, majestic mountains, and warm breeze as well. Then the male voice told me I had stayed long enough; I needed to turn around and go back. I really didn't want to. The music had been so beautiful; everything felt exquisitely warm and loving. I would have been happy to stay right there or to continue on the journey the rest of the way. But, I turned around and returned, as instructed. Almost instantly, along with a rushing sound that tickled my ears, my next memory was the sound of voices singing…

Apparently, while I was unresponsive in the ICU, several people were singing to me and sending me healing. They had been visiting someone else there and offered to do some healing work on me. My friend, who was sitting next to me, agreed. Their singing was really pretty. The sound of their voices was my first conscious memory. My second conscious memory was waking up in the ICU.

Whenever I find myself in a lot of pain, I get a little weepy. On those days, I find myself looking back, living in the past, and wishing I could just go home. I'm not exactly sure what "home" means; perhaps it is home to God. Fortunately, there are days when I can see the progress I am making. I am gradually getting stronger and healthier, and it feels really good. On those days, I'm very happy to be here. I am able to focus on the future instead of looking back at the past.

As a result of my extraordinary near-death experience, I am no longer afraid to die. My fear of death has been totally eradicated. I feel so blessed to have had a near-death experience. Furthermore, it was an experience of God's limitless love. I no longer worry about being good enough. I know God loves me, and one day, he will welcome me home.

SOMETHING BEYOND THE PHYSICAL

Dianne Kessler-Hartnett

During my thirteen years working as an ICU nurse caring for the critically ill, I have witnessed many things that have led me to believe there is something much more than the physical body. Whether it is the visions of deceased loved ones that are often seen by the dying or the things they sometimes privately share, I am deeply honored that my patients feel comfortable enough to share their intimate and sometimes inexplicable experiences with me. One such encounter involved an elderly gentleman by the name of John. I had met John and his family on two prior hospitalizations.

During this admission to the ICU, John was recuperating from a cardiac arrest he had just experienced. Successfully resuscitated by the emergency medical services in the community, he had been transferred to the ICU for monitoring and care. As an ICU patient, John spoke to his daughter, Sherrie, and me about what he had just experienced prior to his resuscitation. In a very calm manner, John described seeing the "most beautiful, bright colors," which were more vivid than anything he had ever seen in his whole life. He spoke of hearing "trumpets playing and the incredible feeling of being calmed."

Then, John turned to Sherrie and requested that CPR never be done on him in the event he ever needed it again; John was no longer afraid to die. The place he had been was *beautiful.* John was discharged from the hospital a week later. About one month passed when, while sitting at the breakfast table with his daughter, John suffered a second heart attack. Remembering their conversation in the ICU, Sherrie did not call 911. She allowed her father to go in peace, just as he had requested. Because of what he had told her, Sherrie felt very comfortable honoring her father's wishes.

A second briefer situation involved a middle-aged man, Harry. He had experienced a cardiac arrest while in the ICU. Fortunately, Harry had been successfully resuscitated there. As his primary nurse in the unit, I had spent considerable time caring for him.

On the day following his cardiac arrest, Harry asked to speak with me. He didn't think anyone would believe him, and he needed to talk with somebody. Harry was somewhat anxious. At the same time, he also felt relieved to finally be able to tell somebody what had happened.

Apparently, during the episode, Harry had experienced himself standing over the head of his bed, watching the medical team resuscitate him! He watched the entire procedure and everything that had been done to his body. Amazingly, Harry did not feel any pain whatsoever during the code, even though the team had used electrical paddles to bring him back to life. No further details were offered. As far as I know, Harry did not speak to any other medical personnel about his experience. Yet, what Harry shared that day has surely confirmed for me that there is so much more to life than just the physical body.

I'll never forget these two patients, John and Harry. Their experiences touched me deeply. Clearly, there are no logical or rational explanations for the things that happened to either one of them. All I know is that each of these men willingly divulged their life-affirming experiences. And, by doing so, they blessed me with a momentary glimpse of something beyond the physical.

Dianne Kessler-Hartnett, RN, wife of Bill and mother of Jenna and Kyle, has worked in critical care, cardiac rehabilitation, and quality management. Also certified in nursing administration, Dianne enjoys teaching as well as offering emotional support to cardiac patients and their families.

BABE, DON'T LEAVE ME

Brian Walsh

⌐────────⌐

As a master engraver and the owner of a start-up jewelry business, I continually worried about whether or not my wife and I would financially make it. Almost every waking moment was spent creating jewelry, getting ready for shows, and fulfilling orders. Stressed to the max, I smoked three packs a day, didn't exercise, and ate mostly fast food. I weighed 280 pounds. With my life chaotic and out of control, it set me up for an experience that was about to change everything.

On October 27, 2000, Vicki and I had spent all day preparing for a craft show. Even though I was anxious about not having enough inventory for the next day's show, we were exhausted and called it quits around 8:00 that evening. Suddenly, the left side of my jaw began to hurt. The pain started to worsen, so I went into the bathroom to splash some water on my face. Then, severe pain started shooting down my left arm. Now, both my left jaw and my left arm were hurting! At that point, I opened the bathroom door. Totally drenched in sweat, I yelled out, "Babe, you'd better call 911! Something weird is happening to me!"

I hurried to the kitchen, quickly took two aspirin and a Rolaid, and barely made it back to the bedroom to sit down. As soon as I did, I began to feel intense pressure and tightness in my chest, as if someone was standing on top of it. Then, I started having difficulty breathing—something was seriously wrong! Vicki dialed 911 and told them she thought I was having a heart attack. Then, she grabbed the holy water her mother had just brought back from Lourdes and splashed it all over my face. She put her rosary beads around her neck and my beads around mine. In about a minute and a half, the fire truck arrived with the ambulance. The EMTs whisked us both away to the emergency room, where the ER doctor administered intravenous clot busters immediately. "One to ten, what's your pain?" he questioned.

"Ten!" I cried out, as it felt like a wrecking ball was on top of my chest. I could barely breathe; the pain was severe, constant, and my left arm felt even worse than my chest. "There's no change!" I blurted out. More clot busters were given and again no change. The doctor said, "It's not working!"

All of a sudden, I got an overwhelming sense that I was going to die. I yelled to the nurse, "Get Vicki in here, *now!*" I urgently needed to tell my wife that I loved her. I *knew* I was going to die.

One of the nurses ran to get my wife, who was in the waiting room with her father. The nurse told them I was having a massive heart attack and that they needed to get to the ER *now*. The urgency on the nurse's face was quite apparent. Vicki couldn't believe it—I was forty-four years old! They rushed in and found me with my eyes wide open, terrified. I really believed I was going to die. Even though Vicki tried hard to reassure me that I would be all right, I knew differently. Scared, I told her, "Babe, I want you to know how much I love you..."

"I know, babe," Vicki said as she tried to calm me down. "I love you, too." Right then, I heard the rhythm of the EKG monitor change from beeping intermittently to one long, continuous sound...My heart had stopped beating! Frantically, the doctors and nurses pushed Vicki and her father aside. "Get out of the way!" the nurse commanded, and she rapidly pulled the curtain closed. The medical team focused all their efforts on saving my life, while, on the other side of the curtain, Vicki and her father remained, intensely praying for my survival.

Despite all their combined efforts, the room went black. In that moment, I felt myself whoosh through a tunnel of pure light. It felt as if I were being propelled in a high-speed elevator through a very long, circular tube of light. The feeling was incredible and my pain was completely *gone!*

The light was everywhere and all around me. It was such a bright white light, yet the brightness didn't hurt my eyes. The light made me feel warm...at peace...calm...and in a perfect situation. The light brought with it a sense of understanding. There were no more questions to ask. It was an automatic sense of knowing. In the light, I was in a state of utter and extreme happiness! Everything felt *perfect*. Even the temperature felt perfect. I found myself in absolutely the safest place I could ever imagine. It was so overwhelming and immeasurable, I can't even put it into words.

Time didn't exist. I saw my entire life literally flash in front of my eyes. I relived *everything* that had happened to me, from the very moment I was born to the moment I died. I felt everything—good and bad—that I had ever done in my life. I relived every decision and every life choice I had made, especially as they had affected others. Once my emotions were fully re-experienced, they dissipated into the light. Finally, all the bad feelings from the past were gone. All that remained was incredible, immeasurable love.

I was greeted by several people who felt very familiar to me. It was so great and wonderful to see them. It was like having family all around me and truly felt like home. Life on this earth is only temporary. Over there is where we all belong. It's like each one of us goes on a trip to earth for a while and then returns back home. From the time I was there, I no longer had any worries about pain or death; they were all gone. A lot was explained to me which I cannot recall. All I know is that I look at life much differently now.

At one point, I found myself facing a being of authority approximately five feet away. The being seemed to be a little larger than me and much brighter in light than all the light that surrounded me. I didn't feel any sense of maleness or femaleness. I felt one with everything and everything felt connected. There was an overwhelming sense of love to a degree that I had never felt on this earth. The being of light seemed to be a spirit in human form, as I could see a head, limbs, and the bright outline of a person wearing a loose robe. I could feel the being's presence so strongly. Then, the being spoke to me telepathically, saying, "You have a choice to go back or stay." It felt so great being there! Believe me, I did not want to go back. But all I could hear in my head was Vicki's voice screaming over and over, "Babe, don't leave me!" Vicki was the only thing I could think about. I couldn't do that to her. She was my whole focus, and I couldn't think of anything else.

When I was told about the choice to stay or leave, the being said, "If you want to go back, do not look into the light beyond me." So I turned around to head back to the tunnel for Vicki. Briefly tempted, I turned around to take one last sneak peak at the light. The being's voice raised louder, "I said, if you're going back, *do not look into the light!*"

Instantly, I was catapulted back to earth, almost as if someone had turned a light switch. I opened my eyes, and the ER doctor's face was in mine. "Hey, what's going on?" I asked. The monitor started to beep in a regular rhythm. I was back, and so was the pain. But, I no longer had a fear of dying. The doctor told me I was having a massive heart attack and I was in the process of being transferred to another hospital. As they rushed me into an ambulance, the ER doctor wished us good luck. By the look on his face, he didn't think I would survive the night. As for me, I wasn't worried whether or not we would make it in time; I was no longer afraid of dying.

At the second hospital, the doctors inserted a bare-metal stent which completely took away the pain I had been experiencing. Following the procedure, I was transferred to the CCU. When the doctors came in to check on me, they told me they had no idea how I was still there. The type of heart attack I had was called the "Widow Maker," for obvious reasons. After they left, I told Vicki about everything that had happened to me and that all I could hear in the background was her screaming, "Babe, don't leave me!" Amazed and laughing, my wife told me that she was silently praying those exact words repeatedly during the code!

Right after my heart attack, Vicki called one of our friends, who lived on Prudence Island. She instructed him to go to the dock when the ferry arrived and tell everybody, including the church ladies, to start praying. My wife knew everyone on the island from having spent summers there her entire life. Vicki also asked that every person tell two people to pray and to concentrate their prayers on me. When Vicki visited me the next day in the CCU, I told her that I could feel people praying for me. I had no idea that she had made the request. Now I know prayer has power—I could *feel* it.

One physician, Dr. Poppas, was particularly curious about what happened to me because my heart had stopped for such a long time. I felt weird describing my near-death experience, something that I had never heard about before. But, the more questions Dr. Poppas asked, the better I felt because I could tell she understood. In fact, I wondered if she'd had a similar experience. When I went to see her for a follow-up checkup, she said, "We don't know why you're here. People don't usually survive that type of heart attack."

It took a year of determination and hard work before I felt myself again. However, that same year, I was faced with a ruptured disk. Inexplicably and miraculously, I happened to slip and fall on the exact spot with the exact pressure needed which caused the condition to self-correct. Even my neurosurgeon admitted that medical science was not capable of doing what happened to me. It was truly a miracle.

Surviving the widow maker, the ruptured cervical disk, and a bout of Legionnaires' disease in 1976 were three miracles that have happened in my life. How did Vicki and I survive all these challenges? Faith got us through. Humor got us through. I'm so blessed to have Vicki as my life partner. From the moment we met, Vicki and I knew it was a match made in heaven. The two of us have been together ever since.

As a result of having died, I now know that God is not a force. God is a spirit, the presence of perfection and the feeling of home. God is there for each and every one of us. We are exactly where we're meant to be. In the presence of God, no negative feelings can remain. Each of us is clean, pure, perfect, and at peace.

I don't know if everyone is given the same choice to come back. However, I knew I had to come back for my wife. Hearing Vicki's voice in my head made all the difference in the world. I am also now certain that people who die or experience near death can still hear the thoughts and prayers of their loved ones.

My heart attack happened for a reason. It was a wake-up call. I needed to start living more. Since I'm only here for a limited amount of time, I no longer worry about taking time off from work. Now, I'd rather go fishing or go for a ride on my motorcycle. I appreciate every moment I have. I'm enjoying nature more. If it's a beautiful day, I want to be outside. I still work hard, but I'm much more focused and productive.

Whenever I get the chance, I share my story of the widow maker with others who are struggling. It often will help get them through the dark times. Also, I no longer wonder if there's something after this life—I know there is. I'm genuinely happy for people who pass away because I know they're in a better place. Life is so short. Enjoy the simple pleasures. Tomorrow is promised to nobody, so remember to make the most of today.

Brian Walsh, master engraver, husband of Vicki, and father of Michelle, enjoys spending time with his family. Originally a lead singer in a number of rock-and-roll bands, including Impact with his brother, brother-in-law, and friend, Brian enjoys riding his Harley-Davidson motorcycle.

II

The Circle of Life

*You have noticed that everything an Indian does is in a circle,
and that is because the power of the world always works in
circles, and everything tries to be round. The sky is round and I
have heard that the earth is round like a ball and so are the stars.
The wind, in its greatest power, whirls. Birds make their nests
in circles, for theirs is the same religion as ours. Even the seasons
form a great circle in their changing and always come back again
to where they were. The life of a man is a circle from childhood to
childhood, and so it is in everything where power moves.*

—BLACK ELK

LIFE IS A CIRCLE TO which there is no beginning and no end. Eternity
is incomprehensible to the human mind. Occasionally, we are blessed
with a transcendent experience, one which reflects the unending nature of life. During sacred moments such as these, we often discover
our relationship to a Higher Power, as well as our connectedness to
the whole. There is no death, for life is eternal. Nothing dies; it simply changes form.

The Circle of Life

Tracey L. Coleman

It was the summer of 1993. I was working at a nursing home in Portsmouth, New Hampshire. Eloise, a ninety-year-old French woman with bone cancer, had been a resident at the facility for about a year and a half. Even the slightest movement was extremely painful, and it was necessary to use morphine to manage her pain. Although reluctant to move, Eloise loved to bask in the hot summer sunlight. She would allow us to prop her up with pillows on the reclining chair and wheel her outside. The therapeutic sunlight was comforting and seemed to lift her spirits.

Because she was unable to reposition herself, the nursing staff turned Eloise often. During the last week of her life, she became totally unresponsive. Early one morning, the night nurse found her awake. Eloise was moving her right arm in wide, continuous circles and repeated this action nonstop for the next fourteen hours. As a home health aide who has cared for many patients with bone cancer, I can say that I have never witnessed anything so extraordinary in my whole life. Even the slightest movement can cause patients with advanced bone cancer excruciating pain. For this very reason, Eloise rarely moved on her own. So, you can imagine the surprise of the entire staff when the word got around that Eloise's arm was in constant motion.

At first, she was unable to speak. Yet, during the last hours of her life, Eloise stated over and over, "I've completed the circle of life... I've completed the circle of life..." These were the only words she spoke repeatedly. At approximately 4 PM that same day, Eloise stopped speaking. She laid her arm down to rest and within minutes, she took her last breath.

Although her body lay motionless in front of me, I could still see her arm moving in wide circles and hear the words she spoke in my mind, "I've completed the circle of life." Eloise had connected into a far greater wisdom than most of us usually experience. A circle represents eternity, which has no beginning and no end. Eloise was communicating the timeless message that death is not an end. Rather, it is only one more beginning in the vast, endless cycle of eternal life.

Tracey L. Coleman has received the Editor's Choice Award from the International Library of Poets and the End-of-Life Caregiver Award from hospice. A nursing assistant for twenty-six years, Tracey plans on returning to nursing school once again.

My Beloved Baba

Ibelle Fouladvand Sebastian

My father, Khosrow Fouladvand, was the truest, most sincere, and considerate person I have ever known. I affectionately called him Baba, which means "daddy" in Persian. Originally born in Iran, Baba and his younger brother were sent by their parents to France in order to pursue their studies. Majoring in political science and law, Baba eventually became a judge. He met and married my mother. Although their first daughter died at the age of two, my parents were blessed with five more; I was the fourth of their five girls. We were raised in Tehran until the Islamic Revolution in 1979. At that time, my family relocated to Southern California while I continued my studies in France. I eventually relocated to Boston to study dentistry.

Since Mom was often busy with my baby sister, my relationship with Baba became quite strong from the start. Family time and family affection were important to Baba, since he had missed so much during his youth from studying abroad. I remember one time when Baba had just left for a business trip. I was only nine years old, and I had suddenly become upset a couple of hours after his departure. I urged my mother to get in touch with Baba right away because I knew something had happened to him. She thought I was just deeply missing him. But, within an hour, the phone rang. Someone at the hospital was calling to tell us that Baba had been in a serious car accident. His car had rolled over several times, and he was hospitalized with multiple fractures. Baba was lucky to be alive. This was just one example of how closely the two of us were connected.

Baba always talked about God. Even though his relationship with God was paramount, he never pressured any of our family members to follow a particular religious path. "Always know there is *only* God," Baba would say. "God is everything." He taught us that whatever we put out in the world needed to come directly from our hearts, as well as from our faith. Baba was my spiritual mentor; he was the source of my strength and faith in myself and in the universe. Baba was my best friend and my most significant life teacher.

On Valentine's Day 2003, my sister called to wish me a happy Valentine's Day. That was Baba's birthday. During her call, I got the strangest feeling in my heart that something was wrong. When she called the next morning to tell me that Baba had been admitted to the hospital, the news affirmed the unsettled feeling I had been having. My sister Shirin informed me the doctors were doing everything they could; she reassured me that Baba was in good hands and that I didn't need to worry. She also told me another sister had spent the night with him. All our family members were taking turns staying with Baba so that he would never be alone.

The next day, Shirin called again, this time upset because Baba's breathing was now labored. He had been placed on a ventilator, and it was becoming obvious that Baba was not getting better. I tried desperately to catch a plane to California, but I couldn't because every airport in the Boston area had been closed for two days due to a blizzard. Finally, I was able to purchase a ticket for the first available flight the next morning. Yet, within four hours of purchasing my ticket, Baba died. Because of the blizzard conditions, I wasn't able to be with my Baba when he passed.

Throughout my entire life, Baba lovingly called me his little *snow baby;* he was referring to the weather conditions under which I had been born. A blizzard had prevented Baba from being with me when I came into this world, and now, a blizzard prevented me from being there with Baba when it was his turn to leave. For the two of us, the circle of life and death in the physical world had been completed. Truly, there is no death, for through the blessing of birth, life continues on in the physical realm. Even with this spiritual awareness and knowledge, my grief for Baba remained. How could I possibly live without him? I did not know how I could survive. Moving in slow motion, I felt numb to the world, barely able to think, eat, or move.

The funeral was an incredible tribute to Baba. My oldest sister and my niece spoke, along with several other family members and longtime friends. A reception was held at a restaurant following his funeral, and several friends accompanied us home afterwards to offer support. My sister's mother-in-law offered a prayer for the first night of Baba's passing. Immediately following the prayer, a huge bolt of lightning lit the evening sky, and a gentle rain began; when she left with her daughter, she called ten minutes later to tell us that the rain had stopped two minutes after leaving our home. Amazingly, the weather had once again responded to a sacred time for my father.

The long, arduous journey of healing from the loss of Baba began. I looked to all sorts of places for love, support, and comfort to help me through those endless days and nights of loneliness and despair. I cannot begin to describe how blessed I was to have the love and support of my beloved husband. Always at my side, Steve was invaluable, especially as an emergency room physician during the last critical days of my dad's life. It was so difficult for me not being there, which haunted me for months to come. At least I knew in my heart that everything possible was being done as a result of my husband's expertise, along with the loving support of my mom, sisters, and our family who kept vigil with him. Also, my sisters continually reassured Baba that both Steve and I were frequently consulting with his physicians, which was a tremendous comfort to my dad.

My friends were a wonderful support for me. My dear friend Elissa, with her love, faith, and encouragement, helped me realize I would still be able to connect with my Baba in new and different ways. Yoga helped me clear my mind and my grief-stricken body. Meditations brought me closer to Baba, as I could feel his presence during those quiet moments. I would pray to Baba and repeatedly ask, "How can I find you? How will I feel your presence?"

I had to embrace my pain and sorrow in order to heal the wounds of grief. I sobbed daily. After a year or so, my weeping had begun to lessen and the knifelike pains in my heart had transformed into a dull ache. As difficult as it was, I was keenly aware of how important it was to acknowledge my pain rather than try to avoid, suppress, or deny it. If pain isn't acknowledged, healing can never happen. And, the only way to heal pain is to simply go through it, one step at a time, in order reach the other side. *Attention* to pain and *intention* to heal are the secrets to healing from loss. Like an eagle, I had to rise above the clouds in order to see the sun.

One of the most difficult things about the loss of my dad was the inability to bring closure. I never got to say goodbye. I never got to tell Baba one last time how much I loved him and how much he meant to me.

The week following Baba's funeral, my husband and I headed to Maui, which happened to be one of our favorite places on this earth. This particular place brought great peace and respite to our souls. While there, I had a dreamlike experience of Baba, my first tangible experience of him since he passed. It is difficult to say whether I was asleep or awake, but all I know is that Baba was with me.

In the dreamlike experience, I was in the same hotel room in Maui that Steve and I were staying in. It was nighttime. Before going to sleep, I got up out of bed to close the television cabinet doors. As I went to close the doors, I noticed Baba's silhouette on the television glass. I could clearly see Baba from his shoulders up; he was wearing a suit and his French beret. I gasped in disbelief. I turned around to my left, and I saw my Baba standing right next to me!

Baba appeared healthy and looked the same way as he always did. Wanting to make the most of this extraordinary moment, I reached out with both my arms, and I embraced my Baba. I could feel the loving and comforting warmth from his body, the same warmth that I felt the last time I hugged him goodbye. I could also smell Baba's scent. This opportunity was exactly what I needed, because I was the only one of his children unable to be at his side when he died. I finally got to say goodbye to Baba; I am so grateful for those few moments we shared.

In my journey of grief, I found myself continuously asking, *Where is Baba? Where did my Baba go?* A few days later while still in Hawaii, I happened to be walking inside an art gallery on the Big Island with Steve. I noticed a large and very familiar-looking painting of a crystal castle in the distance with lots of light surrounding it. I couldn't believe what I was seeing. Instantly, I recalled that I had seen the identical castle in a dream the week *prior* to Baba's passing. With great excitement and curiosity, I asked the art gallery attendant the name of the painting. She went behind the counter and looked up the name…the name of that painting was "Heaven"! This was the answer to my questions. My beloved Baba was in heaven.

Since then, I am occasionally blessed to see Baba in my dreams. I so treasure those moments we share. It feels wonderful to know that whenever I need him, my Baba is still near. All I have to do is ask.

I haven't forgotten Baba. However, I needed to forge a new relationship with him, just as the author of this book had conveyed. This was necessary if I was ever going to be able to go forward in my life again. The loss of someone so significant brings one to a newer and deeper level of living. Relationships deepen, the understanding of life broadens, and the foundation of one's own existence transforms. The experience of profound loss stretches the spirit beyond physical understanding. Baba quoted the legendary Persian poet Rumi often when I was a child. The following words by Rumi bring me great comfort; they offer solace as I continue on my lifelong journey of healing from the loss of my best friend, my spiritual mentor, my Baba:

> *It's good to leave each day behind,*
> *Like flowing water, free of sadness.*
> *Yesterday is gone and its tale told.*
> *Today, new seeds are growing.*

Baba, thank you for awakening the seeds of consciousness within me. You are my inspiration and my angel. I love you for eternity. I await our reunion.

Ibelle Fouladvand Sebastian, DMD, general dentist and clinical Ayurvedic specialist, is a seeker of knowledge and wisdom. Blessed with a beautiful family in California and unbelievable friends, Ibelle adores her husband, Steve, her Bichon, Cosmo, and the family dog, Lucky.

Steffan and the Unicorn

Elissa Al-Chokhachy

My parents divorced when I was just a baby. Dad was in medical school. Single moms were rare back in the fifties. With few resources available to her, our mother struggled to provide for my older brother and me. When she could no longer cope, we went to stay with our aunt, uncle, and six cousins, where we lived for the next nine years. Our cousins became our brothers and sisters. When I was twenty-three, my eldest cousin, Steffan, was killed in an automobile collision at the age of twenty-nine. Fortunately, his pregnant wife and two little boys survived the crash, but it was an extremely difficult time for all.

Two weeks after Steffan's death, I had the most extraordinary experience of my life. Steffan came to me to let me know he was all right. The dreamlike experience is as vivid today as it was thirty-two years ago. It began in the woods, very much like the ones in which we played during our youth. In all directions, the leaves on the trees were a brilliant green. In fact, every color in the experience was accentuated beyond anything I have ever seen in this reality. Every emotion I felt was magnified as well.

I was standing alone in the woods when a beautiful, stark-white unicorn ran right past me down a dirt road from right to left. The color of the unicorn was a luminescent, brilliant, white light, as bright as the sun hitting freshly laden snow on a sunny winter's day. I could not believe I had just seen a unicorn. I remember thinking to myself that unicorns aren't real. "But they must be," I thought, "*I just saw one!*"

I took off in pursuit after the unicorn through the forest and down the long, winding dirt road. Because the unicorn was galloping at a faster pace than I could run, the distance between us naturally widened. Eventually, we came to a large, open field, just like the one next to the house in which we had grown up. By then, the unicorn was on the other side of the field and had completely disappeared from sight.

As I looked across the field directly in front of me, I noticed a solitary male figure standing to the left of our childhood home. To my total amazement, there stood my cousin. I could not believe my eyes. My cousin Steffan was *alive*! How could that be possible? Two weeks earlier, I had attended his wake.

Overjoyed, I tore across the field as fast as my legs could carry me. Tears of joy streamed from my eyes as I ran. When I finally reached Steffan, I hugged him so completely. I absolutely did not want to let him go. "Steffan, you're alive! You're alive! Thank God, you're alive!" I kept saying this over and over, as I intensely wept. I could feel his body so tangibly wrapped inside my arms.

Steffan laughed and laughed, as he continued to hug me with so much love. What a glorious moment! I was in ecstasy. Then, suddenly, I let go of him. I remembered that 95 percent of Steffan's body had been burned in the accident. I was horrified to think that I had forgotten. "Steffan, I'm so sorry," I cried, now feeling deeply ashamed. "I am so sorry. I didn't mean to hurt you. I was just so happy to see you that I forgot…"

Ever so calmly and gently, my 6'2" cousin, who was a foot taller than me, lovingly looked into my eyes. He had an enormous smile on his face and radiated such an indescribable inner peace. "It's okay, Elissa," he said reassuringly. "You don't have to worry. I don't hurt anymore."

I breathed a huge sigh of relief. Thank goodness, I hadn't hurt him. But even more incredible was the fact that his pain was entirely gone. It was almost too good to be true. Then, as I looked at his face, I noticed something was different. He wasn't wearing glasses; all of us wore glasses growing up. "Steffan," I blurted out. "Where are your glasses?"

He laughed out loud, saying, "Elissa, I don't need glasses anymore. I can see!" All of this was almost too much to comprehend. Not only was my cousin alive, he was totally healed and had 20/20 vision! I felt myself intensely wanting to remember this exquisite moment forever. Instantly, a camera appeared in my right hand. "Steffan, can I *please* take your picture?" I pleaded. "I want to remember this moment for all of eternity." He laughed, thinking I was silly, but eventually he humored me. Stepping back, Steffan grinned as I focused the camera. When I pressed the button to snap the picture, the dreamlike experience ended.

Regular Kodak paper could never have captured the emotional or spiritual significance of that experience. At the time, I was still very much in grief over the loss of my cousin. Yet when I awoke, I knew to my core that he was alive, totally healed, happier, and more at peace than I had ever known him in this life. That knowing healed my grief. My experience with Steffan changed me forever: no longer did I fear death, for I knew with certainty that life was eternal. My beloved cousin had given me a lasting sense of hope and inner peace that I carry with me to this day. This knowledge has been a tremendous asset for me in my work as a hospice nurse and when I have cared for the dying and the bereaved.

I believe that Steffan and all of our departed loved ones are alive, well, and filled with God's deep, abiding peace and love. If we were able to hear them speak, I feel in my heart each would surely say, "My dear ones, I love you very, very much. Yes, I am alive, I am happy, and I am at peace. What a joy it was to know and love you. What a joy it is to love you still!"

Dear Reader,

If you would like to share a true firsthand experience affirming the continuity of life beyond death, please send your brief description and contact information to stories@MiraculousMoments.com.

Every submission will be read and reviewed on a first-come, first-serve basis. You will be contacted if your story is a potential submission for the next book. Thank you in advance for your willingness to share. May we bring much hope to many.

Blessings,
Elissa Al-Chokhachy
www.MiraculousMoments.com

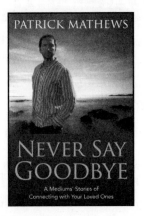

NEVER SAY GOODBYE
A Medium's Stories of Connecting with Your Loved Ones
PATRICK MATHEWS

"I'm a normal guy . . . I just speak to dead people."

When he was six years old, Patrick Mathews came face to face with the spirit of his dead Uncle Edward. As an adult, Mathews serves as a vessel of hope for those who wish to communicate with their loved ones in spirit.

The stories Mathews tells of his life and the people he has helped are humorous, heartwarming, and compelling. Part of his gift is in showing the living that they can still recognize and continue on-going relationships with the departed.

Mathews takes the reader on a roller coaster of emotional stories, from the dead husband who stood by his wife's side during her wedding to a new man, to the brazen spirit who flashed her chest to get her point across. You will also learn step-by-step methods for recognizing your own communications from beyond.

978-0-7387-0353-4
216 pp., 6 x 9 $15.95

BRIDGE TO THE AFTERLIFE
A Medium's Message of Hope & Healing
TROY PARKINSON

What if you could talk to the other side? What would you say? And what messages would the spirits have for you?

Spiritual medium Troy Parkinson, a rising star in the paranormal world, shares fascinating first-hand stories of his communications with the spirit realm.

Channeling spirits was the last thing that Troy Parkinson ever thought he'd do. A North Dakota native and self-described "ordinary guy," he first attended a spiritualist meeting when he was a college student in Boston. After receiving a message that night from his grandmother's spirit, he decided to pursue mediumship training through the world-renowned First Spiritual Temple of Boston. Parkinson now travels around the country, doing readings for large audiences and presenting workshops that teach people how to develop their own spirit-communication abilities. Troy's moving story and amazing messages from spirit will touch your heart, inspire your soul, and remind you that your loved ones are always with you.

978-0-7387-1435-6
240 pp., 6 x 9 $15.95

SOULS UNITED
The Power of Divine Connection
ANN MERIVALE

If you have ever experienced the joy of connecting with your soul mate—or hope to—this book is for you.

Regression Therapist Ann Merivale has researched the lives of ordinary couples who have indeed found their other half. From the glorious moment of instant recognition to shared past life experiences, their true stories illuminate the nature of these intense relationships. *Souls United* explores a wide variety of karmic connections: blissful marriages that revolve around great work; evolved souls who share a telepathic connection; twin souls who suffer a rare break up; and famous figures such as Edgar Cayce, Elizabeth Taylor, and St. Francis of Assisi who were in twin soul relationships.

Authentic and moving, these case studies offer reassurance that every one of us—in this lifetime or another—will reunite with our other half.

978-0-7387-1528-5
336 pp., 5³⁄₁₆ x 8 $15.95

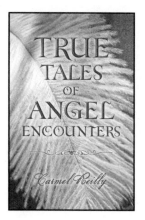

True Tales of Angel Encounters
Carmel Reilly

A distraught mother thinks twice about abandoning her family, a junkie is inspired to kick the habit, and a young man on the verge of insanity makes a remarkable recovery—thanks to the divine intervention of angels.

Ordinary people of diverse faiths, including the non-religious, have experienced the wonder of angels. This inspiring collection of true accounts highlights how these spiritual beings—manifesting as a kind stranger, a radiant figure, a gentle voice, or a comforting presence—have touched lives around the world. Breathtaking and heartwarming, these personal tales offer a convincing glimpse of angels at work—protecting children, offering advice during a crisis, healing babies, comforting the bereft and the dying, bringing messages from loved ones who have passed on, easing pain, and offering strength at the darkest hour.

True Tales of Angel Encounters is a glorious exploration of the human/angel relationship that's sure to reinvigorate your faith in the Divine.

978-0-7387-1494-3
312 pp., 5³⁄₁₆ x 8   **$15.95**

Bringing Your Soul to Light
Healing Through Past Lives and the Time Between
Dr. Linda Backman

What happens after we die? What is the purpose of my current life? Have I lived before?

In this unique and inspiring guide, Dr. Linda Backman answers these questions with compassion, objectivity, and more than thirty years of experience conducting traditional and past-life regression therapy with clients. *Bringing Your Soul to Light* includes a wealth of first-hand accounts from actual past-life and between-life regression sessions, offering readers a compelling and personal glimpse into the immortality of the soul.

Readers will discover the extraordinary universal connections we all share in this lifetime and beyond. They'll learn how they can use this knowledge to heal and grow, both physically and spiritually, by understanding themselves on a soul level and releasing energetic remnants of past-life trauma. *Bringing Your Soul to Light* includes a foreword by holistic healing pioneer and author C. Norman Shealy, M.D., Ph.D.

978-0-7387-1321-2
264 pp., 6 x 9 $16.95

The Case for Reincarnation
Unraveling the Mysteries of the Soul
J. Allan Danelek

What is the purpose of reincarnation? How does it work? What is the role of the soul, free will, karma, soul mates, and God in this wondrous and mysterious process driving spiritual evolution?

Steeped in J. Allan Danelek's signature, scrupulous logic, *The Case for Reincarnation* presents verifiable evidence of rebirth and brings clarity and credibility to an age-old belief. Addressing all aspects of reincarnation—including how the next physical life is chosen, the influence of past lives, the difference between the soul and personality, what happens between lives, the necessity of evil, and the maturity level of souls—Danelek illuminates this beautiful mode for perfecting the soul.

978-0-7387-1999-3
264 pp., 6 x 9 $16.95

SPIRIT GUIDES & ANGEL GUARDIANS
Contact Your Invisible Helpers
RICHARD WEBSTER

They come to our aid when we least expect it, and they disappear as soon as their work is done. Invisible helpers are available to all of us; in fact, we all regularly receive messages from our guardian angels and spirit guides but usually fail to recognize them. This book will help you to realize when this occurs. And when you carry out the exercises provided, you will be able to communicate freely with both your guardian angels and spirit guides.

You will see your spiritual and personal growth take a huge leap forward as soon as you welcome your angels and guides into your life. This book contains numerous case studies that show how angels have touched the lives of others, just like yourself. Experience more fun, happiness, and fulfillment than ever before. Other people will also notice the difference as you become calmer, more relaxed, and more loving than ever before.

978-1-56718-795-3
368 pp., 5³⁄₁₆ x 8 $12.95

Spanish edition:
Ángeles guardianes y guías espirituales
978-1-56718-786-1 $13.95